# Leadership, Nation-building and War in South Sudan

*Peace, Society, and the State in Africa*

Published in collaboration with the African Leadership Centre,
King's College London

Published in association with the African Leadership Centre, this original and necessary series interrogates issues at the intersection of security, conflict and development in Africa, focussing in particular on the relationship between the state and the wider society from which it emerges. Guided by the promotion of Africa-led ideas and respect for independent thinking, the series presents cutting-edge research, fieldwork and theoretical insights into the society-based changes impacting the continent today.

The **African Leadership Centre** (ALC) is an internationally renowned academic unit based within King's College London, with a semi-autonomous research and training centre in Nairobi, Kenya. It incorporates a global community of scholars, whose cutting-edge research on peace, leadership, development and security issues aims to inform and influence intellectual debate, teaching and learning as well as policy discourses both in Africa and globally. Over the years the ALC has attracted some of the most influential African and global thought leaders, diplomats, military personnel, politicians and civil society leaders to speak at lectures and debates with its students in London and Nairobi. Although not exclusively African in its coverage or its student intake, the ALC is nevertheless committed to developing the next generation of African scholars, analysts and leaders.

The series editors are founding Director of the ALC, Professor 'Funmi Olonisakin, and Associate Professor at the ALC, Dr Eka Ikpe.

# Leadership, Nation-building and War in South Sudan

## The Problems of Statehood and Collective Will

Sonja Theron

BLOOMSBURY ACADEMIC
LONDON • NEW YORK • OXFORD • NEW DELHI • SYDNEY

BLOOMSBURY ACADEMIC
Bloomsbury Publishing Plc
50 Bedford Square, London, WC1B 3DP, UK
1385 Broadway, New York, NY 10018, USA
29 Earlsfort Terrace, Dublin 2, Ireland

BLOOMSBURY, BLOOMSBURY ACADEMIC and the Diana logo are trademarks
of Bloomsbury Publishing Plc

First published in Great Britain 2022

For legal purposes the Acknowledgements on p. ix constitute an
extension of this copyright page.

Series design by Adriana Brioso
Cover image: Roberto Schmidt/AFP/Getty Images

A catalogue record for this book is available from the British Library.

A catalog record for this book is available from the Library of Congress.

ISBN:  HB:     978-0-7556-2214-6
       PB:     978-0-7556-2213-9
       ePDF:   978-0-7556-2216-0
       eBook:  978-0-7556-2215-3

Series: Peace, Society, and the State in Africa

Typeset by RefineCatch Limited, Bungay, Suffolk

To find out more about our authors and books visit www.bloomsbury.com
and sign up for our newsletters.

*For my family*

# Contents

# Figures

# Acknowledgements

I would like to acknowledge my PhD supervisors, Prof. Maxi Schoeman and Prof. 'Funmi Olonisakin, for their mentorship and guidance. Without them, this book would not have been possible. Also, I wish to thank all my colleagues and friends who assisted with and facilitated my field research in Juba and Nairobi in varying ways. A special note of thanks is extended to Dr. Majak D'Agoot, Vicky Karimi, and Josephine Chandiru for their help in this process.

*The financial assistance of the National Institute for the Humanities and Social Sciences, in collaboration with the South African Humanities Deans Association, towards this research is hereby acknowledged. Opinions expressed and conclusions arrived at are those of the author and are not necessarily to be attributed to the NIHSS and SAHUDA.*

The financial assistance from the Carnegie Corporation of New York, through the African Leadership Centre, for my field research is also hereby acknowledged.

# List of Abbreviations

| | |
|---|---|
| AU | African Union |
| AUCISS | African Union Commission of Inquiry in South Sudan |
| CPA | Comprehensive Peace Agreement |
| CRA | Compensation and Reparation Authority |
| CTRH | Commission for Truth, Reconciliation and Healing |
| GoNU | Government of National Unity |
| HCSS | Hybrid Court for South Sudan |
| IGAD | Inter-Governmental Authority on Development |
| JIU | Joint Integrated Units |
| NCP | National Congress Party |
| NCRC | National Constitutional Review Commission |
| NDA | National Democratic Alliance |
| NIF | National Islamic Front |
| NLC | National Liberation Council |
| NSCC | New Sudan Council of Churches |
| NUP | National Unionist Party |
| PMHC | Political-Military High Command |
| SACDNU | Sudan African Closed Districts National Union |
| SANU | Sudan African National Union |
| SPLM/A | Sudan People's Liberation Movement/Army |
| SPLM-IO | Sudan People's Liberation Movement – In Opposition |
| SSDF | South Sudan Defence Forces |
| SSIM/A | South Sudan Independence Movement/Army |
| SSLA | South Sudan Liberation Army |
| SSLM | South Sudan Liberation Movement |
| SSNPS | South Sudan National Police Service |
| UN | United Nations |
| UNMISS | United Nations Mission in South Sudan |

# Introduction

## Fault and Fault Lines: Leadership and Identity in South Sudan

'Many people do things on the idea that tomorrow "I will go to another country".'[1]

For over sixty years the people of South Sudan have lived their lives in a near constant state of uncertainty – an uncertainty of livelihood, of governance and of self-definition. Almost fifty of those sixty years were a struggle for the right to define and govern themselves. But when that right was won in 2011, the people within the geographical space of South Sudan found themselves overburdened with the weight of decades of war and the immediate concerns of living. The question of what it means to be South Sudanese was never fully answered. With a troubled sense of belonging to the country, little sense of responsibility between state and citizens, and a bleak economic outlook, it is unsurprising that many South Sudanese are looking for their future elsewhere. But this puts the very notion of a South Sudanese nation in question.

The fault lines that have emerged (or rather re-emerged) since the outbreak of war in 2013 have raised questions on the viability of a South Sudanese nation, fears of a potential genocide, and accusations of ethnic warfare. The fault for this crisis has been laid at the feet of the political elite. How and why did a political, factionalist struggle at the centre degenerate into a civil war fought by a multitude of actors over a multitude of issues, though framed as an ethnic war between two groups? It is my assertion that the question of responsibility for the crisis and the role of identity have been oversimplified to dangerous levels. Framing the conflict as simply either a political dispute or an ethnic war is neither accurate nor helpful.

The political elite of South Sudan did not act in isolation and, more importantly, the leadership process that has produced this crisis is not new in South Sudan's nation-building journey. The leadership challenges facing the country today are similar, if not the same, to those facing southern Sudan since before Sudan's independence in 1957. Blaming individual leaders, without understanding the leadership process that has permitted them to loot, plunder and tear apart their country, gives one the impression that a change of personalities may bring about a change in situation. But this is not the case. Similarly, the identity fault lines emerging are more intricate than a case of historical, or even new, enmity between the Dinka and the Nuer. The patterns of group identification, inclusion and exclusion have been repeated in Sudan like fractals reflecting the same pattern at ever smaller levels, implying chaos but being systematic. Identity in South Sudan's conflict, then, cannot be understood purely as a case of ethnic enmity, nor can it be dismissed as a mere tool for mobilization.

Rather, the history of violence and continued conflict in South Sudan can be found in the contradictions between nationhood and statehood throughout the country's history. The 'national' identity of Sudan and South Sudan have been in constant dispute. This contributes to the narratives of Sudanese and South Sudanese wars as Arab/African or Dinka/Nuer. But the more pressing issue is not that these different identities exist in a collective geographical space, but how they interface with the state. The values, norms, ideologies and beliefs of the people of South Sudan have never been aligned with the state. In fact, collective action, will and responsibility have often been generated primarily in opposition to the state. Meanwhile, the state has been externally constituted, not only in terms of its colonial origin, but through the international community's peacebuilding endeavours. John Young (2021) details how one of the key failings of the peacebuilding process was the international community's assumptions that (1) Sudan's civil war was the result of two incompatible 'nations' in the north and the south, (2) the southern Sudanese people constituted a national collective, and (3) all would be resolved by imposing a Western-style nation state in the south.

This constant tension between social processes related to nationhood (i.e. the framing and reframing of identities, collective building of norms, ideologies and regimes for social governance, and collective action, will and responsibility) and the formal processes related to statehood (i.e. the building of institutions, making of constitutions and defining of territories) have contributed to the violent nature of South Sudan's nation-building process. The source of this misalignment can be found in the leadership process. This leadership process predates the current elite and has outlived many leaders. It is therefore not a simple matter of personality, but a deep-rooted system of engagement between the South Sudanese people and their elites. As this book will demonstrate, this system is created by an over-reliance on coercive and reward power, or identity-based sources of power, which originates from (1) a lack of mutuality between leaders and led, and (2) the interruption of the relationship between leaders and led by external actors.

## South Sudan: In search of nation and state

'Dinka is a name foreign to our language.' This is how a nineteenth-century Dinka reverend characterized the name used to label his identity group (Deng 1974: 108). Today, the Dinka, as one of the largest ethnic groups in South Sudan, have been placed on one side of a conflict that has been framed as approaching genocide.[2] Identity, especially identity used in war, is founded on a story of history. But any past that is called upon for contemporary action is obscured by the present. In the early years of conquest and kingdoms in Sudan, many Arabs sought shelter amongst southerners to escape the demands and constraints of statehood (Johnson 2013: 39). In the early twenty-first century, southern Sudanese were demanding statehood for themselves, and framing the Arab as an enemy. Nations and states change. They are built and broken through conquest, war, politics, social change and economic needs. They are not born out of nothing, and they are not 'eternal' (Hroch 1996: 61). But they are real.[3]

South Sudan's nation-building story begins with the early settlement of the geographical space known by this name, and continues today and in the future. The elements that make a nation – a national identity, a territory, political organization, collective will and collective responsibility – have evolved, shifted and conflicted with each other for centuries. The conversations[4] and contestations around these issues often turned violent. From the earliest cases of inter-communal violence, to anti-colonial and anti-conquest struggles, to civil war with Khartoum and civil war within South Sudan, war and conflict in South Sudan gravitates around an unanswered question: What does it mean to be South Sudanese? This has fuelled multiple debates around questions like: What are the physical and social boundaries of the nation? What identity markers distinguish members from outsiders, those deserving of protection and those not? What institutions and structures ensure societal order? What values and norms drive interpersonal action and ensure societal trust? Who determines all of this and how?

This last question is the main concern of this book. For example, who decides what identity markers matter, when and how? How is this negotiated? Did elites simply dictate the boundaries of Sudanese and South Sudanese society? In a way, yes. Much has been said of the colonial roots of the Sudanese conflict.[5] Of particular note is the colonial policy of separate administration between north and south. But other examples of elites driving (or attempting to drive) identity narratives include the Khartoum elite seeking to impose an Arabic Muslim identity across Sudan and the use of ethnicity in intra-South Sudanese conflicts as a mobilization tool. None of these elite efforts, in and of themselves, determined which identity fault lines would grow into irreconcilable and destructive divisions. Some watered existing seeds of communal identity, others provided the foundation and rationale for embedded identity narratives, while others were rejected outright, often violently. How and why an identity story gained traction was influenced by context, situation, lived experiences of the targeted audience, competing narratives, leaders' tools and tactics, and the relationship between the driver of an identity narrative and their sought followers.

Similarly, who determines what territory is included in the nation? Is territory given by right or taken by force? Is the idea of a homeland built from myth or is it a *de jure* administrative boundary imposed from above? In South Sudan, one sees examples of both. Again, the colonial legacy stands out. The decision to incorporate southern Sudan into an independent Sudanese state, despite previous plans to separate the two at independence (Nasong'o & Murunga 2005: 59) and amidst objections from southern Sudanese (Natsios 2012: 40), appears a clear case of artificial border making. The truth is not as simple, however, as will be explained in Chapters 1 and 2. Within South Sudan, ethnic groups are closely associated with certain geographical areas for historical reasons (Thomas 2015: Ch. 1), generating demands for federalism and identity-based administrative boundaries (Frahm 2015: 261; Pendle 2014: 237). Most importantly, in Sudan and South Sudan borders determine not only who is governed by which structures and who has access to which resources, but whether the leaders within a territory are big fish in a small sea or small fish in a big sea. As a result, leaders and their followers have used narratives of right to territory (sometimes factual, sometimes myth-based) or claimed territory by force, often times both. Importantly, this includes not only the right to reside in a specific territory but the right to rule it and how.

Who determines the structure and institutions of this rule? How does a political entity – be it a state or other form of autonomous rule and political organization – decide on the norms and rules governing a society and their enforcement? Are these negotiated or imposed? If they are imposed, by whom? If they are negotiated, how? Sudan and South Sudan have wrestled with these questions since independence, and even before. Key fault lines of note included the role of religion in the state, the language of the state, the dispersion of state resources, the share of power between the centre and periphery (e.g. federalism) and more. In addition, Sudan and South Sudan have faced dual and contradicting forces of national identity and statehood. Where the state tried to guide and mould national identity through its institutions and representatives' rhetoric, competing national identity narratives have often pushed back against the state or rejected it outright. Negotiating these forces proved difficult and could turn violent due to a problematic leadership process which did not permit an exchange of influence between the leaders within the state and the followers they were meant to represent.

Finally, who decides the direction a society will take and how? Who defines the norms and values that guide social life and ensure social trust and responsibility? Who ensures that there is unity within the nation and how? This has proven elusive in South Sudan and subject to rapid shifts based on elite interests. From the Mahdi revolution in in the nineteenth century, to the 2013 civil war in South Sudan, the ability to reach a collective decision and the will to pursue a representative agenda has been rare. Instances of collective cooperation are evident, within and across various identity fault lines. Members of southern Sudanese groups fought with the Mahdi against Turco-Egyptian rule (Collins 1962: 23, 29; Deng 1995: 10–11). Northern Sudanese political parties and militant groups cooperated with the SPLM/A during the Second Sudanese Civil War, through the National Democratic Alliance, for example (Deng 2006: 158; Nasong'o & Murunga 2005: 67). Southern Sudanese banded together against Khartoum in the struggle for independence. What these examples share is not a similar identity or value system that determines collective action, but shifting interests, usually of elites. Interests of both differing identity groups and leaders and followers converge and diverge throughout South Sudan's history. A common trend, however, is that when leader interests are met or change, follower interests are usually set aside by those with agency. The result is a society with shifting loyalties and responsibilities and people who most often turn to what is evident and most reliable in their daily lives – a smaller, narrower identity group rather than an abstract and absent nation and state.

## Understanding nationhood and leadership

As the newest country to enter the international community of states, South Sudan presents a unique and important opportunity to interrogate the idea of the 'nation state' – meant to form the building blocks of our international order. It is this very notion of the 'nation state' that has generated such violence and contestation. In Europe, sovereignty emerged before nationalism, and it was only when the people began to demand their inclusion in politics through the American and French revolutions that the nation state was born (Ringmar 2017: 12–14). The nation, then, emerged as a result of an internal (often violent) conversation between elites and the people about the relationship between the people (nation) and the state. In Sudan and South Sudan, this conversation was had between elites, and between elites and external actors.[6] How and why did this exclusion of the people in such a people-centred issue occur? The answer can be found in the leadership process within South Sudan. But first, a few points on how this book understands both the nation and leadership are necessary to understand the structure of subsequent chapters.

## The nation

What is the nation? What are its sources and how does it emerge? What is the relationship between nation and state? These are not resolved issues. Guibernau (2007: 14–17) categorizes the debates surrounding nationhood into three key issues: (1) whether nations are an ancient or more recent phenomenon, (2) whether they are natural or constructed, and (3) whether they are driven by the masses or elites. Many argue that a historical basis is critical for the emergence of nationhood (Guibernau 2007: 10, 14; Smith 1998: 196; Weber 1994: 22). This historical foundation, however, need not always be based on the objective truth, but can be constructed through myth building (Eley & Suny 1996: 8). Chapter 1 of this book will illustrate some of the historical foundations of South Sudan's nation-building myths, as well as some of the fissures in both Sudan and South Sudan's nationhood processes. It argues that the perceived identity fault lines are not as clear-cut as popularly perceived. Rather, these were dramatized by an elite-driven political process before and after Sudanese independence (as shown in Chapters 2 and 3).

The question of a nation's historical roots feeds directly into the question of its natural or constructed nature. This book takes the view that nations are socially constructed entities. They are 'imagined communities' (Anderson 2006). These social and mental constructs are built on certain attributes or identity markers – markers that can be subjective or objective, that can expand or contract, and that are relational (Guibernau 2007: 12; Horowitz 2001; Mann 2001: 208). This means that nations are defined by the myriad of relationships between attributes both within the nation (e.g. how racial and religious identity interact/overlap to form a national identity) and without (i.e. in contrast to others) (Eley & Suny 1996: 32; Guibernau 2007: 10; Hroch 1996: 61). This latter point – the ability of the nation to distinguish itself from others – is a critical yet problematic element of nationhood (Weber 1994: 21–2; Deutsch 2010: 11), as the example of South Sudan clearly demonstrates. The persistent use of 'the other' to manufacture nationhood and drive collective action would prove unsustainable (as Chapters 4 and 6 will demonstrate).

But who drives the nation-building process? Renan famously said that a nation is an 'everyday plebiscite' (Renan 1994: 17). In doing so, he not only rejected the prevailing notion that nations are natural entities but also brought into play the element of choice (Laitin 2007: 29–30). In other words, nations are chosen, not predestined, and a nation only exists when the defined members believe it exists (Norman 2006: 4–5). Who makes this choice and how? Nations do not spontaneously emerge from the masses.

Intellectual and political elites have often been viewed as critical in the emergence of nations. This can be through the political and instrumental use of identity for mobilization purposes (Guibernau 2007: 12; Hutchinson & Smith 1994: 47-48; Stewart 2008: 8), or the more critical role of building consciousness of national identity amongst a group of people (Eley & Suny 1996: 4, 14; Horowitz 2001: Chapter 1; Hroch 1996: 63; Laitin 2007: 41). On the other side of the coin, an elite analysis leaves much unexplained, particularly why identity – and especially ethnic and national identity – holds such emotive and mobilization power in the first place (Horowitz 2001; Hearn 2006: 55–61). The way in which identity is internalized and drives collective action is not sufficiently explained by an elite 'puppet masters' view (Guibernau 2007: 12). Rather, there is something between the top-down and bottom-up processes of nation-building that remains unresolved. You will see throughout this book how, in South Sudan, a disjuncture emerged between elite-level conversations around Sudanese and South Sudanese national identities and the lived experiences of identity amongst the people.

Identity and nationhood, then, is understood as complex, subjective, relational, fluid, contextual and constructed. When such a concept is linked to the equally complex, fluid and contextual processes of war and conflict, teasing out the relationship between the two can be quite difficult and subject to reductionist thinking. Identity difference does not cause war, this we know.[7] War is too complex to be reduced to such a cause and identity too fluid and subjective to hold the burden of war all on its own. The Sudanese wars were not about an incompatibility between Arab-Muslim and African-Christian identities. But when thousands, hundreds of thousands and even millions are killed in a genocide or ethnic cleansing, we cannot dismiss the importance of identity either. While 'ethnic conflict' may be comparatively rare in relation to the number of plural societies who live in peace, and the concept itself disputed (Gilley 2004; Laitin 2007: 9–11), the atrocities committed when identity-related conflicts do occur bring to bear the importance of understanding these conflicts (Brubaker & Laitin 1998: 424; Mann 2001: 207).

The immense suffering caused by identity-related killings and human rights abuses in South Sudan are not easily explained away by the notion of political disputes.

Nation-building and war often intersect. Von Bogdandy et al. (2005: 586) defines nation-building as 'a process of collective identity formation with a view to legitimising public power within a given territory', while Mylonas (2012) defines it as 'the process through which governing elites make the boundaries of the state and nation coincide'. Nation-building, then, is by nature a contentious and often violent exercise because of its intersection of the political and social identity. This book uses five elements of nationhood, found in the various definitions of the nation in the literature.[8] It argues that the more contradictions that emerge between these elements, the more violent the nation-building process is likely to become. In the case of South Sudan, the contradictions abound, and were driven by the historical leadership process in the society. The five elements are:

a) National identity: This can be determined by a range of attributes that provide shared norms, beliefs and values.
b) Territory: A nation requires a territorial link of some sort, whether a perceived homeland or state borders.
c) Political organization: A nation lays claim to some form of political organization and self-government.
d) Collective will: A nation has the ability to form a collective will.[9]
e) Collective responsibility: A nation's members hold a collective responsibility that lays certain rights and responsibilities on its members and ensures mutual trust.

It must be said that this is an ideal type and that few, if any, nations will fulfil all these obligations and contain coherence amongst them. These five elements are seen to emerge in three key processes: identity construction (element a), statehood and state-building (elements b and c), and the formation of collective will and collective responsibility (elements d and e). Of these various elements, some are easier to achieve than others. For example, fostering loyalty and trust amongst group members and between group members and the government is far more difficult than formalizing the state, its borders and its institutions. Ensuring collective will and building a sense of belonging through identity are similarly much more difficult than establishing a *de jure* state. While the eventual creation of the South Sudanese state as a legal, sovereign entity was not easy, the subsequent war shows there were other similarly pertinent but more complex processes that also needed to be instituted. Indeed, the imposition of a Western-styled state is one of the greatest failings of the peacebuilding process (Young 2021: 153–4). Even harder still is to get all five elements to complement, rather than contradict, one another.

## Leadership

Many observers and commentators of South Sudan's current crisis choose to place blame on the country's leaders (Interview B 2017; Interview C 2017; Interview D 2017; Kisiangani 2015: 3). Fault can be given to the nefarious practices of corruption and patronage, power-hungry leaders and the all-encompassing but vague concept of 'lack of political will', but placing blame on individual leaders is reductionist at best. The violent trajectory of South Sudan's nation-building story crosses several generations and various leaders. The leadership problem that tends towards violent nation-building is more systemic than the 'good' or 'bad' characters of select individuals who find their way to positions of power. What structures exist that permit this situation? To understand this, and thereby better understand the fault of leaders in the ongoing conflict, we must understand leadership as a process. Leaders do not act in isolation. Leadership is defined as a relationship between leaders, their followers and the situation or context, allowing for an understanding of leadership that is not limited to an individual (Pierce & Newstrom 2011: 4–6). This is the leadership process.

The relationships between leaders and followers are particularly useful in understanding the nation-building project and its relationship with violence and peace. First, the way in which influence is exchanged is important in understanding where leadership occurs, between who, and what pathways of influence are used to build and frame the nation. If this exchange of influence does not include all members intended to be within the nation, then it is likely that conflict will arise, as the case of South Sudan will illustrate. It is crucially important to note that peaceful nation-building requires collective will and collective responsibility, and this can only be achieved if all members of the proposed nation feel part of this process, requiring the exchange of influence to flow both ways. A two-way influence is important between leaders and followers (Graen & Uhl-Bien 1995: 223). In other words, followers also influence and shape the leadership process (Oc & Bashshur 2013: 919–20). Throughout this book, the ways in which influence was exchanged or hampered between leaders and followers, and the effect this had on war and nation-building, is evident.

The nature of this exchange of influence is often determined by the degree of mutuality between leaders and followers. Mutuality refers to the presence of a common situation confronting both leaders and followers, who therefore hold a common goal or purpose and exchange influence in a meaningful manner based on common values and visions (Bass 2008: 21; Burns 2012: 10, 13–14, 20–1; Northouse 2016: 6). This mutuality, however, requires more than a convergence of interests. Interests are transitory, and mutuality requires a stronger foundation. In South Sudan, this lack of mutuality becomes evident every time the situation changes, such as after the 1972 Peace Agreement and after secession.

Another important determinant of how influence is exchanged is that of power. French and Raven identify five sources of power: referent power (followers follow because they identify, or want to identify, with the leader); expert power (followers follow because the leader is competent in the field or situation at hand); legitimate power (followers follow because of 'internalized values' that legitimize a leader's right to rule and obligate others to follow); reward power (followers are enticed to comply and follow through a system of rewards); and coercive power (leaders use force and sanctions to gain followers' compliance and loyalty) (French & Raven 2011: 136–41). The use of power in South Sudan's nation-building project is extremely important. Leaders have often relied on coercive or reward power, due to the lack of mutuality, which has proven unsustainable and ineffective in embedding any true sense of nationhood.

In addition to this, the leadership process allows for a situational understanding of leadership. Leadership does not occur in a vacuum. Leaders are influenced by and a product of the situation they, and their followers, face (Hollander & Julian 2011: 15). Their response to this situation also creates a feedback loop which alters or influences the situation (Pierce & Newstrom

2011: 5). This is why this book takes a historical view of the South Sudanese conflict. The challenges of today are viewed and formed through previous events and leadership responses. The understanding of the nation and its future have been directed by previous interpretations of nationhood.

A final note must be made on the nature of the leadership discussed in this book. As the focus remains on understanding the nation-building process, and South Sudan's violent contestation between nation and state, the leaders discussed are primarily those who operate at this level: the politico-military elite. Of course, in a context like South Sudan, other types of leaders, such as traditional and religious leaders, play an important role in societal relations. These are primarily discussed in terms of how they related with the 'national' or 'state' leadership, or when their actions influenced nation-building processes.

## Chaos or pattern: The fractal-like nature of South Sudan's nation-building trajectory

While South Sudan's experience, especially post-2013, appears to reflect a chaotic spiral of disintegration, I argue that the current crisis is the product of a repeating leadership and nation-building pattern. The various contradictions within the Sudanese and subsequent South Sudanese nation that have resulted in conflict, violence and war are repeating at ever more localized levels. This is best illustrated using the geometric principle of fractals, particularly Koch's snowflake (see Figure 1).

In the illustration, I show how contradictions between the various nation-building processes have resulted in a move further and further away from broader, cohesive social communities to ever smaller groupings, often in a violent manner. Examples from the Sudanese case are given to demonstrate this. The ideal nation-building process is one where a leadership process, based on sustainable forms of influence and mutuality, is able to manage these tensions and contradictions between identity, state and the moral community, and thereby keep the nation relatively stable (see Figure 2). Throughout this book I will illustrate that the source of the contradictions in South Sudan that leads to this fragmentation lies in a leadership process that relies on coercion and reward power to impose broader national and state visions, which is

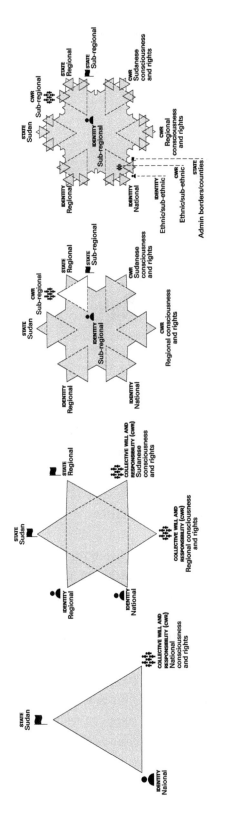

**Conctradictions**

**STATE**
Separate development between Northern and Southern Sudan.

**IDENTITY, STATE & CWR**
'Sudanism' vision vs. separatist goal in Southern Sudan under Garang

**IDENTITY & STATE**
Unitary Arab/Islamic state imposed over a racially and religiously diverse population at Sudanese independence.

**IDENTITY & CWR**
Separate rights provided to Muslim and non-Muslim citizens in pre-colonial era.

**IDENTITY & CWR**
SPLM/A support determined by sub-regions within Southern Sudan during second civil war.

**IDENTITY & STATE**
Division of Southern Sudan into three states during interim period and 23 states after ARCSS sparking overlapping border and identity conflicts

**IDENTITY & CWR**
SPLM/A split in 1990s and post-secession, resulting in more localised factions and conflicts.

**IDENTITY & CWR**
County and local border disputes, coupled with ethnic identity.

**IDENTITY & STATE**
Use of ethnic militias in national political conflict.

**Figure 1:** The fractal nature of the Sudanese and South Sudanese nations, using Koch's snowflake

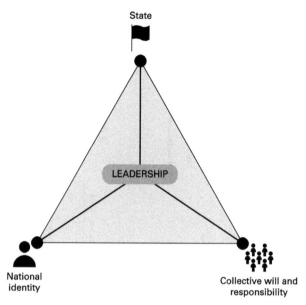

**Figure 2:** The 'ideal' nation-building process

unsustainable; while prototype leadership, based on identity (Hogg 2001), fuels greater identification with the local rather than the national.

## A note on methodology and structure

This book stems from my doctoral research conducted between 2015 and 2018 and is based on an extensive review of the literature, archival research, and interviews with members and former members of government, civil society members, and members of international governmental organizations, conducted in Juba and Nairobi in June 2017. The book traces South Sudan's history from its pre-colonial era to the 2015 Agreement on the Resolution of the Conflict in the Republic of South Sudan. Chapters are divided into specific periods in South Sudan's history, and each period is discussed within the context of the key components of nationhood (identity, statehood, and collective will and responsibility), followed by a discussion of the role of the leadership process in these issues. As the reader moves through the chapters, they will see the repetitive and fractal nature of the leadership process, war and nation-building in South Sudan.

## 'All along living a refugee life'[10]

As one respondent lamented, South Sudan has not known peace since 1955, and its people have been 'living a refugee life' throughout that period (Interview D 2017). The country's quest for nationhood began centuries ago and has been marred by violence. This book therefore takes a chronological view of South Sudan's leadership and nationhood trajectory and traces key moments of identity formation, state-building and collective will and the moments where these failed or shifted. I will demonstrate the key leadership patterns that have emerged and entrenched themselves in South Sudan's nation-building project and how these patterns have contributed to the continued leaning towards violent nation-building. Most importantly, a crucial disconnect in the leadership process has resulted in action being driven by momentary intersections of interests, while mutuality and exchanges of influence are found between elites and with external actors, rather than between leaders and their people, or between the state and society.

## Notes

1   Interview B 2017.
2   In November 2016 the UN Special Adviser on the Prevention of Genocide, Adama Dieng warned of a potential genocide in South Sudan. See United Nations (UN) 2016.
3   The debate on the origins of nations is an immense one that cannot be discussed in depth here. For further reading on this topic see Smith 1999; Guibernau 2007; Hearn 2006; Weber 1994.
4   See Olonisakin, Kifle & Muteru (2021) for a discussion on 'conversation' in nation-building, peacebuilding and state-building.
5   See Copnall 2014: 2; Young 2012: 3; Idris 2005; Johnson 2011a; Nasong'o & Murunga 2005: 58–9.

6  It has been pointed out that one of the gravest assumptions made by the international community was that the SPLM/A represented the broader southern Sudanese population (Young 2021: 150–2).

7  See Laitin 2007 and Gilley 2004 for a discussion on this.

8  The following elements are drawn from and found in definitions from the following sources: Smith 1998; Laitin 2007; Deutsch 2010; Weber 1994; Guibernau 2007; Eley & Suny 1996; Hearn 2006: 31; Miller 2000: 127; Norman 2006: 5; Ting 2008: 457; Weilenmann 2010: 33, Anderson 2006: 6–7; Breuilly 1993: 1, Gellner 1983; Mazrui & Tidy 1984.

9  Weilenmann (2010: 43) defines collective will as a society's ability to reach collective decisions and act upon them.

10 Interview D 2017.

# Part One

# Origins: The Southern Sudan as People, Polity and 'Problem' (*c.* 1821–1983)

1

# Conquest and Colonization

## Introduction

The question of South Sudan's troubled journey towards nationhood must start with its first encounters with the modern state. As a frontier region to various early Sudanic states, there was little driving the formation of a strong, centralized state. In fact, the region became a haven to escape the state (Johnson 2013: 39). Diverse communities and groups lived within different governance systems based on varying social, economic and geographic needs – from decentralized, loosely knit groups governed by social norms and traditional practices, to more centralized kingdoms with hierarchical political structures (Johnson 2011a: 11–13; Thomas 2015: Ch. 1). But, with the encroachment of the modern state in the form of Turco-Egyptian conquest in 1820, Mahdist rule from 1883 to 1898 and Anglo-Egyptian colonialism from 1899 to 1956, a tension arose between identity, later nationhood and the state.

This tension was born out of opportunities the colonial state provided to elites and the restrictions it placed on the populace. It manifested in the way groups and communities were defined and bounded for political purposes and in the way policies and institutions were developed in service of external powers. This is the origin of the fractured mutuality between leaders and followers in South Sudan, preventing the development of a social contract. Throughout this book, we will see how leaders within South Sudan have been steered more by their relationship with the 'external' than with their purported followers. The lack of influence between leaders and followers encourages the use of narrow identity markers to garner support. These narrow identity markers also find their origin in South Sudan's early history.

## Identity construction: The birth of 'the other'

Sudan has variously been portrayed as a bridge or a frontier between the Arab and African world (Copnall 2014: 6–11; Nasong'o & Murunga 2005: 57–9; Sidahmed & Sidahmed 2005: 8). But to what degree is this a truthful representation of the Sudanese identity landscape? How did the complex social landscape of early Sudan, characterized by a multitude of overlapping and multilayered identities, come to be reduced to a binary story of north/south, Arab/African, Muslim/Christian? This dialectic narrative and its associated myth-building fuelled many of the perceptions that supported conflict and war between northern and southern Sudan. How and why was this dialectic formed, and what role did leadership play? Three key processes – migration and trade, slavery, and colonialism – interacted in complex ways, creating the foundation for this narrative.

First, migratory and trade patterns between today's northern Sudanese Arabs and southern Sudanese Africans date back to the seventh century (Iyob & Khadiagala 2006: 22). Yet, as state power emerged, an increasingly distinctive Arab and Muslim identity was formed, in parallel with the Islamization of the state; political, spiritual and social legitimacy and power became intertwined with 'Arab' and Muslim identity (Deng 1995: 35–68; Johnson 2013: 38–9). Genealogies, often stretched or interrupted, were used to trace Islamic and Arabic heritage to build this legitimacy (Deng 1995: 40; Johnson 2013: 38).

Leadership was then determined through a process of prototype leadership. This leadership theory argues that group members who are seen to best represent the typical and most valued characteristics of the social identity are perceived to have more influence, through referent power and other social identification processes (Hogg 2001). Political and spiritual influence was given to those seen to represent the 'ideal' of the identity group. But the cost of this prototype leadership, as well as attempts to represent the 'ideal' Arab, was to create a false distinction between Arab and African. Also, while Arabic descent was used to signal social status, the racial distinction in Sudan was much more blurred due to intermarriage and migration (Idris 2005: 28). More importantly, it created a sense that one was superior to the other, with greater right to political power.

Slavery was another process that fuelled this distinction and hierarchy of identities. In 1963, William Deng and Joseph Oduhu, leaders of the Sudan African Closed Districts National Union (SACDNU) liberation movement, wrote:

> It is unfortunate that half a century of Anglo-Egyptian rule did not succeed in dissipating the impressions left by the slave trade on Northern and Southern Sudanese alike; the former tend to regard themselves as born masters, and the latter surround themselves in a stockade of suspicion which has proved to be well founded.
>
> Oduhu & Deng 1963: 11

Slavery began in northern Sudan when smaller kingdoms would raid hinterlands in the north, and to a limited degree the south, for slaves (Johnson 2011a: 2–3). As the state became more prominent, slave soldiers were used to exercise and maintain state power (Johnson 2011a: 3–4). At first, slavery was less clearly aligned with racial and religious distinctions, with Muslims also being enslaved (Idris 2005: 27–8). But this would shift as Islamic states used *Shari'a* law to distinguish 'between "enslavable" infidels and those who belong to the *umma*' (Iyob & Khadiagala 2006: 25) and non-Muslim territory became the raiding ground for slaves (Johnson 2013: 42).

Slavery's legacy was a narrative of superiority in the north and oppression in the south. Those of African descent were freely referred to as '*abeed*', meaning slave, well into the twentieth century (Deng 1995: 5; Copnall 2014: 24–5). Northern Arabs were seen as oppressors. They would be referred to as '*Jallaba*', a term for Arabic traders that would evolve into a derogatory term for northerners as a whole (Young 2005: 536). This sense of 'otherness' between northern and southern groups was largely subjective. Northerners of the twentieth century are more likely to have descended from slaves than southerners (Deng 1995: 5–6). Those who suffered the fate of slavery were often assimilated into northern Sudanese culture through conversion to Islam and the learning of Arabic (Sikainga 2000: 35). As a result, former slaves held a complex and ambivalent identity that shared with other non-Arab groups a history of oppression and discrimination, but also provided them with greater opportunities than other said groups (Sikainga 2000: 35). As one respondent indicated, 'those taken into slavery became elites themselves' (Interview F 2017).

The same challenges of subjectivity that exist between north and south exist between different identity groups in the south. The various identity groups in southern Sudan are diverse in political, social and economic structure. Colonial structures attempted to generate distinct lines between these groups using colonial ethnic interpretations (e.g. pastoralist vs sedentary groups, centralized vs decentralized groups, 'warrior' groups, administrative groups, etc.) (Collins 1962: 4–5; Johnson 2011a: 12–15, 17–18). In reality, however, the distinctions between these groups are not as clear-cut as colonial administrators perceived.

For example, while ethnic groups are often distinguished by their economic activities (e.g. Dinka, Nuer and Murle as pastoralists and others as agrarian), there are those within the traditionally pastoralist groupings that also engage in agricultural practices (Thomas 2015: Ch. 1). Another distinction is that of geography or language. Certain groups were largely associated with certain territories or regions, and remain so (Johnson 2013: 54; Interview B 2017; Thomas 2015: Ch. 1). The previously fluid territorial boundaries between these groups were often arbitrarily assigned by the colonial government, and people resettled to make these regions more homogenous (Justin & De Vries 2019: 66). Furthermore, the word 'tribe' itself (often used to identify these various ethnic groups) has no clear equivalent in South Sudanese languages (Thomas 2015: Ch. 1).

As such, fluid identities within Sudan as a whole were crystallized and demarcated through a series of processes related to migration, state formation, conflict and contestation. The dominant narrative of slavery and oppression has thereby come to define the shared memory and history of southern Sudan, which would go on to play a central role in constructing the southern identity. At the same time, similar processes at the local level were embedding identity distinctions that would create a fractal-like identity landscape, prone to conflict at multiple levels (community, regional and national).

## Statehood in early Sudan

Modernist nationalism scholars view nationhood and statehood as closely interlinked. Gellner (1983) argued that nations primarily emerged out of the modern industrial process, while other scholars linked these modernization processes closely with the state (Hearn 2006: 74–80). In short, it was the state that gave birth to the nation. The modernization processes of mass media, language, education, civil society, modern militaries and bureaucracies generated a sense of cohesion and shifted the relationship between government and people.[1] Yet the state-formation process in Sudan tells a different story.

A fundamental challenge for future nation-building in Sudan would be finding an aspect of Sudanese society which would act as the centre of gravity for political thought, consciousness and action. This is where agency is very important. In a complex society such as Sudan, leaders, as the managers of meaning, can influence the narrative that drives a society in one direction or the other. However, they are also restricted by changing situations and existing sentiments amongst the population. The trajectory of state formation in Sudan will illustrate that leaders often centred their ideologies for the future Sudanese state on narrow political interests rather than broader societal goals. This stemmed from an inherent lack of mutuality between a very small intelligentsia and a large, diverse populace. One of these centres of gravity was religion, particularly Islam, which was able to transcend ethnic groups, but only in the north (Khalid 2003: 40). As a result, a significant portion of the future Sudanese state was excluded from the foundational ideology of that state. The future leadership of Sudan would embed rather than shift this ideology. For now, a brief overview of early state formation processes is illuminating.

Sudan's early history of statehood entails the presence of several smaller kingdoms and states. Through commerce, exchange and migratory patterns, many of these states' leaders converted to Islam and began to adopt Islamic legal principles (Johnson 2013: 38). The Funj kingdom in particular (located in central Sudan) was one of the first to institutionalize Islam as part of the state, also beginning a long tradition of identity-based politics (Idris 2005: 26). At the same time, a distinction emerged between states and their peripheries. Different legal frameworks, rights and social status were applied based on one's territorial origins, generating different experiences and relationships with the state (Johnson 2013: 38–40). This 'centre/periphery' distinction would continue into the modern era, hindering the development of a social contract between state and citizen, and mutuality between leaders and the populace.

Southern Sudan, however, remained outside the reach of any state for much of its history, in large part due to the resistance provided by the Shilluk and

Dinka (Johnson 2013: 41). It was only with the conquests of the nineteenth and twentieth centuries that this began to change. Prior to becoming an independent state, the conquest and centralization of state control in Sudan took the form of three key phases. The first was the Turco-Egyptian conquest that lasted from 1821 to 1885, when it was replaced by the Mahdist government of 1885 to 1898. Both governments had very little presence in what is South Sudan today (Arnold & LeRiche 2013: 9). Yet, the Turco-Egyptian regime reached further into southern Sudan than any of the previous Sudanic states, opening the door to greater economic exploitation and slave raiding, and setting the foundation for a north/south divide (Johnson 2013: 41–2).

Further complicating the state-identity landscape was the use of slave soldiers as a tool of coercion in an oppressive state (Sikainga 2000: 24). This policy of using slave soldiers significantly increased the slave trade in southern Sudan during the Turco-Egyptian rule (Dekmejian & Wyszomirski 1972: 201). In the West, the military has often acted as a focal point of nation-building (Mann 1995). Naturally, the use of slave soldiers would not result in the creation of patriots. At the same time, being part of the military influenced their social identification processes. While they lacked loyalty to specific regimes, they were socialized by the military to 'identify themselves with the government', and were also distinct from the society they would enter upon leaving the military (Sikainga 2000: 24). In this case, then, a key state institution served to generate distinctions amongst the society rather than resulting in a more cohesive populace. In this example, we see how the early leadership processes, reliant on coercive power rather than mutuality, would serve to embed societal fissures across social status, territorial origin, race and religion.

Meanwhile, dissatisfaction with Turco-Egyptian rule resulted in an uprising led by Muhammed Ahmed Ibn Abdalla in 1885, and a short-lived theocratic Mahdist state. Confronted with a situation of economic decline, social upheaval caused by migration, and religious conflict, the Mahdi promoted a religious message of Islamic puritanism and, eventually, *jihad* to his in-group followers[2] (Dekmejian & Wyszomirski 1972: 201–6). The Mahdi, however, was able to adjust his message to the needs and beliefs of his audience, developing a wide support base in northern Sudan at least (Dekmejian & Wyszomirski 1972: 206, 210–11). This uprising was joined by southern groups such as the Dinka, Nuer and Shilluk, out of frustration with the government's oppressive nature (Collins

1962: 23, 29–30). The Mahdist government would turn out to be oppressive towards southerners as well (Arnold & Le Riche 2013: 9). This cooperation was not the result of the 'Mahdist influence', but an alliance against a common enemy (Collins 1962: 29–30). Such transactional type of leadership[3] founded on transitory goals against a common enemy, without a common vision driven by mutuality, foreshadows the experience of the South Sudanese struggle and post-independence war.

What this event and other, albeit rare, instances of cooperation between northerners and southerners illustrates is the flexibility of identity and its relative animosities. Many of the animosities that would follow between northerners and southerners were instigated by certain situations and exacerbated by leaders who saw these situations as opportunities to further political interests. However, in situations like this, where mutual interests were present amongst diverse followers, collective action was possible. It is also important, however, to note that most instances of mutual cooperation across perceived identity divisions were in opposition to the state. This indicates that Sudan has always struggled to find a system of political organization (statehood) suited to the society.

The brief life of the Mahdist state was followed by the Anglo-Egyptian condominium. Many of the post-colonial challenges of Sudan and the current problems in South Sudan have been traced to this period. The administrative policies of the British are said to have contributed to the divisions not only between north and south but also amongst southerners themselves. The first is often attributed to the Southern Closed Districts Ordinances Act, which prohibited contact, cultural exchange and trading between north and south (Nasong'o & Murunga 2005: 58–9). Another method of separating northern and southern Sudan was through creating two separate legal communities, one influenced by *Shari'a* law (in the north) and the other by customary law (in the south) (Pendle 2019: 36). The original purpose was to unite southern Sudan with British East Africa, but this did not happen at independence (Nasong'o & Murunga 2005: 59). Of course, another reason for this separation was due to British fears of southern Sudan being influenced by increasingly nationalist and revolutionary leanings in Egypt and Sudan (Pendle 2019: 35–6).

One respondent identified this moment as the start of the rift between northern and southern Sudan and an orientation away from a growing Islamic and Arabic culture in the south (Interview A 2017). In other words, British colonialism can be perceived as an interruption of an Islamization and Arabization process that was already occurring organically in the south. Similarly, development initiatives (both political and economic) were targeted to the north's riverain core, largely excluding the south (Young 2012: Introduction). The development of state and governing institutions was deliberately neglected (Interview C 2017). Yet, some have cautioned against overstating the role of the British attempts at state engineering in Sudan's identity crisis (Arnold & LeRiche 2013: 2–3, 8–9). In this argument, the narrative of an imposition of a single state over two clearly separate entities is exaggerated and neglects the long history of contact between northern and southern Sudan (Arnold & LeRiche 2013: 2, 8–9). Similarly, it has been argued that the Closed Districts Act was never fully implemented (Arnold & LeRiche 2013: 8–9).

Concurrently, British indirect rule identified and cemented boundaries within southern Sudan. Between 1910 and 1930, this type of rule relied on colonial interpretations of southern Sudan's ethnic landscape to impose administrative structures, resulting in stricter boundaries and more centralized administrative structures than those traditionally held in some communities (Poggo 2009: 22–3; Zambakari 2015: 73–4). This is evident in the institution of separate legal codes for different ethnic groups ostensibly based on said group's customary laws, though traditional variance of laws within ethnic groups was suppressed in order to create more unified legal ethnic communities (Pendle 2019: 37–40). As such, these identities shifted from primarily cultural and social identities to political identities (Idris 2005: 23). A natural inability to exert influence over a population due to its external nature resulted in a 'divide and rule' situation under British colonialism – a strategy that would not be forgotten by Khartoum. In the absence of a reliable and sustainable source of power, state control was maintained by actively preventing the development of a national identity. But this generated a fissure between state and citizen, and between citizens themselves, that would hamper the social contract for generations to come.

This ethnicization of the state translated into the southern armed forces. Originally, in the Turco-Egyptian and Anglo-Egyptian condominium, military recruitment centred around ethnic stereotypes of good 'warriors', often belonging to non-Arab groups, but this created fears in the British colonial government that the military was leading to a re-socialized, de-ethnicized military that could promote Egyptian nationalism (Sikainga 2000 26–7). While this type of military-born nationalism was a critical component of how the nation state emerged in Europe (Mann 1995), it was not conducive to the aims of a colonial government. So, this system was replaced with 'territorial units', including the Equatorial Corps in southern Sudan, which divided companies and units according to ethnicity and stationed them in their own communities (Poggo 2009: 30–1; Sikainga 2000: 27–30). This furthered the problem of colonial governments creating *de jure* 'states' on the continent that did not match identified and constructed 'nations'. More than this, the state-building and nation-building processes directly contradicted each other.

Another key component of both state-building and nation-building is education. Diverse education policies would result in a populace with differing perceptions of and relationships with the central state. Northern and southern education systems under the colonial regime differed in terms of organization (in the south, education was delivered in more ad hoc form through the use of missionaries, compared to a more centralized education system in the north), language (Arabic in the north and a combination of English and local languages in the south), and purpose (to educate skilled workers and administrators, along with minimal education of masses, in the north, and to spread Christianity and educate a small number of administrators for the colonial administration in the south) (Deng & Daly 1989: 167–70; Deng 1995: 19; Seri-Hersch 2017: 4–5; Sharkey 2008: 33). Therefore, this education provided little in the way of nation-building as it (1) did not target the broader population but only a select few, and (2) did not aim to promote a collective ideology through, for example, educating southerners on a shared history or developing a national language.

A small community of southern leaders with a southern consciousness did emerge in this space, nevertheless, and would go on to represent the south at the national level (Howell 1973: 168–9). This, however, created a gap between the future leaders and followers in South Sudan. A quote by Andrew Wieu, discussing a dispute between the students of his school and its headmaster regarding regulations compelling students to wear their traditional dress, is illuminating:

The students argued that 'we should not be halfway between our people and civilisation. Either we are recognised as mixed or left to be like our people, but we should not be kept halfway, neither with civilisation nor completely with the traditional way of life.'

Deng & Daly 1989: 170

What is of interest here is that the students at a very young age began to identify themselves as different and apart from their fellow southerners, albeit not completely separate.

The purpose of the above overview is to illustrate two key points. The first is a theoretical observation: state action and structure can influence the ways in which identity is constructed. It can either promote a national identity (as seen in Europe) or fragment the society into smaller sub-national identities. Sudan's history illustrates the enduring effects of identity divisions, however false, that are constructed by processes of state formation. However, the story of South Sudan also illustrates how imposed state structures can be rejected by its citizens. The imposition of a state therefore does not equate to the building of a nation and if the leaders of said state hold little influence over the populace and are required to use coercion to do so, it is likely that the narrative underpinning said state will be unsustainable.

As the state tended to be external to southern Sudan, perceptions of other groups and the state became conflated in the minds of many southerners. This is illustrated in the following quote:

*Tueny* could be a white man, an Egyptian, or a Northern Sudanese; he could be any person who wore clothes and carried a gun or had government authority over others ... It made me bitter against whoever was in charge of what you call the government, whether white men or other men. I didn't have any idea in my mind as to the racial identity of the government at that time. But later on, I learned that the government was British.

Deng & Daly 1989: 165–6

This sheds light on the perception of foreigners and the state in colonial southern Sudan — namely that they were synonymous. In this instance, distrust of 'the other' was first developed due to lived experiences, after which racial identities were superimposed on the oppressors. In other words, southern Sudan has faced oppression under the state by various regimes of different social and group identities. However, as the conflict would progress, historical and contemporary perception of the enemy would be framed as the Arab North, reducing several complex processes of oppressive state formation and exploitative economic practices to an oversimplified and constructed identity division.

One can contrast this state-building and nation-building process with that in Europe as theorized by modernist scholars. The notion of the state being instrumental in the formation of a cohesive and conscious nation does not hold in southern Sudan, where the state-building processes, driven by external actors, and its accompanying institutions promoted the development of separate nations within one future state. Instead of creating a sense of 'us' and 'them' between nation states (as seen in Europe), the state-building process created insiders and outsiders within the state itself.

## Challenges for collective will and collective responsibility in early Sudan

Collective will and collective responsibility in nation-building are both important and elusive. Determining the level of support for political actions taken a century ago, and the degree to which group members felt loyalty to one another, is difficult. However, some tentative assertions can be made by an analysis of known events. First, the people of southern Sudan were largely isolated geographically, economically and politically until the Ottoman Empire began to reach into Sudan (Poggo 2009: 21). Such a context and situation required little collective will or action amongst southerners as a whole. It is possible that since the situation did not demand a unified response, no sense of unity emerged, and no leader either to build such unity. This would change as the situation changed. Even then, collective action did not come easily.

Situational leadership argues that leaders emerge in response to a problem, and those that emerge are those best suited to address that situation (Murphy 1941: 674). When foreign powers began to infiltrate what is South Sudan today, some communities would often collude with these powers to invade other communities whom they perceived as the 'traditional enemy' (Interview F 2017). In addition, these imperial conquests were not 'felt across the country at the same time' (Interview F 2017). In other words, the context was not favourable for the emergence of a leader who would drive collective will.

As seen above, the notion of Arab in Sudan is more a historical than racial distinction (Sawant 1998: 345). In this case, then, one of the key attributes that would be used to distinguish between northerners and southerners is largely subjective. It could therefore be argued that the immense loyalty given to these groups, and the distaste of 'the other', is largely non-rational. Yet, as will be shown in the following chapters, the distinction between Arab and African was engrained through a leadership process in which leaders often responded to situations out of an interest in their own political needs or that of a select group of followers, rather than a mutuality with their followers or the society as a whole. As discussed, relations between Muslims and non-Muslims during this early period were not inherently conflictual and were even cooperative at times. For example, during the rise of the early Sudanic states, Muslim pastoralists averse to state control would seek refuge with non-Muslims beyond the reach of the state, including the Dinka (Johnson 2013: 39). In addition, northerners and southerners banded together to overthrow the Turco-Egyptian presence in Sudan (Deng 1995: 10–11). Thus, cooperation and collective action was often dependent on context and the situation to which people were responding.

## Conquest and colonization in early Sudan: The leadership challenge

This historical context, of a subjective, constructed but deeply felt fissure between social identities, provided a ripe ground for leaders to emerge using manufactured mutuality. Colonial economic and political structures would go on to generate a deep divide between the centres and the peripheries, urban and rural, formally educated and uneducated. The mutuality between the urban, intelligentsia, political class and majority rural population would be broken. How does one mobilize support in such a case? Identity, based on these early divisions, would provide a quick and easy way to order the political space and narrative.

Prototype leadership would become a key form of leadership emergence. This created a feedback loop in which leaders were chosen using identity-based criteria, who would go on to further embed identity-based societal boundaries. Hogg (2001: 194–5) also identifies three 'pitfalls' of prototype leadership, some of which would come to characterize the leadership process in Sudan and South Sudan. These are:

1. The 'distancing' of leaders from followers once they are placed within a position of power, leading to abuse and the use of coercive tactics to maintain power.
2. Leadership based on prototypicality rather than leaders with the most appropriate solutions and decisions for the situation.
3. A tendency to exclude minorities from leadership and 'hierarchical leadership structures' prone to abuse. (Hogg 2001: 194–5)

All three of these trends will be observed in the South Sudanese case in the subsequent chapters.

Another key factor in leadership emergence was the situational context. The Mahdist rebellion of 1885 was able to generate cooperation between a northern leader and southern peoples by manufacturing short-term mutuality in opposition to a common enemy. Once the situation had changed, and the moment had passed, the brief instance of mutuality was lost. No lasting sense of common identity, destiny or purpose was formed in that situation.

Sudan's case illustrates one of constant tension between the nation and the state. As will be shown throughout this book, leaders' response to this situation was often to either try and alter the state or alter the nation. One or the other, however, would often be rejected by either all or a significant group of followers. In each case, the seed for future contestation of the state or the nation was laid in these responses. After Sudanese independence, northern leaders tried to alter the nation through Arabization while southern leaders sought to alter the state borders or structure. This context resulted in an untenable situation as 'othering' practices became the norm in discussions surrounding the state. In Sudan's early years, the rejection of the state by smaller identity groups was the norm, particularly in the south (Gray 1971: 1; Poggo 2009: 25). This was largely due to the external nature of the state, however, resulting in a situation where state and nation were incompatible.

Local leaders and followers, then, were often in agreement when challenging the state. However, external rulers (particularly the colonial government) were able to leverage local leaders by bringing them into the fold of the state, creating a mutuality gap between leaders and followers. These leaders then developed their own interests and have been perceived as colonial 'puppets' (Interview F 2017). The independence process discussed in the next chapter illustrates this more clearly. In addition, the external state often had to rely on coercive power to ensure compliance. The use of military oppression, legal restrictions and heavy taxation were institutional tools that ensured short-term adherence to the state but not long-term loyalty based on a sense of collective destiny, identity and responsibility. In other words, the leadership of the colonial regimes was often transactional. Transactional leadership, however, is not based on a shared understanding of the nation and the state by leaders and followers and therefore does not contribute to building a sense of nationhood.

An important point that has not been discussed is that of followership, which is central in creating collective action. Without supporters, nationalists' views would rarely leave the halls of academic institutions. The followership in southern Sudan, however, faced certain challenges arising from this period. In contrast to the riverain core in northern Sudan, the British administration was primarily concerned with security rather than development (Young 2012: Introduction). Administrators, despite being obliged to learn the customs and languages of the communities they governed, were both scarce (no more than thirty over the colonial period) and often on leave (being given three months' leave a year) (Poggo 2009: 23). The north and south were also exposed to different educational policies, as discussed above.

This, of course, would have an impact on leadership emergence and the influence process. First, it would limit the emergence of leaders in the south who would be able to provide vision and leadership towards collective action. Little to no effort was made to build up a southern Sudanese elite class who could exert influence using expert power. It was only late into the colonial period that a limited number of southern Sudanese were educated in such matters in order to ensure representivity in the Legislative Assembly after the 1949 elections (Poggo 2009: 24). Secondly, the people in the south were not exposed to a single, coherent education system that would build a sense of collective consciousness. The followers in the south would therefore be much harder to unite post-independence.

The ability to compel people to act as a collective (collective will) and to create loyalty beyond narrow identity groups was often situation-dependent. The Mahdist revolution and the independence movement show contradictory examples of being able to do this, or not needing to due to the situation, respectively. What is most illuminating in this case, from a leadership perspective, is the depth of collective will and responsibility shown once situations changed. For example, the cross-group collective will raised by Mahdi was unsustainable once the Turco-Egyptian state was no longer a threat. This is a theme carried throughout Sudan and South Sudan's history, as will be shown in the next chapters regarding the transition to independence, the period following the Addis Ababa Agreement and South Sudan's secession.

Another aspect of leadership is the ability of followers to be conscious of and able to choose alternative leaders (Burns 2012: 4). Naturally, this did not exist in the colonial regimes and the brief Mahdist interlude suggests followers exerting their choice in leadership as a response to this. As a result, it is not possible to suggest that actions taken by the Sudanese state during this time can be perceived as an example of collective will. Rather, collective will was often found in the actions of rebellion, such as the Mahdist revolution and the resistance to Anglo-Egyptian rule by southern Sudanese groups. However, due to the circumstances and the coercive power used by the colonial regimes, there was little room for these examples to develop into a national collective will across multiple identity groups. The move towards independence provided a brief opportunity to develop such collective will, but leaders failed to respond to this situation or the needs of their followers as a whole.

## Conclusion

Many of the nation-building and state-building contradictions that would plague Sudan and South Sudan in future are mirrored in these early processes. The fluid and complex identity landscape was 'panel-beaten' into concrete and oversimplified identities to suit the imposition of the structured state and the leaders at the helm of these states. The state formation process, dominated by colonialism and conquest, was not conducive to the formation of a cohesive nation. The 'leaders', capable of driving policy and state action, were either external to the nation, or lacked mutuality due to their distance from the populace, both geographically and in terms of lived experiences. As a result, those driving the state formation process (the leaders) had separate interests and values from the members of the future nation (the followers), resulting in a state formation process that fractured rather than formed the nation. Also, as a result of the leadership process, collective will was often transient and situational, and a moral community with collective responsibility was lacking, as 'citizens' were given access to different rights and freedoms based on their origins, identities, proximity to leaders and more.

## Notes

1   For in-depth explanations of these theories see Anderson 2006; Hearn 2006: 67–94; Mann 1995.
2   For an explanation of in-group and out-group followers see Bass 2008: 63.
3   See Burns 2012: 3–5 for a discussion on transactional leadership.

# Independence and Rebellion

## Introduction

Sudan became a fully independent state, in the eyes of international law, on 1 January 1956. This followed a relatively subdued independence process, in comparison to some of the more bitter and bloody independence struggles on the African continent. This process, however, would result in a disconnect between people and state. One South Sudanese official, Steven Wöndu (2011), recounts his experiences with the early Sudanese state. In one instance, following a school fire, he recollects the way in which the governor of Equatoria Province confronted the students: '[The Governor] spoke as if we were beneficiaries of the generosity of a society to which we did not belong' (Wöndu 2011: 38–39). Two questions emerge from this quote, which would persist throughout Sudan and South Sudan's history. First, what was the relationship between the state and its citizens? Second, who belonged to the state and why?

After independence, we see that the Sudanese state became a tool of coercion, rather than a source of protection, unity or service delivery. Without a sustained independence struggle, or a leadership process that encouraged a meaningful relationship between the political leadership and the citizenry, the relationship between state and citizen remained fractured. What followed was decades of political instability, civil war and an antagonistic nation-building process. Sudan would experience two military coups within its first fifteen years of independence: in 1958 (followed by Ibrahim Abboud's rule until a popular uprising in 1964) and 1969 (followed by Jaafar Muhammad an-Nimeiry's rule until another uprising in 1985). Ismail al-Azhari was at the helm as Sudan's prime minister when independence was ushered in, and he would return briefly as president in between Abboud's and Nimeiry's rule.

Meanwhile, unrest in the south began before independence and would become a perennial challenge for successive Sudanese leaders.

The question of who belonged to the Sudanese nation took a volatile turn towards identity politics. The dominant process of leadership emergence, prototype leadership, contradicted the way in which official state leadership emerged. External relations with former colonial powers drove this process. This lack of influence between the country's leadership and the citizenry forced the leadership to rely on coercive and reward power to maintain order and support. The source of this coercion and reward power they found in the state itself – its institutions and its resources. The state became a tool to impose the elite's identity onto the citizenry from above, using Arabization and Islamization policies. Meanwhile, southern Sudan began to agitate against the state as soon as it was created. A shared sense of oppression drove collective action and the emergence of a southern political consciousness as 'different from' the Sudanese identity being pushed by Khartoum.

## Identity construction and contestation in modern Sudan

A critical period of any nation's identity formation is that of an independence struggle – when the nation becomes an independent state (or when the state creates the nation). Two key 'variables' influence the direction this process will take: the nature of the independence struggle and the nature of the elite leading it. Nationalist thinking is often driven by an elite, educated class.[1] Sudan's independence process was more a matter of political expedience and manoeuvring than a call for collective action and self-determination. The state formation processes of the conquest and colonization era generated a small and separate elite to lead this process. The average person living in the future Sudanese state had little say in the process.

Elites or an intelligentsia class play a central role in nationalism and nation-building. They are often central to ideating and collating the knowledge, values, history and vision of an identity group with nationhood and statehood ambitions. Sudan's intelligentsia, however, was narrow in its representativity, being largely Arab and Muslim, and framed the Sudanese nation in these terms (Sharkey 2008: 30). Even non-Arab soldiers, whose education received in the army led to their inclusion in this class, were overshadowed by the dominant Arab-speaking blocs (Sikainga 2000: 31). Officers who remained in urban areas maintained the identity instilled in them by the military, separating them from the communities they came from originally (Sikainga 2000: 31).

In the 1940s and 1950s, the Graduates' Congress sought to develop a nationalist ideology and movement. Members included high school graduates from northern Sudan (already excluding southern Sudanese graduates), and the ideologies that emerged argued for a Sudanese identity above all others, while also viewing ethnic groups in the peripheries as unworthy of 'being treated as nationalities' (Khalid 2003: 46–7). Not only is the mutuality gap evident in terms of education, economic development and access, but elites had a clear sense of superiority over other groups, rather than viewing themselves as representative of those groups. Consequently, any attempt to build a nation inclusive of a cross-section of the future citizens of Sudan was dead in the water.

As a result, the nationalism that underpinned the independence process reflected the identities of a select few (Khalid 2003: 46), as shown in the following quote from *Al Fajr*:[2]

> Belonging to the country, rewriting Sudan's history so as to cleanse it from flawed notions, upholding the pillars of religion, shunning tribalism and parochialism and attending to Arab language with a view to ensuring the supremacy over all other languages.
>
> Quoted in Khalid 2003: 48

In fact, 'Arabs' as understood in Sudan reflected a minority of a country that was predominantly of African descent (both in the north and south) (Abbas 1973: 34).

Compounding this situation was the geopolitical situation, which resulted in Britain's relative willingness to grant independence without an armed struggle. In a growing confrontation between Britain and Egypt, Egypt had been pushing for recognition of its rule over Sudan, which the UK could only counter by invoking Sudan's right to self-determination under international law (Johnson 2011a: 21–2). The intelligentsia and future leaders of Sudan did not require the support of the populace, so did not rely on mobilization tools (common narratives and symbols) that both build a movement and the foundation for a collective sense of shared identity (Khalid 2003: 42).

But a nation cannot be imposed by force, and an identity cannot be constructed from thin air. A failure to resonate with the everyday experiences, values and attributes of the Sudanese populace would shift them from being members of a group to outsiders, and from citizens to subjects. This relationship, a broken social contract, would require coercive power to maintain order, an unsustainable source of influence.

After independence, this narrow view of Sudanese identity would continue. Abboud's military regime sought to ensure unity in Sudan through a process of Arabization and Islamization in the south, using educational and religious institutions (Beshir 1968: 81). For example, Islamic education was introduced and the language of instruction was changed to Arabic (Natsios 2012: 43). Some reports indicate that chiefs and government employees were pressured to convert to Islam (Abbas 1973: 35). Sudan as an Arab country was reiterated in government ministries and foreign policy (Abbas 1973: 34, 40). In other words, the government sought to ensure a congruent nation and state by speeding up the process of identity construction through the coercive imposition of a broader identity. It used oppressive tactics, including arresting Catholic leaders, expelling missionaries (only from the south, not the north) and driving southern intellectuals out of the country (Beshir 1968: 81–2). Despite the overthrow of the military regime, the successive governments of 1965 to 1969 continued the Arabization and Islamization policies (Natsios 2012: 46).

The assimilation of smaller groupings into a larger identity group is not unheard of.[3] However, it did not work in this case. The use of coercive power, specifically targeted towards the south, in this nation-building initiative would instead foster resistance. An interesting example of this is the increased number of conversions to Christianity after these policies (Natsios 2012: 43). Sharkey (2008: 35–6) points this out when questioning why the Anya-Nya leadership preferred to implement education reminiscent of the colonial system when both colonial and Arab education employed similar practices of assimilation:

> The major difference after 1956 was that the national government was no longer officially colonial, and educated Southerners aspired to a share in national power. Moreover, what Northern politicians regarded as policies of national unity, many southern intellectuals regarded as cultural colonialism, precisely because they had no choice or voice in the matter.
>
> Sharkey 2008: 36

The post-independence Sudanese government, then, lacked influence over the southern Sudanese population. As citizens surrender some rights to the state in exchange for protection through the social contract,[4] followers must surrender influence to the leader, but will not do so if they receive nothing in return. Smircich and Morgan (2011: 20) argue that leaders are granted 'the powers to shape and define [followers'] reality', but that when a situation results in competing definitions of reality, leaders vie for this power, resulting in 'loosely coupled networks' and group members 'feeling disorganised because they do not share a common way of making sense of their experience'. While Khartoum's leaders were seeking to influence the south, they were offering little in return in terms of vision, rights or protections. As such, their ability to influence the nation-building process was limited and competing definitions of the Sudanese and southern Sudanese state and polity began to emerge, hindering the formation of a collective sense of community.

Similarly, choosing two attributes – race and religion – that were a key source of division to try and unify the nation was ill-conceived from the start. It is representative of the lack of mutuality between leaders and followers. The Arab and Islamic identity did not provide a source of common history or values between elites and followers but rather highlighted their lack of a shared history.

The social and historical distinction between northerners and southerners grew deeper, along with the assumed religious, linguistic and cultural stereotypes associated with those groups. By independence, geographical origin often determined one's primary identity, even when some attributes would overlap with those of another region (e.g. a Muslim graduate from Khartoum would still identify themself as southern if originating from this region) (Gray 1963: 1–2). But these overlapping categorizations and groupings also generated fractured and conflicting identities. For example, former slaves from the south who had assimilated and settled in the north were excluded from southern political clubs and associations for not being 'genuine Southerners' (Sikainga 2000: 34).

As a result, by this time, the north was already viewed as the common enemy of the south, which would form the foundation of southern identity. Joseph Lagu (quoted in Natsios 2012: 41), the leader of the armed rebellion against the north, wrote of Sudanese independence: 'It was not a true independence for the South, but the start of another colonialism by the North, *their traditional enemy*' (emphasis added). Furthermore, Abboud's policies and oppressive tactics fostered further resentment in the south (Howell 1973: 173). One respondent argued that the civil war between the north and south stemmed from a disagreement over how the south would be governed, rather than a difference in identity (Interview A 2017). Yet, southern leaders also perpetuated the notion that the challenge was one of identity difference in their framing of the crisis. In response to claims by some northerners that the differences between northerners and southerners were 'imaginary' and constructed by British colonial policies, southern politicians Oduho and Deng (1963: 17) stated simply: 'The differences are so apparent as to require no proof.'

An analysis of Oduho and Deng's (1963) language also illustrates a construction of northern identity from the southern perspective as primarily Arab. Notably, they often use north(ern) and Arab interchangeably. For example, at one point they describe the army in the south as being 'overwhelmingly Northern', while a few paragraphs later they instead refer to it being 'overwhelmingly Arab' (Oduho & Deng 1963: 18–19). At the same time, it is important to note that some southern leaders were hesitant to frame the conflict as religious. This is seen in a statement by the Sudan African National Union (SANU), which agreed with the Commission of Enquiry's findings that the 1955 disturbances were caused by political rather than religious reasons, highlighted the inclusion of southern Muslims in the rebellion, and criticized Khartoum for blaming missionaries for the crisis (SANU, No Date). At the same time, the statement does make extensive and unquestioned use of the labels of Arab and African (SANU, No Date). So, at this time, where identity was used to frame the conflict, it tended to lean towards a racial and territorial framing rather than a religious one.

The Anya-Nya (the armed wing of the southern rebellion against the north) capitalized on the fear of an Arab colonialist regime to build support for the rebellion. A background paper published by the Anya-Nya highlights the dangers posed by the north. Importantly, the paper identifies the enemy repeatedly as Arab, an identity that does not encompass the entire northern Sudan, rather than the north or the Khartoum government (South Sudan Resistance Movement, No Date). This further framed the conflict as an identity-based conflict. Key excerpts include:

The Army ... if left unchallenged ... would have turned the South into an Arab colony. Arabs were settled in strategic areas of the South, and all culture save Arab culture was suppressed.

Towards the end of 1960, a government plan to move 1.5 million Arabs to the Southern Sudan, to be preceded by the mass arrest of all Southern former parliamentarians, was revealed to Southern leaders by an Arab informant.

[A] tribal people ravaged and torn for over a hundred years by Arab slave-traders and political and military oppression.

Until all Southern Sudanese are free, energies had best be devoted to fighting the common enemy.

[T]he Anya-Nya, armed with traditional weapons ... were able to drive out the Arabs from their posts ... and to send Arab settlers fleeing back to their country – thus removing the threat of Arab colonisation of the South.

The Southern Sudanese people face an enemy bent on exterminating them unless they accept virtual serf status in an Arab country.

South Sudan Resistance Movement, No Date

The paper goes on to claim significant atrocities committed by Arab troops under both Abboud's and Nimeri's regimes. In addition to this, the Anya-Nya showed an understanding of the role of conflict in nation-building. In the same publication they state:

Armed struggle is a revolutionary means of accelerating national unity. The blood and tears of Dinka, Anuak, Bari and Azande which have washed the soil of southern Sudan are producing a new generation, undivided by earlier tribal and political differences ... Armed struggle is making southern Sudan more united and cohesive than many veteran African countries.

South Sudan Resistance Movement, No Date

This view would later prove premature but, in this way, conflict predictably created further divisions between northern Arabs and southerners and a sense of commonality amongst southerners, which fostered further conflict. Steven Wöndu (2011: 42), a member of the future Sudan People's Liberation Movement/Army's (SPLM/A) struggle and government, details the horror of witnessing the violent repression during the Anya-Nya movement and the rumours of atrocities committed by the local Arab commander. He says: 'In those circumstances, it was impossible not to hate the government and the Arabs who represented it' (Wöndu 2011: 42). In response to several alleged massacres in 1965, a southern leader of the Azania Liberation League stated: 'The moderates have now joined the extremists. Those of us who believed in a federation ... no longer think this is possible. The only policy now is to make the Southern Sudan into the independent State of Azania' (*The Observer* 1965).

Similarly, in December 1964, shortly after Abboud's military regime was overthrown, riots between northern and southern Sudanese broke out in Khartoum. In response to false rumours that southern leader Clement Mboro had been assassinated, the crowd that had gathered to welcome him back to Khartoum began to attack members of the Arab community (Natsios 2012: 45). This sparked extensive rioting and violence between northerners and southerners, resulting in four thousand southerners seeking refuge in a football stadium, hoping to be given safe passage to the south (Tayar 1964). Such inter-group violence indicates that the perceived boundaries between north and south had crystallized and were likely further cemented by these events. It was also clear that southerners viewed themselves as a separate social and political entity who could only be represented by a leader from the south and could only find safety and belonging in the southern region. At this stage, and indeed for many years to come, it seemed as though mutuality between leader and follower was dependent on mutual identity, defined along north–south boundaries. Had a leader emerged from the north who was responsive to the situation in the south and addressed their needs and interests, would this have been the case?

However, southern Sudan needed more than a conflict with the north to build a collective identity. Leaders appeared conscious of this, if incapable of actualizing a vision for a national identity in southern Sudan. For example, in May 1969, the Anya-Nya leaders declared southern Sudan as the Nile Republic and Gordon M. Mayen as its president (Voice of Southern Sudan 1969: 1). This period illustrates a short but interesting phase in the nationalism of southern Sudan. The deliberation over the name of an independent southern Sudan was in itself an exercise in identifying the characteristics of the southern Sudanese nation (Interview F 2017). After rejecting 'Southern Sudan' due its origins in colonial history and rejecting Azania due to a 'more legitimate claim' for this name being found in East Africa, the leaders settled on the Nile Republic (Voice of Southern Sudan 1969: 1). This showed a superficial, and largely unsuccessful, attempt at creating a sense of nationhood through the use of symbols. In addition, the southern Sudanese leaders attempted to minimize internal identity differences. They critiqued those who highlighted inter-ethnic differences in southern Sudan, including the Khartoum government and the press in neighbouring countries (Voice of the Nile Republic 1969a: 1, 3–4).

It is interesting to note, however, that despite the constructed nature of northern and southern identities, leaders tended to adhere to this reading of Sudanese society rather than explore alternative visions of a unified Sudan. Where this did occur, it was rarely successful. For example, a fledgling vision of a unified Sudan began to emerge in the early 1970s within the Southern Sudan Liberation Movement (SSLM). In a critique of Nimeiry, an official statement by the organization 'call[ed] upon all patriotic Sudanese from North, West, East-Central and South Sudan to work together to bring down the dictatorial regime of Nimeiry and to restore to the Sudan the independence and democracy which have been betrayed by this gang of human butchers' (deGarang 1971). This statement, along with earlier ones made in the same publication, is a rare example of the narrative extending beyond the north/ south dichotomy which was more commonly used in such publications.

## The opposing forces of state-building and nation-building in modern Sudan

The structure of the new Sudanese state was a matter of intense debate prior to independence. In the north, the primary issue was whether Sudan would unify with Egypt, while in the south, the concern was the self-government of the region (Sidahmed & Sidahmed 2005: 29–30; Howell 1973: 166–7). In 1953, negotiations were held in Cairo to determine the future of Sudan's independence. After the exclusion of southern representatives from this meeting, ostensibly because they had no official party, the Southern Party, which would become the Liberal Party, was formed (Abbas 1973: 33). In response, southern leaders gathered at the Juba Conference to debate and state their position: that Sudan should not be unified with Egypt on the condition that southern Sudan should be given self-determination either through federation or independence (Natsios 2012: 40). This position was largely ignored by Khartoum politicians in the plans for independence, and the independence process turned into another colonization experience for southerners (Poggo 2009: 32–9).

The Sudanization process similarly excluded southern elites. This process, whereby administrative and bureaucratic control was shifted from the British to the Sudanese, resulted in only six out of eight hundred posts being granted to southerners, even in the south itself (Poggo 2009: 35–6). In Parliament, only twenty-two out of ninety-seven seats went to southern Sudan (Poggo 2009: 34). From local administration to national representation, southerners were excluded from government. Not only were they excluded, but their new rulers were seen as oppressors due to the slave trade.

The formation of the state then interrupted one of the dominant leadership processes, prototype leadership, by placing many citizens under the authority of those who were not even seen as members of the same identity group, never mind the ideal 'prototype' of that group. As a result, these leaders would be rejected, and leaders would emerge in the south who had the referent power ('likeness' to southern identities) to continue the process of prototype leadership. So, independence was seen as a 'change of masters' for the south, not self-determination (Report of the Commission of Enquiry 1956: 117).

Due to the long history of 'othering' that had occurred between north and south, this resulted in a distinct leadership crisis. The gap between elites and followers created by this separation of Arab and African in the consciousness of the people meant there was no exchange of influence or mutuality. Therefore, the state could not and did not act as the usual agent of nationalism that it had in the development of the European nation state. At the same time, there was a mutuality problem within the south. Southern leaders in the Sudanese Legislative Assembly (the predecessor to the 1954 Parliament) had little widespread southern support outside their individual communities, and while a sense of 'Southernness' was forming amongst these leaders, the same political consciousness was lacking in the southern population (Howell 1973: 164–5).

Sudan gained independence on 1 January 1956. Political power was already in the hands of a Sudanese government elected in 1953, and the shift to independence has been characterized as an 'anti-climax' (Holt & Daly 2000: 145). By the time the British had left Sudan, key questions on the future of the state, including federalism for the south and the role of Islam in the state, were still unanswered (Natsios 2012: 42). The Khartoum elite chose to structure independent Sudan as a unitary, Arab, and primarily Islamic state, engendering a southern identity that stemmed from resistance to being forced into such a state (Arnold & LeRiche 2013: 3). Even beyond the south, many groups in northern Sudan outside Khartoum (such as Nuba and Darfur) would come to support federalism as the structure of the Sudanese estate (Abbas 1973: 35).

Sudan was now a legal state on the international stage, but a nation had barely been cultivated. While state institutions can be used to cultivate nationhood, the first prime minister, El-Azhari, used these institutions as a means of coercive power. In a statement to counter growing discontent in the south, he said: 'The Government must use all its force and strength ... the Government shall not be lenient ... it has army, its police and all its might' (quoted in Poggo 2009: 39). The state cannot build a nation, despite holding the tools to do so (such as education, bureaucracy and the military), if leaders deploy these institutions using coercive rather than legitimate and referent power. Renan (1994: 17) argues that the nation is a 'daily plebiscite', a choice to see oneself a part of a wider community (Laitin 2007: 30). Leaders must rely on mutuality and an exchange of influence not based on coercive power but rather on expert, legitimate and referent power that persuades people of their common destiny, is founded on common norms, and inspires people through a common vision. In other words, while leaders can manipulate nationhood, it cannot be forced upon a society when there is no influence exchange between the leader and the people.

On 17 November 1958, a *coup d'état* installed Major-General Ibrahim Abboud as the new prime minister. The coup stemmed from a deteriorating political and economic situation and was instigated in part to suppress growing expressions of discontent from outside the government (Beshir 1968: 80; Holt & Daly 2000: 145, 148). But this did not change the social and political landscape drastically in terms of leadership. The coup was led primarily by members of the 'Three Tribes' (the leading Arab groups of the riverain core) – a community that would continue to dominate the political, economic and military spheres through 'tribal-military power' throughout Sudan's history (Natsios 2012: xxii, 42).

Abboud's Arabization policy intensified the southern rebellion, now named Anya-Nya (Abbas 1973: 35). In 1963, SADNU (later the Sudan African National Union (SANU)) declared its intention to seek independence for southern Sudan (Beshir 1968: 83). A brief period of civilian rule returned following the October 1964 revolution, sparked in part by criticism of Abboud's handling of 'the Problem of Southern Sudan' (Deng 1995: 143). But another military coup occurred in 1969, eventually installing Jaafar Muhammad an-Nimeiry as president of Sudan.

In its early years, the second military regime, under Jaafar Mohamed an-Nimeiry, held some promise for the south. A man of modest upbringing, Nimeiry supported a 'secular, socialist pan-Arab ideology', pursued negotiation with the south and was open to decentralized rule for the south (Natsios 2012: 47–8). Using a southern minister in his cabinet, Abel Alier, as an envoy to engage church leaders and probe the appetite for a settlement in the south, Nimeiry was able to hold peace talks in Addis Ababa between 1971 and 1972 (Natsios 2012: 49–50). While Nimeiry's engagement with southern Sudan initially suggests a willingness to listen to the needs of the south, his moves were largely of a pragmatic nature. The urgency of solving the 'southern problem' was less about solving the challenges faced by the southern people than the challenges he faced to cementing and maintaining his own rule (Abbas 1973: 43; Johnson 2011a: 36). As with the Mahdi revolution, it was a situation of temporarily aligned interests rather than mutuality guiding leader and follower engagement.

The Addis Ababa Agreement promised the south regional autonomy, a return to English as the language of instruction and government, and religious freedom (Addis Ababa Agreement 1972). But regional autonomy was poorly defined in the agreement, and in practice fell short of a federal system (Johnson 2013: 101–5). Discontentment would follow the agreement. Many southerners viewed Alier as an 'accommodationist' and Lagu (the leader of the Anya-Nya movement) as an opportunist who had traded true southern independence for a high-level position in the Sudanese army (Natsios 2012: 51). By this time, the 'bitterness' created during Abboud's rule meant that 'the federalist cause was coming to be seen as a compromise, if not a betrayal' (Howell 1973: 173).

This reveals the power of the idea of the nation state in the twentieth century, where self-determination was a global ideal. While southerners have historically resisted the state, and later demanded a federal arrangement when statehood was imminent, once the idea of a southern independent state entered southern consciousness, it could not easily be rejected. This was true even if their leaders may have seen potential benefits in remaining in Sudan. Both the nation and the state evoke powerful images in people's imaginations, be they viable or not. Leaders, therefore, hold the responsibility of managing these images responsibly. In the case of Lagu, promising independence and then backing down from his stance led to his losing some of his influence. The drive for an independent southern state may also have precluded any development of a united Sudanese nation. Southern leaders, therefore, through their factionalism and own opportunism (perceived or real), failed to build a narrative in southern Sudan that was durable and flexible enough to confront the complex identity landscape of Sudan and the political realities of the international scene (which was averse to any separatist movements). However, the leaders' ability to manufacture mutuality with southerners, based on a shared sense of oppression, planted the seed for a long journey to statehood.

## The emergence of collective will and responsibility and its continued challenges

The articulation of a desire to become an independent state, and the action of becoming one, is in itself a representation of collective will (Weilenmann 2010: 43). Sudan's independence, and southern Sudan's war for autonomy, reflect a measure of collective will. But the will driving Sudan's independence came from above, not below, and was organized through the National Unionist Party (NUP) and the Umma Party (Poggo 2009: 31). Southern and African elites organized themselves in political groupings and parties, such as the Black Bloc in the north and the Liberal Party for the south, just prior to independence, but were given little space in the Legislative Assembly and faced significant opposition from northern politicians (Abbas 1973: 32–3; Poggo 2009: 32). The Khartoum, predominantly Arab, elite also worked towards preventing the formation of a unified African ('Black') political movement, precluding the registration and operation of political parties claiming to represent African Sudanese across northern and southern Sudan (Abbas 1973: 32–6).

The Black Bloc (*Kutla as-Suda*) emerged from a group who supported former soldiers and slaves in the urban north (Sikainga 2000: 32). Dr Adam Ahdam, descended from a Darfur slave family, originally founded the organization in an effort to unite all black Sudanese, but the organization was forced to maintain its official position as a social organization when the British denied registration as a political organization, under the pressure of the dominant Arab parties (Abbas 1973: 32–3). Support for the Black Bloc would sometimes be split, however, with a militant opposition emerging in a group called the Black Liberals (Sikainga 2000: 33) and factions emerging within the Black Bloc itself (Abbas 1973: 33). Competition for support would sometimes lead to resorting to monetary rewards to gather popular support (Sikainga 2000: 33). The Black Bloc used both rewards power and referent power, resulting in a mixture of transactional and transformational leadership.[5] Eventually, the Black Bloc would fail as a result of poor organization, internal fragmentation and suppression (Sikainga 2000: 34: Abbas 1973: 32–3).

Southern leaders' main policy objective was federalism, but they were divided on other issues (Gosnell 1958: 415). For example, in the 1958 Sudanese elections, southern representatives' votes in the Legislature for the new government were split between the Umma Party's coalition and the NUP opposition (Holt & Daly 2000: 148). But when the Umma Party proposed a new constitution promoting a centralized Islamic state, the southern MPs caucused together to oppose the constitution and present a federal proposal (Abbas 1973: 34–5). A contemporary academic wrote at the time (1958) that 'No Liberal [Southern] representative would risk appearing to be lukewarm or opposed to Federalism' (Gosnell 1958: 415). Despite having been promised consideration for a federal arrangement in exchange for southern MPs' vote for Sudanese independence, these proposals were summarily rejected by the constitution committee (Abbas 1973: 35).

Eventually, the desire for a federation was expanded to include the support of the southern people. The Liberal Party courted the support of southerners in this endeavour and traditional leaders and their followers rallied behind this demand in fear of Arab oppression (Poggo 2009: 37). El-Azhari tried to garner the loyalty of southerners but failed. During his tour of the south in 1954 he was met with ridicule and a mass walkout of one of his speeches by the Juba population, led by southern leader Daniel Jumi Tongun (Poggo 2009: 38). Tongun's decision to lead the walkout was driven by El-Azhari's promotion of a unified Egypt and Sudan, which was against southern wishes (Poggo 2009: 38). After this response from southerners, El-Azhari reportedly first tried to gain southern support by offering higher salaries and, when this failed, resorted to repressive tactics (Oduho & Deng 1963: 26). This southern discontent resulted in El-Azhari and his circle viewing the south and Tongun as 'agitators' hostile to the north, precipitating his aggressive stance towards the south (Poggo 2009: 38). This is a case of using first reward power, followed by coercive power, neither of which build mutuality; they rather represent a form of transactional leadership. El-Azhari made no effort to understand and confront the beliefs and needs of southerners, nor to build or communicate a vision of Sudan that included those needs.

This illustrates a clear challenge in building collective will and responsibility. It requires a sense of mutuality amongst group members and with those who are meant to represent them. In this instance, El-Azhari lacked an understanding of southern needs and therefore was unable to build mutuality with them, resulting in a lack of influence exchange. Due to this lack of influence, the prime minister was unable to build collective will with the southerners to garner their loyalty in pursuing his vision for a united Nile Valley. Tongun, on the other hand, understood the current situation and needs facing the southerners (the fear of another colonization) and was therefore able to motivate collective political action.

The post-independence leaders of Sudan also failed to face and plan a solution for the 'southern problem' (as it was described by the north) (Beshir 1968: 80; Natsios 2012: 45). This illustrates a clear failure to recognize and address the situation at hand – a necessity of leadership. It is important for leaders (be they intellectuals or politicians) to be sensitive to the broader context in which they seek to build a nation and a state. Unfortunately, Sudanese nationalists failed to recognize the importance of including southern ideas in their conceptualization of the Sudanese nation and northern politicians were remarkably indifferent to the needs of southerners. Had these leaders been more attuned to the context in which they were operating, the results may have been significantly different.

Little else indicates the presence of collective will and loyalty than the willingness to go to war for one's nation. It is, however, also a weak measure, since crisis elicits loyalty and unity easier than peace does (Weilenmann 2010: 41). The true test of collective will and responsibility comes in peace. Still, the first rebellion provides some insights into leadership and collective will. The first signs of violent resistance were seen in 1955, when southern discontent with the independence process led to rioting and a mutiny in Torit by the Equatorial Corps (Natsios 2012: 41). These were unorganized expressions of discontent, however (Natsios 2012: 41), and did not yet represent a collective will amongst southerners. Small and isolated incidents of resistance continued to crop up in the southern countryside but remained disparate and unorganized (Beshir 1968: 84). In short, it took several years and the continued oppression of the south 'as a collective' to generate national appeal for the rebellion (Interview F 2017). At this point, the south lacked the leadership necessary to channel and frame the discontent of southerners into collective political action. Also, despite similar discontentment amongst Sudan's other predominantly African peripheries, a unified rebellion in the south and north against Khartoum did not emerge, in part because Africans from these peripheries were used to fight against the south in the Sudanese Army, fuelling mistrust (Abbas 1973: 36).

Rebellion leaders tried to instil a sense of collective responsibility and collective will in its followers. One example of this is the critique of southern Sudanese youth who had fled to neighbouring countries, arguing that it was their 'duty ... to free their own country from Arab occupation' (Voice of the Nile Republic 1969a: 3). Unfortunately, it is difficult to determine exactly how widespread the support for rebellion was amongst ordinary southerners. However, it is suspected that the majority of troops in the Anya-Nya rebellion originated from Equatoria (the southernmost region of southern Sudan) (Arnold & LeRiche 2013: 1). This raises two possible questions. First, while the rebellion claimed to be speaking for all the peoples of southern Sudan, to what degree did the movement and its leaders command the loyalty and attention of all southerners? Second, if those willing to fight were largely from a single region, does this indicate a lack of collective will amongst southerners as a whole? When combined with the arguments that the south lacked unity from the start, it seems creating a collective will indicative of a nation was an early problem in the south.

By 1963, the rebellion grew more organized under the Anya-Nya rebellion. This rebellion rose out of a dissatisfaction and impatience with SANU's peaceful tactics and diplomatic efforts abroad, while SANU condemned the rebellion's use of force (Beshir 1968: 85). As such, there is a question to be raised here regarding mutuality. First, leaders tended to emerge from a small, educated elite – those educated in missionary schools. While their schools provided them with the space to grow their political consciousness, they also created a gulf between the educated and the less-educated that made it more difficult to communicate and transfer their views to the majority of southerners (Howell 1973: 168). Gray (1963: 1) notes this in an overview of Sudan's identity landscape: 'The educated élite of [the north and south] have, in many ways, far more in common with each other than with their illiterate fellows; there are Marxists, democrats and totalitarians on both sides.' Secondly, many leaders spent significant periods of time outside the country (Poggo 2009: 66–8; 115–16; Howell 1973: 171).

Their experiences, then, were markedly different from those of the ordinary southern Sudanese. This does not automatically negate their ability to lead, but it would present a significant distance between leaders and led that would hamper the exchange of influence. Beshir (1968: 84–5) uses the fact that 'SANU did not have a close relationship with the sufferers of the South' to explain why the Anya-Nya rebellion garnered more sympathy and support. Similarly, this is a trend that would carry throughout southern Sudan's history and will come to the fore after its secession, when the common enemy of the north is no longer present to manufacture mutuality between leader and led. The recent conflict in South Sudan has placed in the limelight the significant gap between followers and leaders in South Sudan.

In addition to this, disunity amongst the southern leaders was a common problem. During the first Juba Conference of 1947, the southern leaders brought together found 'they had little in common with one another' (Howell 1973: 164). After the 1964 riots, a peacemaking conference failed in part due to southern factionalism (Natsios 2012: 45). During the conflict, southern leaders struggled to build a 'united political movement', resulting in the Anya-Nya forces 'operat[ing] quite independently of the politicians and their factions' (Ruay 1994: 154). After Abboud's departure, this factionalism and disunity amongst southern leaders increased as they competed for positions and relevance in a new electoral system (Johnson 2011a: 32). Similarly, the Anya-Nya forces themselves faced disunity (Ruay 1994: 154). The organization itself acknowledged the lack of leadership and the need for a single, visionary leader who would act as a 'brand figure' in the movement (Voice of the Nile Republic

1969b: 2). Mayen was described by the *Voice of Southern Sudan* (the mouthpiece of SANU) as 'one of the most popular men in southern Sudan' in the hope that he might emerge as such a person (Voice of Southern Sudan 1969: 2).

This did not occur, and the leadership remained fragmented until Israel became involved in their training in 1969, when the Israelis also chose Joseph Lagu as the leader of the forces (Ruay 1994: 154). This demonstrates again the way in which the relationship between leader and led was often interrupted or determined by external actors and interests. Lagu was able to emerge as a leader primarily because of his access to Israeli weapons and supplies, which he used to garner support from military leaders and build a strong military force that outmanoeuvred and overshadowed southern political leaders (Johnson 2011a: 37). Natsios (2012: 46) sums up the leadership challenge as follows:

> The first leadership of the South in the First Civil War was hampered by several constraints. No single figure emerged with the moral authority, experience, intellectual capacity, or fighting ability to lead Southern forces in the civil war. The poisonous Southern tribal rivalries were reflected in the factional intrigue among Anya-Nya commanders and politicians, who were unable to form a unified military command structure or political organisation, advance a single political ideology, or develop a coherent plan to defeat the North. The division between the military commanders in the bush and southern exiled political figures – whom the commanders often dismissed as armchair rebels – weakened the effectiveness of the Southern forces.

The preference for federation was reportedly held by the majority of southerners, across all leaders (including the educated political class and the traditional leaders) and down to their respective followers (Oduho & Deng 1963: 27). The broad acceptance of this vision stemmed from a collective fear of the Arab North (Oduho & Deng 1963: 27). Therefore, the dominant experience that was used to build mutuality in order to drive collective will was a response to an external threat. There are two key challenges with such an approach. First, while identity is relational, an identity that is primarily dependent on 'the other' is likely to be fragile as context changes. It also lacks the peace-supporting elements of nationhood, such as norms and behaviour that foster collective responsibility and create a sense of 'predictability'.[6] This will be illustrated in the fluctuating sense of unity and internal strife identified throughout this book.

Secondly, this strategy used by southern leaders throughout the struggle (as illustrated in the following chapters) was often effective in the short term but lacked vision. In other words, it was responsive to the situation at hand but failed to prepare for a changed situation once their actions yielded results, as seen in South Sudan's post-secession experience. The shared history of oppression, the common enemy in the north and the mutual goal of self-determination provided the foundational blocks for a nation to emerge. However, without leadership based on true mutuality with the people of the south and with each other, this failed to mutate into collective will and political action. It also failed to translate into a sense of collective responsibility to one another as southerners that would surmount other identity divisions. At this point, southerners had a collective goal but not a collective will, in large part due to a leadership crisis.

## Independence and the First Civil War in Sudan: Leadership and power in a shifting context

In the previous chapter, the Mahdist revolution was used as an example of how certain situations and challenges can engender cooperation. The independence process in Sudan is a different example of how situations can build divisive identities rather than unifying ones. This is because the situation did not demand this of leaders. Instead of forcing leaders to build support by appealing to the common experiences, beliefs and identities of a wider populace, the independence process favoured leaders who were politically adept at navigating regional and global geopolitics. As a result, the situation did little to call for a sustained process of national identity construction and rather allowed leaders to raise support based on narrower identity groups and traits. This would set the foundation for leader response after independence, as the need for a unified nation-building project became ever more apparent.

In other words, while the situation prior to independence may not have required leaders to raise broad collective will and responsibility, their continued survival as leaders did demand this post-independence. Their inability to maintain this loyalty and sense of unity resulted in a tumultuous political system with multiple coups and struggling democratic periods. Therefore, the move to an independent Sudan signalled a change in situation, while at the same time many continuities remained. Sudan was now an independent state, theoretically capable of ruling itself after over a century of external rule. However, while the context had changed, the leader/follower relationship remained fraught with the same challenges – namely, followers were fragmented and remained fragmented due to leaders' mobilization tools; leaders sought to exert influence primarily through coercive and reward power; and mutuality between the leaders and the led remained weak.

In addition, the leader/follower relationship can shed some light on identity construction processes. Sudan's geographical, political and social experience resulted in a highly diverse group of potential followers. The Sudanese people ranged in terms of educational background, socio-economic status and demographical make-up. As a result, leaders did not only have in-group and out-group followers at the political elite level,[7] but were also able to split their followers in society amongst those whose needs, beliefs and interests they represented and those they did not. This was a pattern established in Sudan's early years that has been carried throughout its history. Unfortunately, as leaders and followers were largely chosen based on narrow identity lines (which often overlapped with socio-economic and political divisions), this severely hindered the development of a national identity. As a result, mutuality was seen to exist when leaders and followers bore the same narrow identity markers used to determine group identity at the time (prototype leadership). This, unfortunately, is a superficial mutuality that rarely extends beyond early mobilization, although it holds significant emotive power. The continuation of this pattern of leader/follower relationship in Sudan would pose significant problems in the future.

Regarding the construction of identity, it has already been noted that, due to contextual factors, Sudan's independence and nationalist process did not instil the same sense of collective identity that other national struggles have done in the past. The nationalist struggle in the south, however, did foster a sense of collective southern identity. This is because, due to northern opposition to southern independence or autonomy, leaders had to mobilize a broader segment of the respective population than northern leaders had to prior to

Sudan's independence. In order to mobilize sufficient support to meet this challenge, leaders had to create a sense of collective identity.

This collective identity was based on a sense of collective oppression, which was felt by most southerners across various ethnicities, and by most leaders. As a result of this mutuality, southern leaders were able to exert their influence in constructing southern identity and southerners were able to accept the narrative offered. However, beyond this, leaders faltered in building a sense of national identity amongst southerners due to internal strife and the large gap between leaders and followers. Therefore, the experience of oppression, while holding a certain emotive power, lacked the depth of shared experiences, values and beliefs that would build a sense of collective identity. This is a trend that would continue throughout South Sudan's history and come to a head in the 1990s and in 2013, discussed in Parts Two and Three of this book.

With reference to the state, it is clear that the borders of Sudan were not constituted to encompass a fully fledged nation. However, the idea that modern Sudan was created by the attachment of two entirely distinct entities is also not true (Arnold & LeRiche 2013: 2, 8–9). As discussed in the previous chapter, engagement between northerners and southerners was limited but not non-existent prior to conquest. The type of state(s) that would have emerged in this geographical region without external conquest is impossible to predict. Nevertheless, Sudan was undergoing a long and slow state-building and nation-building process whose trajectory was likely altered and sped up by external intervention. Therefore, upon independence, Sudan was faced with a classical nation-building challenge of ensuring the borders of the state and nation coincide.

The state is often equipped with the institutional tools to build a sense of nationhood, such as educational establishments, mass media and the military.[8] However, the way in which these tools are employed is determined by leaders. In Sudan, the state apparatus was used by leaders to impose a narrow perception of national identity on followers. This suffered two key challenges. First, the identity pushed by leaders through the state reflected only a segment of the population – Arab and Muslim. In other words, the cultural identity of a specific in-group of followers was being promoted over the identity of others, creating resentment rather than unity. Secondly, the use of coercive power to build national identity rather than expert, referent or legitimate power, for example, created opposition to rather than acceptance of said identity. In fact, it likely furthered an existing distrust of the state rather than fostering identification with and loyalty to the Sudanese state. This illustrates the importance of understanding the leader/follower relationship in nation-building. The example of slave soldiers given in the previous chapter illustrates that assimilation into northern Arab culture was possible. Yet, despite their efforts, leaders were not able to manipulate southerners into assimilation, not because they did not identify with the cultural values being imposed, but because of the act of imposition itself. Therefore, the process by which nations are built is as important as the characteristics used to delineate it.

Finally, despite facing a situation of collective oppression, southern leaders struggled to form a movement that was unified in its efforts and illustrative of collective will and collective loyalty. The goal of an independent southern Sudan was fairly widely held, as discussed above. This solution to the nation-building crisis in Sudan was founded on a perception of northerners and southerners as inherently different. This narrative was promoted by southern leaders' rhetoric and reinforced by northern leaders' inability to respond to southern needs. But it was the followers who chose to reject northern leaders' influence and accept that of southern leaders on this matter, leading to their support in the rebellion. This example of collective action was founded on mutual oppression on the part of both leaders and followers. However, the oppression felt by leaders and followers, while originating from the same collective enemy, permitting the illusion of a collective identity, was often different between leaders and followers. The educated classes in southern Sudan rebelled largely due to their political and economic exclusion. As discussed above, they were marginalized in the Sudanization process, administrative and military positions and political representation of the south in Khartoum and other national forums. The oppression faced by the everyday southerner was likely of a different sort.

The lack of a shared experience between leader and led would in future conflicts become a serious challenge. In the First Civil War, it resulted in an inability to find a cohesive leadership accepted by the broader southern population, leading to fragmentation of the movement. Without such a leadership, southern Sudan was unable to build a vision that looked not only towards the past oppression but also to the future southern Sudanese nation.

In other words, there was little engagement with what the nation would entail beyond self-government, as this was the primary concern and interest of southern leaders. Therefore, nation-building requires a reciprocal exchange of influence between followers and leaders. Leaders need followers to accept and internalize the narrative of national identity they promote, which followers can and do at times reject. At the same time, followers require leaders that can frame social reality to guide the group in unified action towards a shared goal.

## Interlude between wars: The Addis Ababa Peace Agreement and the 'return' to conflict

The period from 1972 to 1983 held several elements of continuity in Sudan. The nature of the Sudanese state remained a matter of great debate. Sudanese identity remained highly contested. And Sudan's leadership process continued to suffer from a flawed relationship between leaders and followers. This resulted in leaders often taking action and framing issues based on political situations that confronted their own interests rather than the social and economic situations facing the Sudanese people as a whole. The divisive process of identity construction continued in this period; the structure of the Sudanese state became a bargaining chip in political competition rather than an expression of the Sudanese nation, and southerners grew increasingly suspicious not just of the north but of their own leaders as well.

While the shared suffering of conflict did not yet generate a mass nationalist movement in the south, it provided the foundation for the formation of a southern identity and its associated political goals (Howell 1973: 175). The capitulation on regional autonomy for the south also furthered the perception of the south as a separate political entity (Rolandsen 2011: 555), based on the perception of southerners as a separate identity group. As a result, the period between the First and Second Civil Wars did not drastically change the path of identity construction in the country. The south remained divided from the north and political discourse and actions continued to fuel this divide. Southern demands for an independent state persisted. In fact, a splinter group opposed to anything but self-determination formed a second rebellion in 1978, referred to as Anya-Nya II (Young 2005: 538).

In addition, the debate in the north about the character of the Sudanese state continued on its identity-based path, with religion becoming an increasingly divisive issue. The historical memory of the Mahdi played a role in this continued relevance of Islamic ideology in Sudanese politics. For example, when exiled Islamist poitician Hassan al-Turabi returned to Sudan, he was likened to the Mahdi himself, and he was instrumental in the development and imposition of *Shari'a* law (Natsios 2012: 54–5). The narrowing of Sudanese identity to not only religion, but a specific interpretation of religion, would create significant rifts in society. It is impossible to know the true motivations of individual leaders who pushed for an Islamic state, but it is clear that they were largely disengaged from the citizens in the south at the very least.

This lack of mutuality between northern leaders and the south also manifested in economic policies. Nimeiry's development schemes primarily targeted the north, and in some cases held potentially detrimental consequences for the south, as seen in the Jonglei Canal (Johnson 2011a: 45–7; Natsios 2012: 52). In addition, the discovery of oil would exacerbate the fragile truce between north and south. Southern leaders and their followers wanted an oil refinery built in the south, but Nimeiry and his colleagues chose to build it in the north, without consultation (Natsios 2012: 59). This sparked protests amongst southern students (Natsios 2012: 59). Consequently, many southern Sudanese, particularly the elite, felt frustration with their inability to raise their social status, which was exacerbated by the return of many refugees from Uganda in the late 1970s and early 1980s (Johnson 2013: 108).

This is one of the typical preconditions of nation-building – where frustrated elites who find their path on the socio-economic ladder blocked raise and pursue a nationalist agenda to further their cause (Horowitz 2001: Ch. 1; Hroch 1996: 66–7). Southern leaders had managed to slowly build southern consciousness by invoking the common enemy of the north, but they failed to build a common vision beyond this at the time. In addition, by the 1970s, political and ethnic divisions within the south had deepened significantly (Johnson 2013: 108), while the two key leaders, Alier and Lagu, faced accusations of tribalism (Mayen 1982: 9–11, 17–19). This would lead to nationalist politics often being driven by situational factors, such as the discovery of oil, and political factionalism, rather than by engaging in a robust project to identify commonalities amongst various Sudanese, or even southern Sudanese. The use of the common enemy of the north as the defining characteristic of the south, as opposed to creating awareness amongst southerners of common values, histories and a future, therefore also pre-empted any solution to Sudan's identity crisis beyond separation.

Shortly after the Addis Ababa Agreement, Nimeiry drafted a new constitution that was secular in nature and 'declared Sudan to be both Arab and African' (Natsios 2012: 52). Nimeiry's secular stance, however, united factional Islamic parties against him, eventually forcing him to change tactics (Natsios 2012: 52). As a result, the fragile peace of the Addis Ababa Agreement came under threat when Nimeiry welcomed back several Islamist politicians who sought an Islamic state (Nasong'o & Murunga 2005: 66). Over the years, Nimeiry had failed to gain popular support, alienated the Islamic parties and maintained power through repression (Natsios 2012: 52–6).

When it became clear that he was losing his grip on power, Nimeiry changed his secular approach for Sudan to an Islamic one, and traded his commitment to the Addis Ababa Agreement for an alliance with his opposition (Natsios 2012: 54). As a result, Nimeiry and his government reinstated Islamic law across Sudan in 1983, including the south (Nasong'o & Murunga 2005: 66). At the same time, due to ongoing tensions between various ethnic groups in the south, there had been a debate regarding the division of the south into separate provinces. One side viewed it as a way to prevent Dinka domination while the other feared it would allow the north to practise a divide-and-rule strategy (Natsios 2012: 60). The Equatorians in particular sought this division through what they termed *Korkora*,[9] to escape Dinka domination, but this caused fears amongst the Dinka that they would eventually wish to secede, in the same way the south sought to secede from Sudan (Young 2021: 147). In the end, Nimeiry single-handedly divided the south into three provinces with his signing of Republican Order Number One, which largely undid much of the political and cultural autonomy that had been given to the south in the peace agreement (Natsios 2012: 60). He did this because he was 'Anxious to weaken the south and respond to the opposition of northern political parties to the Addis Ababa Agreement' (Young 2021: 147).

As a result, while the Addis Ababa Agreement provided a space to re-engage the Sudanese state and its correlation with a Sudanese nation, leaders' commitment to its content and the space it provided was superficial at best. At this point in time, the state had become a tool for leaders to gain political and economic access rather than a mechanism for the nation to assert its collective will on itself and the outside world. In addition, the inconstancy in Nimeiry's approach to the south illustrates a failure in leadership that would have disastrous consequences. His shift in ideology indicates an inability to build a narrative that was inclusive and resonated with the Sudanese people, while also confronting the volatile political climate. It also indicates that his interests were centred on regime security rather than the needs and interests of the Sudanese nation, indicating a lack of mutuality. Finally, his source of power depended on coercion and therefore was unsustainable. In the end, Nimeiry's vision for Sudan was ill-suited to the context at the time and his approach to building this vision was flawed in its coercive nature.

Many southerners were unhappy with the outcome of the First Civil War. The compromise made by accepting regional autonomy rather than full independence was not well received (Young 2005: 538). In addition, many in the south viewed the Addis Ababa Agreement with suspicion and cynicism (Johnson 2013: 101; Natsios 2012: 58). These fears proved well-founded. The regional autonomy granted to the south did not allow the south to govern itself in its own manner, preventing the exercise of collective will. There also did not appear to be a significant increase in responsibility and loyalty to the southern government or between southerners. Despite being granted regional autonomy, Nimeiry maintained a tight control over the south's political and economic future, which was strengthened by the factional fighting between Alier and Lagu (Natsios 2012: 57–8).

Alier and Lagu struggled during their respective terms as president of the southern region. Both courted Nimeiry's support in their competition with each other, indicating implicit acceptance of Khartoum's interference in southern politics (Johnson 2013: 107). Alier lost popular support because of his inability and/or unwillingness to stem northern interference in the south (Johnson 2013: 107–8). His leadership was rejected when he appeared to side with Nimeiry's oil policies (Mayen 1982: 10.) Lagu, on the other hand, came into conflict with the legislature and judiciary due to his 'unconstitutional use of power' (Johnson 2013: 107–8). Gordon M. Mayen (1982: 19) suggests that the corruption scandals surrounding Lagu forced him to rely on identity politics to maintain his position. This indicates another problematic gap between southern leaders and their followers. After the agreement, their interests no longer aligned as clearly with the southern people's interests. Therefore, both leaders were unable to build and maintain mutuality with their followers, resulting in their use of other sources of power to maintain their influence. Unfortunately, this highlighted ethnic difference, illustrating the challenges of maintaining collective will and a sense of collective identity that was not initially built on a strong foundation of mutuality.

## Interlude between wars: The leadership gap becomes evident

Similar to the transition to independence, the Addis Ababa Agreement, while meant to signal a new situation, did not result in a significant change in the leadership process. First, the mutuality gap between leaders and followers persisted. The widespread distrust of the peace agreement amongst southerners contrasted with the actions of the leaders, who began to compete with each other for the positions the agreement offered. Nimeiry's fluctuation on his policies were driven by elite political competition rather than being dependent on the challenges confronting the Sudanese people. These examples illustrate the problem of mutuality in Sudan. As a result, southern leaders were unable to formulate a vision for southern Sudanese, while Nimeiry's secular vision of Sudan proved to be superficial and unable to withstand a threat to his own individual interests.

A lack of exchange and mutuality between leaders and followers can be particularly problematic in a peace deal. Peace agreements often provide a road map for the post-conflict state structure. The structure of the state should ideally reflect the needs, values and interests of its citizens (i.e. the nation). However, peace deals often shift the state-building process from a conversation between the state and its people to a negotiation amongst elites. This was reflected in the Addis Ababa Agreement. In this case, although independence had been the goal, southern leaders acquiesced to regional autonomy (Young 2005: 538). However, this arrangement and the subsequent state structure was rejected by southern followers for the reasons discussed above. This challenge of leaders' interests being addressed in a peace agreement but not that of followers would be repeated in subsequent peace agreements. The rejection of the agreement was also likely linked to the promises of independence made during the civil war by southern leaders and the further division between north and south cemented by the violence.

Therefore, the experience of conflict probably deepened the division between northerners and southerners. The violence and its associated rhetoric fostered resentment, embedded the differences between the north and the south in collective consciousness, and reinforced the view that southerners would never be free under northern Arab rule. The resolution of the conflict furthered the perception of north and south as two separate nations (Rolandsen 2011: 555). So, by this time, much of the debate about the Sudanese state became centred on a contestation of Sudanese identity. However, rather than searching for and building a secular, inclusive identity, leaders and their respective followers chose exclusive identity attributes such as religion, race and region. These attributes, though constructed, were perceived as inflexible. As these markers became associated with the state, the potential for an inclusive state structure became all the more elusive.

# Conclusion

The instability and unrest of Sudan's early independence years is indicative of a new post-colonial state attempting to define itself. Olonisakin, Kifle and Muteru (2021) introduce the notion of inter-elite and society-elite conversations in state-building. Post-independence Sudan was having a conversation about the identity, nature and structure of the state and nation, but it lacked depth and sufficient society-elite conversation. The competing visions proposed by elites was often a reflection of elite competition rather than the result of engagement between leaders and followers. This engagement was often non-existent (as seen in the independence process), confrontational (as seen in Abboud's leadership), or superficial and transactional (as seen in Lagu's and Alier's leadership). As a result, no leader emerged who was able to confront the needs of the situation an independent Sudan posed, nor the needs of its new citizens. This is most evident as one views the fluctuating use of power and influence in the shifting context that these years present. Both northern and southern elites are culpable for engaging with their respective followers in a transactional manner. This occurred when popular support was needed to achieve political objectives – we see this during the war. But where support is not needed, as seen in independence and in the interim period, influence shifts from a leader/follower relationship to an inter-elite exchange. This pattern would be repeated after the Second Civil War.

## Notes

1  See Eley & Suny 1996: 4, 14; Horowitz 2001: Ch. 1; Hroch 1996: 63
2  A journal produced by a Sudanese 'intellectual study group' (Khalid 2003: 48).
3  See Horowitz 2001 Ch. 2 for a discussion on assimiliation.
4  See Wolff 2006: 43–5.
5  See Burns 2012: 3–5 for a discussion on transformational and transactional leadership.
6  See Hopf 1998: 174.
7  For an explanation of in-group and out-group followers see Bass 2008: 63.
8  See Anderson 2006; Hearn 2006: 67–94; Mann 1995.
9  *Korkora* means 'a separation into two parts' (Young 2021: 147).

Part Two

# The War Continues: The Fight for Nation and State (1983–2002)

# 3

# War and New Leadership

## Introduction

On 16 May 1983, following Nimeiry's policies retracting the Addis Ababa Agreement, an order was given for southern troops to transfer to the north — a further violation of the peace agreement that resulted in a mutiny by the former Anya-Nya soldiers of Battalion 104 in Bor and Battalion 105 in Ayod (Nasong'o & Murunga 2005: 67). The government responded with force (Nasong'o & Murunga 2005: 67). This was the spark that reignited sustained armed conflict in South Sudan. The Second Civil War would last until the signing of the Comprehensive Peace Agreement (CPA) in 2005. During this period, the identity issue in the country would grow even more complicated. Race, religion, ethnicity, region and class would clash to generate shifting, volatile narratives. While these narratives were often fanned by leaders and elites for strategic, interest-based reasons, they reflected deeply felt experiences and grievances of the people.

The mobilizations strategies, policies and ideological narratives adopted by leaders, however, were more a reflection of an inter-elite or elite-external engagement than an influence exchange with followers. Inter-elite competition for the apparatus of the state and appeasement of foreign supporters would often override the wants and needs of the populace. This occurred even in the south, where a fight for self-determination was ironically guided by external actors. As in the past, the relationship between leaders and their followers was founded on coercion and reward. Even John Garang, who used charisma and persuasion to solidify his position (especially amongst external powers), had to rely on some degree of coercion and reward to maintain support amongst southerners.

## Fluctuating narratives and perceptions of identity
## in the midst of conflict

The Second Civil War was sparked in large part because of Nimeiry's imposition of *Shari'a* law (Deng 1995: 12–13; Interview D 2017; Interview G 2017). This was the spark and not the cause, however, as tensions and conflict predate this (Interview A 2017). Nevertheless, this war would take on a more religious dimension whereas the previous conflict leaned towards dramatizing racial differences. Perspectives differ on the depth, reality and source of these tensions. One interviewee (Interview A 2017) argued that people of different religions lived in a state of peaceful coexistence in Khartoum. Another respondent (Interview G 2017), on the other hand, describes the treatment of southerners in Khartoum and the north as that of 'second-class citizens' and that people were being 'forced' into an Islamic tradition. In addition, the tensions surrounding race and language remained (Deng 1995: 13; Sharkey 2008: 36–7). Racism was reportedly widespread in northern Sudan, with Arabic literature promoting Arabic cultural superiority, and southerners or African Sudanese often being referred to as *abeed* (De Waal 1998: 140; Sharkey 2008: 40). Some have argued that this sense of superiority, which resulted in the Arabization project, stems from a place of insecurity amongst Sudanese Arabs, who were in fact a minority in Sudan and whose Arab heritage was called into question outside Sudan (Sharkey 2008: 40). Nevertheless, due to this perception of superiority, to Arab northerners, the conflict in the south was portrayed as part of a 'divine duty' and a 'manifest destiny' (Martin 2002: 121).

This is important to note, because it highlights the way in which an identity is accepted and rejected not by its intrinsic qualities but by circumstance and leadership. The acceptance of Christianity as a central part of nation-building and Western ideals as the foundation for the political organization of that nation (discussed below) indicates that the south's opposition to an Arabic and Islamic identity does not only stem from its external nature. Rather, it relates to a failure on the part of the Khartoum elite to exchange influence with southerners, and the deeply entrenched narratives of oppression. This was rooted in a lack of mutuality, forcing Khartoum to adopt a coercive strategy. The southern elite and church leaders, mostly educated by Western missionaries, were able to relate, to a degree, with the everyday struggles of the southern people. As a result, they were able to frame the struggle within the narratives of Western democracy and religious persecution.

The tactics used by Khartoum also furthered the perception of the conflict as a religious and racial one. Arab militias, such as the *Murahaliin* in the southwest, were mobilized to target southern populations with whom they often had existing grazing disputes (Martin 2002: 117). However, the perception of the south as a unified identity was also not fully formed yet. In its early years, the SPLM/A support was ethnicized and regionalized. The 'proud owners' were considered to be those from the Bahr el Ghazal and Upper Nile regions, such as the Dinka and Nuer, while Equatorian members were seen as 'supporters' and 'sympathisers' (Wöndu 2011: 144). At the same time, the SPLM/A was not immediately popular in Equatoria and thus Equatorian SPLM/A supporters 'risked being shunned by [their] fellow Equatorians' (Wöndu 2011: 144). Even the Dinka and Nuer experienced the SPLM/A very differently. During early mobilization, Dinka recruits passed through Nuer lands on their way to Ethiopian training camps, often committing violence that left a lasting impression (Pinaud 2021: 72–4). Within the SPLM/A, discrimination favouring the Dinka and disadvantaging other groups, including the Nuer, was evident in the way soldiers were treated, trained and promoted (Pinaud 2021: 73–80). These ethnic narratives would continue and influence post-independence struggle 'credentials' and ethnic politics (discussed in Chapter 6).

Meanwhile, accusations of slavery were laid against the Arab militias during the war. In 1987, the Sudan Relief and Rehabilitation Association (associated with the SPLM/A) released a report on the Dhein massacre, which included accounts of slavery (Mahmud & Baldo 1987). Considering the central role of slavery in the narrative of oppression, this only served to entrench southern fear of northerners (De Waal 1998: 140). Mistrust between fellow citizens was deepened, and the existence of separate nations within the state was further confirmed.

The narrative of slavery also served to simplify the relationship between northerners and southerners, providing a historical foundation for southern identity and a justification for independence from those who had enslaved them (De Waal 1998: 146). As a result of this historical relationship between those who engaged in the slave trade and those who suffered its consequences, which appeared to be repeating itself in the 1980s, the rift between north and south was deepened. The history of northerners and southerners, while intertwined, was one of confrontation that developed opposing narratives of self and group destiny. The use of these narratives in a contemporary conflict only served to further this division.

An important shift in the thinking of Sudanese identities occurred in this period, however, as the leading intellectual guiding SPLM/A ideology, Garang, developed his philosophy of Sudanism. Sudanism championed the diversity of identities in Sudan and discouraged the use of such identities in politics (Idris 2013: 98). It is possible, and the norm, that multiple identities can coexist (Laitin 2007: 9–11). The chosen identity markers of a nation can vary from ideological to ethnic and other markers (Horowitz 2001: Chs 1 & 2; Norman 2006: 4–5; Weber 1994: 22). Certain identity markers such as religion, ethnicity, language and race can be separated from the public sphere (i.e. the state) and therefore the nation. Garang often advocated for a 'multi-nationality country, separating religion ... from the state' (Novicki 1989: 46) within a political system that respected the 'democratic and human rights [of] all nationalities and guarantees freedom to all relgions [*sic*], beliefs and outlooks' (Garang ed. Khalid 1992: 23).

This presented a significant change in Sudanese nationalist thinking which had been driven by narrow and exclusive identity markers (Idris 2013: 98). Garang also aimed to build what he often termed a 'new Sudanese identity' and a 'new Sudanese commonality' (Novicki 1989: 44; SPLM 1994a: 15). Therefore, he went further than mere multiculturalism in his attempt to build a new 'national identity which embodies its own unique historical and cultural heritages' (Idris 2013: 99). In short, he embarked on a nation-building endeavour. His rhetoric underscored an understanding of and need for nation-building not previously demonstrated in Sudanese politics.

Part of this nation-building is the need to build a sense of collective loyalty. In an interview with Novicki (1989: 44, 47), Garang on several occasions refers to the need to build a 'Sudanese commonality to which we all pledge our allegiance and our patriotism'. However, while the theory regarding identity construction appears sound, it is difficult to implement in practice due to the multitude of uncontrollable variables. The secession of South Sudan and recent events indicate that Garang was unsuccessful in this project. This failure also serves as further evidence that leaders do not act in a vacuum. They cannot easily act as puppet-masters in the nation-building process. The following discussion will seek to trace his efforts and understand why his vision failed.

A final note must be made regarding religion and identity. As mentioned, this would be a prominent feature of the Second Civil War. While southern opposition to Islam was clear, a tension between secularism and Christianity was also evident in the south. For most of the 1980s, the SPLM/A, driven by its Marxist ideology, was hostile to not only Islamization but Christianity as well (De Waal 1998: 143). This hostility manifested in the kidnapping and arrest of religious leaders (Akol 2003: 53; De Waal 1998: 143). Part of this antagonism stemmed from the church's threat to SPLM/A legitimacy as the sole representative of the southern people (Rolandsen 2005: 76–7). Yet, the church was a key institution at the local level and played an important role in the organization of social life (Rolandsen 2005: 75). In addition, Christianity gained significant ground in this period and in the 1990s (when foreign missionaries returned to southern Sudan) (De Waal 1998: 143; Rolandsen 2005: 75–6). This growth can be attributed to multiple factors: the adaptation of Christian teachings with traditional values, the need for spiritual and religious meaning to explain the suffering of southerners, and the role of the church in relief and aid operations and activities (De Waal 1998: 143).

In addition, the growth of Christianity has been described as a reaction, and a form of protest, to the Islamization policies of the state (Sharkey 2008: 24–5). This was one of the reasons the SPLM/A softened its stance on the church, believing it would solidify a southern identity as a counterpoint to northern Islam (Rolandsen 2005: 76). Eventually, in the 1990s, the SPLM/A shifted its stance on the church in recognition of its humanitarian role, but some leaders retained a distaste for religion (De Waal 1998: 143). Christianity also took on a form of myth-building, with the southern struggle often being compared to Biblical stories and the southern people being directly linked to Biblical prophecies (Guarak 2011: 562; BBC News 2013; Copnall 2014: 31). This type of myth building is typical of a society building a nation and constructing an identity. It is also not surprising that the source material for such myths would be a religion that both crossed ethnic boundaries and – remembering that identity is relational – represented a resistance to the historical 'enemy' in the north.

The above discussion illustrates the importance of influence in the formation and construction of identity. The Khartoum elite lacked significant influence amongst southerners, and what little they had relied on coercion as its source of power. Their attempts at expanding the Arabic and Islamic identity therefore failed. The southern elite, whose power stemmed from more mutuality with the southern population, was able to exercise more influence amongst southerners. Their mutuality allowed them to construct a narrative of oppression and exclusion, drawing on a historical experience that was used as the basis for southern identity. However, there were tensions between southern leaders and their narratives. The population was often influenced more by the leaders and structures that held a presence in their lives, primarily the church, traditional leadership (based on ethnicity) and later humanitarian organizations (see Chapters 4–6). As these leaders held more influence amongst southerners, their identity narratives often held greater sway.

Similarly, while Garang rhetorically promoted Sudanism, little was done to actually build this Sudanese identity (as will be shown throughout the discussion below). Rather, his rhetoric often reiterated the history of oppression and exclusion, while his vision for the future centred on the state and socio-political structure of the 'New Sudan'.[1]

The first, his rhetoric, resulted in a superficial southern identity that would easily falter and reinforced divisions between north and south. The second, his vision, failed to build a national identity and promoted a vague political vision that few southerners believed in. In short, identity construction is determined by the influence relationships within a society. Identities are constructed by the leaders who can exchange influence with a population, and this requires mutuality.

## Contradictory narratives of statehood and nationhood

While the crisis of identity between north and south had reached perhaps insurmountable levels in Sudan, the violence that emerged was driven, in no small part, by the continuities and contradictions between state and identity. First, identity was used to indicate a level of belonging to the state, with non-Arabs being seen as 'subjects' (Sharkey 2008: 42), or as one respondent put it, 'second-class citizens' (Interview G 2017). Religion, similarly, was seen to 'determin[e] who gets what from the system' (Deng 1995: 16). Second, the question of the identity of the state had reached a tipping point. The debate in the First Civil War, while it included religion, was centred on the question of race. But since independence, an Islamist ideology propagating the establishment of an Islamic state had slowly gained significant ground. It originated with the Muslim Brotherhood and culminated in the National Islamic Front (NIF) party under the guidance of its ideologue Hassan al-Turabi (Glickman 2000: 273). While Islamization and Arabization policies were not new in independent Sudan, the NIF brought a new fervour to the project (Natsios 2012: 55, 72–3).

The NIF came into power on the back of a military coup on 30 June 1989. Nimeiry had been overthrown in 1986, but the subsequent democratic regime did not last long before the 1989 coup. Following the popular overthrow of Nimeiry in 1986, the new leaders neglected to address the grievances surrounding the economy, the civil war and Nimeiry's policies, and instead diverted their attention to winning elections (Khalid 2003: 168). This was a trend in Sudan as seen in the brief democratic period after Abboud's rule (Abbas 1973: 39–40), and would continue into the post-CPA period. Once in power, the NIF, which would later become the National Congress Party (NCP), was led by Omar al-Bashir and Hassan al-Turabi. The NIF was founded on militarism and Islamism, reflected in these two leaders, respectively (Iyob & Khadiagala 2006: 102). *Shari'a* law embodied Khartoum's efforts to merge religion and state. It signaled an assumption of what the Sudanese nation was and/or should be. This did not ring true with southerners' perception of themselves and the state they wished to reside in. The SPLM/A, in response, strongly advocated for secularism. Al-Turabi, however, viewed religion and the state as inseparable (Glickman 2000: 273), and other leaders in Khartoum, such as Ali Osman Taha, maintained a firm belief in the Islamic project (Johnson 2011b: 15).

However, southern grievance was not only centred on the issue of religion and state. Rather, it was representative of a wider concern in which the state was controlled by and served to benefit a select group of people who were identified by their ethnic and racial identity. In other words, there was debate on both the role of the state in identity (e.g. the issue of *Shari'a* law) and the role of identity in access to the state. While this may have resulted in the racialization of the conflict at the grassroots level (see above and Chapter 2), Garang was more nuanced in his explanation of the conflict. He viewed the situation in a more holistic manner and sought to reform the governance structures in Sudan as a whole (Interview A 2017).

A recurring theme in Garang's rhetoric is that of the power structures of Sudan. In various speeches and interviews he refers to the movement's aims to achieve 'a radical restructuring of the power of the central government' (Garang ed. Khalid 1992: 26) or 'the restructuring of power in Khartoum' (Novicki 1989: 44, 47). He also identifies the '*Jallaba*' as the 'real enemy' due to their hold on 'economic and political power' and 'state organs' (SPLM 1994a: 14). Garang, in this case, explained that the '*Jallaba*' referred to the ruling class who viewed themselves as Arab (SPLM 1994a: 14–15). However, '*Jallaba*' evolved into a derogatory label used for all northerners – it was used to personify the enemy of the struggle, despite Garang's more inclusive rhetoric of 'New Sudan' and 'Sudanism' (Young 2005: 536). Therefore, while Garang often reflected a nuanced and intellectual understanding of Sudan's challenges, his followers also framed the struggle narrative based on their own experiences (e.g. the militia raids and cases of slavery).

Regarding the more fundamental question of whether Sudan should constitute one state or two, in a departure from the Anya-Nya rhetoric (Ayers 2010: 161), the SPLM/A's stated objective was 'the liberation of the whole Sudan, and to the unity of its people and its territorial integrity' (Garang ed. Khalid 1992: 26). In a symbolic expression of this vision, the SPLM/A would refer to the territories under its control as 'New Sudan' (Johnson 2011b: 12). This vision drove the SPLM/A towards seeking support and alliances outside the south. Its main political ally was the National Democratic Alliance (NDA), a coalition of opposition parties and movements in Sudan, while the movement also allied with militant groups in other marginalized regions outside the south throughout the war (Deng 2006: 158; Nasong'o & Murunga 2005: 67; Rolandsen 2011: 553). Writing in 1995, Deng (1995: 13–14), expressed reserved optimism for this 'vision of a united, pluralistic, democratic Sudan', as it had begun to gain ground in the north and provided Sudan with a 'counterforce' to Khartoum's Arab-Islamic vision of the state. But this was not popular with all southerners. Wöndu (2011: 181) summarizes some of this discontentment:

Some delegates felt that the struggle should have focussed on the liberation of Southern Sudan from the hegemony of the North. They complained that the blood of the South was being shed unnecessarily to liberate the whole Sudan. If some people in the North needed liberation, they should join the fighting like our brothers and sisters from the Nuba Mountains and Southern Blue Nile. If the Northerners did not rise and wage war against the government, we must conclude that they were not oppressed and that they were in fact the oppressors.

Some have argued that Garang's approach, rejecting separatism and promoting a vaguely Marxist ideology, was influenced by Ethiopian leader Mengistu Haile Mariam, a key supporter of the SPLM/A (Young 2005: 538). Mengistu was facing his own separatist demands at home and therefore could not be seen to support a secessionist movement (Young 2005: 538). In addition, just like most insurgencies, the SPLM/A needed international support in a global climate that was opposed to secession (Deng 1995: 20). Wöndu (2011: 169–70) details how Garang explained this to him personally by arguing that 'New Sudan' was a 'strategic [and] tactical conceptualisation' used to garner international support, counter the Sudanese government's narratives, and address the 'problem of the centre of power in Khartoum'. Nevertheless, most leaders within the SPLM/A favoured self-determination[2] as the end goal, but refrained from opposing Garang directly (Young 2005: 539). This demonstrates a consistent complexity in Sudan and South Sudan's leadership, the tension between the influence being exchanged between elites and the international community, and between elites and the southern population. It is seen again, especially during peace processes (discussed in Chapter 5).

Deng (1995: 21) describes how structures of political organization and ideologies have evolved in Sudan. The north moved from traditional structures to sectarianism to the Islamist ideology exemplified in the NIF. The south, on the other hand, underwent a transformation in the educated elite with Christian missionary education that eventually evolved into an ideology with significant Western elements. This resulted in competing visions of the Sudanese state: one Arab-Islamic and the other a Western secular pluralistic model (Deng 1995: 21). However, neither vision seemed appealing to their respective targeted followers, as will be discussed in the next section. In theory, the state should act as a form of political organization and governance for the nation and society within its borders (see Introduction). However, in this case, the state became a tool in political competition. The visions propagated by both sides were driven by situational factors that influenced leaders' political position rather than followers' aspirations. As a result, ideologies and allegiances were often momentary and a cohesive ideology of the Sudanese state that was coherent with a Sudanese nation failed to develop.

## The emergence of collective will and collective responsibility?

Despite the portrayal of 'the north' as a monolithic enemy, it was hardly united or homogenous. This is seen in the repeated cycles of coups, popular revolts and short-lived democratic regimes. The growth of Islamism as a political ideology could also be argued to reflect elite politics rather than the cultural and religious orientation of the majority of Sudanese (Glickman 2000: 274). Al-Bashir aligned with the NIF and its Islamist ideology for largely political reasons, having alienated most other political powers in Khartoum (Martin 2002: 113). And while the NIF/NCP was able to gain power and dominate the political sphere for decades, just prior to the party's coup, it had only received 6 per cent of the 1986 vote (Martin 2002: 113).

In addition, the implementation and uptake of the government's Islamization policies and the values they espoused was slow due to a lack of support amongst the society and everyday Sudanese (Martin 2002: 120). Finally, the NIF/NCP vision was opposed by many sides, as seen in the NDA's composition of sectarian, secular, northern and southern parties, who were divided in their visions of Sudan but united in their wish to end the NIF/NCP regime and replace it with a pluralistic society (Deng 1995: 21). The NDA signed the Asmara Declaration with the SPLM/A in 1995. It indicated the goals of the parties as that of democracy, regime change and a new constitution, followed by a referendum on secession; yet it also entailed a commitment to unity (Young 2012: 84–5).

The south was also not united in its political vision. By the start of the Second Civil War, political consciousness had spread to the local population, where conversations on political events in Sudan were far more common than in the colonial and pre-colonial era (Rolandsen 2005: 33). This consciousness crossed ethnic boundaries and leaders were able to mobilize southerners beyond their individual ethnic groups (Interview F 2017). This demonstrates an initial shift from prototype leadership as the norm, which emerged during the colonial and pre-colonial period. However, while political consciousness had spread, there were some differences of opinion on the vision for southern Sudan. This in itself is not problematic — collective will does not require the entire population of a nation to agree all the time. It does, however, require structures and norms that permit the nation to reach a collective decision (Weilenmann 2010: 43). Yet Nyaba (2000: 33) states that 'From the outside, it appears the SPLM manifesto of 1983 was not intended for the people of South Sudan ... but rather to gain acceptability in the eyes of outsiders'. Where was influence being exchanged in this scenario? How was collective action being determined? It appears influence was being exchanged between different leaders rather than with followers, which hinders the formation of a national collective will. Thus, this collective will appears to have been lacking in the struggle. For example, while the SPLM/A would go on to become the prominent leader of the struggle, its legitimacy was hard-won. And, by some accounts, this legitimacy never reached the majority of southern Sudanese, but was rather a legitimacy granted by the international community (Young 2021: 148).

Some accounts indicate that the SPLM/A's early mobilization was driven by local inter-communal conflicts, arising from border disputes that emerged out of Nimeiry's policy to divide the south, rather than in response to a call for liberation (Nyaba 2000: 25-26). The SPLM/A used these conflicts to recruit soldiers, who initially joined the movement to get access to weapons they could use in such inter-communal conflicts (Nyaba 2000: 25-6).

Loyalty to the SPLM/A was also purchased through a marriage economy, as detailed by Pinaud (2016). She explains how resources acquired through predation were used to pay bridewealth prices for commanders and their officers to marry. This 'patronage of marriage' ensured the loyalty of troops and communities by building paternalistic and familial bonds, even across ethnic lines (Pinaud 2016: 245–8).

In addition, the Second Civil War began with multiple rebel movements in the south which had to be co-opted or defeated by the SPLM/A, including Anya-Nya II (Rolandsen 2005: 29, 36). Anya-Nya II was a predominantly Nuer movement, which was forcefully defeated by the SPLA, including the killing of their leader Samuel Gai Tut (Young 2019: 5). Some of these soldiers from other movements held little loyalty to SPLM/A leadership and would join the future rebellion against the movement (Rolandsen 2005: 36). Grievances persist about the way in which the Dinka-dominated SPLA took leadership of the independence struggle using violence against the Nuer (Young 2019: 5). The story of the SPLM/A's emergence as the leader of the South Sudanese rebellion is not one of mobilizing a collective southern Sudanese nation on the basis of shared goals. Rather it is one of competition and violent defeat of alternative leaders, visions and groups.

It is therefore important not to assume that the SPLM/A had universal support because of its prominent role. Indeed, according to some reports, the atrocities committed by SPLM/A members threatened the movement's credibility and recruitment capacity (Wöndu 2011: 140–1, 144). Resentment grew in the Equatorian regions amongst smaller ethnic groups, particularly as a result of rape and forced marriages by the SPLA, to the point that some viewed the Dinka-dominated SPLA as a colonizing force (Pinaud 2016: 248–9). This resentment, also driven by the use of Equatorian farming lands for Dinka cattle, spurred the organization of counter-SPLA militia groups (Young 2019: 5). The multi-ethnic but Nuer-dominated South Sudan Defence Forces (SSDF) was the most prominent of these movements (Young 2019: 5). In this way, the SPLM/A initially emerged as the leader of the south through a process of coercion and reward. It would go on to gain legitimacy through other means.

Garang's southern followers largely rejected, or were at least sceptical of, his vision of 'New Sudan' (Idris 2013: 100–2; Young 2005: 538). This vision did, however, resonate with other marginalized communities in Sudan, specifically in Darfur, the Nuba Mountains and the Blue Nile, who would join the SPLM/A in armed struggle (Idris 2013: 100–1). Deng (1995: 20) summarized this tension of objectives as follows:

> Tactically, the leadership of the SPLM-SPLA is following a multifaceted policy that does not exclude and indeed discreetly prefers separation as the ultimate goal. What is remarkable is the degree to which the leadership has made the rank and file understand and accept this rather complex reasoning and strategy. At one point, the rhetoric of liberating the whole country seemed to be taken seriously and was emphatically reflected in the SPLA

morale-boosting martial songs. But the driving force for the fighting men and women has clearly been separation. This was often expressed in the words, 'We know what we want', a popular response to the question, 'What is the SPLA fighting for?'

In fact, despite its official rhetoric, southerners are said to have conferred legitimacy on the SPLM/A on the tacit understanding that it would pursue an agenda of self-determination (Rolandsen 2011: 555). In this situation, an exchange of influence is apparent between the SPLM/A and the southern population, which permitted the south to exercise collective action. Despite the complexity of the unity or separation question, leaders were able to generate a sense of collective purpose and will in the pursuit of a common goal, even though it was in an implicit manner. Internal disagreement about the movement's vision, therefore, did not prevent the SPLM/A from winning significant military victories in the 1980s, nearly capturing Juba before the movement fractured in 1991 (Hutchinson 2001: 307–8). Therefore, while collective will was lacking in the north, there was more unity of purpose in the south, which allowed for initial success.

## A return to civil war: A leader emerges

Once again, a key dimension of the leadership process approach that sheds light on these dynamics is that of the leader/follower relationship. The competing processes of identity construction, disparate visions of the Sudanese state and challenges of collective will and loyalty often reflected a leader/follower gap. In particular, the discussion above illustrates the various ways in which leaders and followers struggled to influence each other in their search for a nation that would serve their values, needs and interests. This may stem from a lack of mutuality, illustrating a fundamental challenge in Sudan's leadership process that would plague the nation-building process throughout its history. It is seen in the way that both Garang and the Khartoum elites' visions were rejected, though the first less violently than the latter.

Nevertheless, John Garang provided what southern politics had lacked until then – a strong leader who 'virtually personified the struggle of the South' (Young 2005: 535). However, there are competing narratives of his leadership. On one side, he is portrayed as the undisputed, charismatic, principled leader of the south, while others highlight his dictatorial and authoritarian tendencies that prevented the emergence of other leaders (Johnson 2011b: 9–13; Martin 2002: 121; Young 2005: 539). One respondent indicated that 'Garang was a strong leader but he did not nurture a democratic culture' (Interview C 2017). Garang himself emerged as a leader through skilled networking inside and outside southern Sudan (Johnson 2011b: 10). His strategy to use marriage as a form of patronage and means to create kinship ties in the SPLA also played a role (Pinaud 2016).

When the SPLM/A was first being formed in Ethiopia, there was tension between the military elite and the political/intellectual elite, the latter being seen as the 'bourgeoisie' (Nyaba 2000: 36). Garang straddled these two camps, holding credentials in both (Nyaba 2000: 36). In addition, Rolandsen (2005: 29) states that 'John Garang used force and intrigue to bolster his position as supreme leader of the Movement'. Opponents were 'purged' by Garang's inner circle, made up of Salva Kiir and Garang's wife Rebecca (Pinaud 2021: 78–80). This is linked to the way the SPLA used force to take leadership of the independence struggle, as detailed above. Garang's heavy-handed leadership style is affirmed by Hilde Johnson (2011b: 1, 11), who had a 'close relationship' with the leader. She says: 'In [Garang's] view, a liberation movement and army could not take decisions by consensus' (Johnson 2011b: 11).

While this may be true, Garang's use of coercion and reward raises questions about his legitimacy, his vision and the SPLM/A in general. In other words, was his vision rejected because of an inability to exercise influence based on mutuality? As discussed above, Garang's vision for a 'New Sudan' was not widely accepted by southerners. Similarly, a Marxist ideology did not resonate with a southern population composed primarily of small landholders and 'fiercely independent pastoralists' (Young 2005: 538). In fact, the Marxist ideology was quickly set aside in the 1990s as its utility wore out (Young 2005: 539). Therefore, southerners' acceptance of Garang's vision was temporary and stemmed from political necessity rather than a mutual belief in the value of a 'New Sudan'. While interests converged momentarily to allow Garang to influence the population, the needs, beliefs and values remained distinct. This, therefore, reaffirms the school of thought which argues that nations cannot be created solely by elites.

This can be seen in many of the processes discussed above. While Garang attempted to construct a more inclusive and broad-based Sudanese identity, competing realities on the ground (such as the use of identity-based militias) and historical narratives (such as slavery) allowed followers to accept a different narrative of their identities. The political expediency driving many of the narratives espoused by the SPLM/A also led to some contradictions. For example, the SPLM/A used the contentious issue of slavery to mobilize international support (De Waal 1998: 145–6). This use of the slavery narrative by the SPLM/A has been criticized by De Waal (1998: 145–6), who saw it as a reactive narrative that could hinder peace and unity. It produced sentiments and identity narratives that ran counter to the Sudanism ideal.

Therefore, while Garang provided the charismatic leadership[3] needed to mobilize and guide the struggle, he did not develop an ideology suitable to the local context, due to his need to balance a complicated array of interests at the local, sub-national, national, regional and international level. Followers and other leaders were also able to assert their own choices in the identity construction process. This is perhaps best exemplified by the growth of the Christian Church, which ran counter to the SPLM/A's rhetoric. This occurred because of the responsiveness of the church to the local context and situation – another important aspect of the leadership process.

Similarly, the effort to make the nation and the state congruent appears to have been an exercise in power and not influence exchange. This is most clearly seen in the continued imposition of an Arabic-Islamic identity from Khartoum, but is also reflected in the south with regard to Garang's almost unilateral framing and dispatch of the SPLM/A vision. The visions espoused by either side also often stemmed from an orientation to a regional and international audience rather than a negotiation with Sudanese society. In short, while followers often sought to influence the Sudanese state through popular uprisings and revolt, they were largely excluded from the negotiation of state and nation. The result — a continued inability of the state to understand and reflect the nation — led to persistent instability and failure to foster a sense of collective will and loyalty to the state.

## Conclusion

As war returned to Sudan, strategic decisions (e.g. using militias) and competing visions of the state (i.e. Islamism, Sudanism and separation) served to further entrench identity differences on one hand, and generate a new collective will on the other. Ethnic, racial and religious divisions were hardened as a result of the Kharoum's divide-and-rule strategy and the SPLM/A's mobilization tactics. At the same time, competing visions, not just between parties to the conflict but within these parties as well, complicated this identity landscape. As a result, contradictions abound and would foreshadow serious fault lines as the conflict would continue.

Yet, the Second Civil War indicates an important shift in the leadership process – that of leadership emergence. Where most leaders in Sudan and South Sudan had emerged through legal, if not entirely legitimate, means (i.e. holding positions of legal power), coupled with coercive and reward power, Garang was able to emerge as a leader using referent and expert power as well. He proposed a vision not seriously considered before, and used his charisma to promote it. But, as will be shown in the next chapter, the actual source of his influence is not clear-cut, which would have implications for the formation of the Sudanese and South Sudanese nations.

## Notes

1   For examples of the first, see Novicki (1989: 44), SPLM/A (1994a: 9–10, 13–15, 17), Garang ed. Khalid (1992: 19–21, 50). For examples of the second, see Novicki (1989: 44, 46), SPLM/A (1994a: 21–2, 25–6), Garang ed. Khalid (1992: 26–7).
2   The term self-determination in this case was used to refer exclusively to secession (Young 2005: 539).
3   See Weber 1978: 215.

# 4

# Inner Turmoil

## Introduction

In August 1991, several senior members of the SPLM/A – Riek Machar, Lam Akol and Gordon Kong – staged a failed coup against John Garang (Hutchinson 2001: 308, 317). The decade that followed was characterized by elite factionalism and widespread south-on-south violence. Stated reasons for separating from the SPLM/A included disagreement with Garang's official policy on unity and self-determination, his failure to implement democratic reforms, and a fear of Dinka domination in the organization (Arnold & LeRiche 2012: 44–5; Nyaba 2000: 1–3; Rolandsen 2005: 35). But official narratives obscured the elite interests at play. As the increasingly divergent elite interests produced a fracturing political movement in the south, the limited bonds uniting southerners disappeared in the face of more immediate needs and realities.

This was a product of the gap between leaders and followers. While leaders pursued elite concerns around leadership of the movement, followers were concerned with the day-to-day of living in an insecure environment. In this environment, the constant sources of security, order and cohesion could be found in the ethnic rather than the regional or national. The only point of convergence between elite interests and followers' needs was the ethnic. As a result, prototype leadership returned. Popular support, leader emergence and military engagement was centred around the ethnic. Political debate on the nature of the state became secondary. Collective will, action and loyalty was determined by a transactional relationship between followers and leaders. Military support was exchanged for the means to protect one's own ethnic and sub-ethnic communities. As a result, while high-level conversations were being had on the nature of the Sudanese state, southern Sudanese society fractured into a fractal-like pattern. The nation and state were diverging.

## A multiplicity of identities: New fault lines (re-)emerge

The resulting conflict in the south, while it was centred on elite interests, significantly affected the civilian population. In the months following the coup attempt, Nuer militias loyal to Machar targeted Garang's home region of Bor, killing and displacing civilians and provoking similar attacks on Nuer communities (Hutchinson 2001: 308). Ethnic identity was subsequently used to identify, target and attack civilians in a vicious circle of revenge attacks (Jok & Hutchinson 1999: 126, 131). The dominant rift occurred between Garang's Dinka ethnic group and Machar's Nuer ethnic group (Gerenge 2015: 94). However, other ethnic militias also emerged, especially when the Nasir faction split and Lam Akol sought support amongst his own ethnic group, the Shilluk (Rolandsen 2005: 37–8).

Ethnic-related conflict in southern Sudan was not new. But this conflict escalated violence significantly because of the use of advanced weapons and entailed attacks on non-combatants and property of a scale never seen before (Jok & Hutchinson 1999: 130–3). The extended nature of the conflict and its political as opposed to economic motivations also demonstrated a shift in inter-group relations (Jok & Hutchinson 1999: 130–3). Quickly overshadowing the north/south conflict, this period witnessed more deaths in south/south violence than north/south violence (Copnall 2014: 26).

The dominant narrative of this conflict, while certainly containing an ethnic dimension, is that of SPLM/A elites manipulating ethnic identities in a political dispute (Jok & Hutchinson 1999: 126, 130–3; Nyaba 2000: 6). Previous conflicts between the Dinka and the Nuer were not driven by a competition for political power, due to the lack of a centralized political organization or state (Jok & Hutchinson 1999: 132–3). Leaders armed their respective ethnic groups in an effort to erode the support bases of their opponents, and raised their own support by inciting fears that 'tribal wealth was under threat' (Jok & Hutchinson 1999: 134). This indicates a return to prototype leadership when other forms of influence failed, which demonstrates a lack of mutuality beyond similar identity markers.

In the view of southern politician Peter Adwok Nyaba (2000: 6), ethnicity was a 'straight jacket' for southern intellectuals. He says: 'They have become so conscious of it that they exploit it in the struggle to satisfy their petty needs and ambitions' (Nyaba 2000: 6). As violence escalated, so did the narrative. Two Dinka commanders of the Nasir faction stated in their resignation that 'we will not be able to explain why we continue to be part of a force that kills our mothers' (Akol 2003: 88–9). In the end, the Nasir faction argued that they were fighting 'Dinka domination', while the Nuer were labelled as 'enemies of the Southern revolution' (Jok & Hutchinson 1999: 133). Elite narratives coalesced with strongly felt ethnic ties to create a volatile situation. At the same time, Khartoum stoked this and similar inter-communal conflicts by arming ethnicity-based militias in a strategy of 'divide-and-rule' (Ayers 2010: 166).

While this conflict raged in the south, the north/south conflict continued. The rhetoric of *Jihad* was used to muster support amongst the Muslim youth (Martin 2002: 117). This provided a religious and identity-based justification for a political war, which is not easily reversed and is likely to entrench differences. However, warlords and militia leaders have been said to lack this *jihadist* fervour and rather viewed the militia as 'an extension of business' (Johnson quoted in Ayers 2010: 167). In this way, the north/south and south/south conflicts mirrored each other's use of identity rifts to instigate significant violence on behalf of leaders whose interests and motivations were often divergent from their followers' needs. As expected, the conflict therefore hardened racial and religious rifts (Deng 1995: 15–16). Religion, in particular, became a key fissure in Sudanese society and provided further fuel for the separatist agenda (Deng 1995: 13). As these societal rifts hardened and crystallized, politics and conflict in both the north and south became driven by fundamentalist and radical ideologies (Deng 1995: 15–16). This ran contrary to Garang's vision of mending rifts to form a new Sudanese identity.

The events described above seem to endorse the instrumentalist view of identity and conflict.[1] However, one must also interrogate why identity proved so instrumental for leaders to mobilize large groups of people. As one respondent indicated, ethnicity is the most efficient way to raise awareness around a set of interests, which is aggravated by a lack of education (Interview D 2017). Some respondents also view these as historical conflicts (Interview A 2017; Interview B 2017; Interview E 2017). While this is debatable, due to the constructed nature of ethnic identity, the perception of ethnic identities and conflicts as historical is important. In the south, social and political life was largely structured on the basis of ethnic identities, through the traditional leadership instituted by the colonial regime (discussed in Chapter 2) and as a result of the dominant kinship networks (Deng 1995: 16–17). It is plausible that ethnic identity, therefore, provided an easy and ready conduit for leaders to exchange influence. However, this influence exchange lacked mutuality. Prototype leaders can have very limited mutuality with their followers in terms of interests and needs once they are given a leadership position (Hogg 2001: 194–5). This was the case here. As a result, the ability to influence the population was momentary and driven by short-sighted elite interests, which would prevent the development of a future-looking and widespread ideology and identity. Instead, a divided society was fractured further.

## Statehood and nationhood in the midst of war

The Khartoum elite continued their drive for an Islamic state in the 1990s. The Comprehensive Call (*da'wa*) between 1992 and 1996 sought to implement and enforce an Islamic ideology across all sectors of society (De Waal 1998: 140; Rubin 2010: 46–7). This included the forcible relocation of African Sudanese to 'peace camps', where they were provided with severe working conditions and taught the Qur'an (De Waal 1998: 141; Rubin 2010: 46–7). It also entailed the abduction or relocation of children to Qur'anic schools, where they were forced to convert to Islam and indoctrinated with the NIF's Islamist ideology, thereby producing military recruits for the Popular Defence Forces (De Waal 1998: 141). However, while the south was facing internal factionalism, the NIF was plagued by political rifts and competition between elites. In a political battle between Hassan al-Turabi, the party's ideological leader, and President Omar al-Bashir, its political leader, al-Bashir emerged the victor, resulting in a shift from fundamentalism to pragmatism in the early 2000s; yet some members, such as Vice-President Ali Osman Taha, did maintain an Islamist ideology (Johnson 2011b: 15; Rolandsen 2011: 553).

Garang grew more open to the idea of secession – a shift some attribute to Mengistu's downfall, though this is uncertain (Young 2005: 539; 2012: 81–2).

The first time the SPLM/A openly introduced the idea of secession was during negotiations in Abuja in 1992, almost a decade after the conflict had begun (Young 2012: 82). The shift in position is clearly seen in Garang's rhetoric. In 1986, Garang stated that 'if anybody wants to separate even in the North, we will fight him because the Sudan must be one. It should not be allowed to disintegrate or fragment itself' (Garang ed. Khalid 1992: 137). At the first SPLM/A National Convention of 1994, Garang's speech, while still promoting unity, demonstrated a softening of this position, promoting self-determination as a viable option if unity fails (SPLM 1994a). In one instance, he says:

> ... it must be categorically stated that a solution within the context of one Sudan is only possible if the cardinal issues are addressed, and if and only if the Sudan moves away from its present basis of Old Sudan to the New Sudan, for otherwise the country will break up and none of us in the SPLM/SPLA would shed any tears.
>
> SPLM 1994a: 37

Garang continued to promote his vision of a unified New Sudan but ensured that secession was a viable option both for bargaining purposes and to ensure support from southerners, as discussed below.

At the same time, the SPLM/A, with significant territory under its command and in positioning itself as future rulers in a united Sudan or of an independent South Sudan, had to look towards implementing its vision of a democratic state. It is in this area, however, that Garang received perhaps the most criticism. In its early phase, the SPLM/A, driven by its Marxist ideology, largely dismantled the traditional institutions that formed the backbone of local society and served as the bridge between state and people (Young 2005: 540; Leonardi 2013: 8). Nevertheless, in many areas in southern Sudan, the chieftainship system, which was hardly universal, proved resilient and the only system of governance (Rolandsen 2005: 72–3). These institutions were often responsible for providing services and organizing communities around public projects (Rolandsen 2005: 72). The weakening of these institutions, however, would have a significant impact on future peacebuilding challenges (see Chapter 5), which demonstrates how institutions are influenced by the leadership process. While these traditional institutions were dismantled in response to a specific situation (the need to maintain foreign support through a Marxist ideology), leader actions in this regard would have an important impact on future state-building and institution-building efforts.

In 1994, the SPLM/A held a national convention in Chukudum that established, at least on paper, key structures reflective of a democratic and functional state. Allowances were made for the wartime context in which they were operating. This included the proposal of executive, legislative and judicial bodies within the SPLM/A and the south (SPLM 1994b: 1–8, 10–12). Some identify this as a watershed moment that sparked a shifting and more open culture in the SPLM/A (Nyaba 2000: 4–5; Wöndu 2011: 182). Others see it as a political and somewhat disingenuous manoeuvre. It has been read as a propaganda move used to win support in the competition with the Nasir faction (Rolandsen 2005: 39). Garang viewed the establishment of more robust institutions as a threat to his authority and reportedly opposed this convention, prevented much of it from being implemented, and blocked any subsequent conventions from occurring (Young 2005: 540–1). The convention itself has been accused of lacking representation and holding 'pro forma' elections (Rolandsen 2005: 82).

Nevertheless, the SPLM/A attempted to establish some institutions, such as elected 'liberation councils', which served to instil a degree of inclusivity in the SPLM/A movement for the southern population, even though these were widely seen as ineffective, poorly organized and in competition with other local structures (Leonardi 2013: 159). In short, it could be argued that these moves were driven by political factors and a need for the SPLM/A to maintain its supremacy, rather than an effort to form a state that was responsive to citizens' needs. This indicates that if leader and follower interests are not in sync, then the state (driven by leaders) and the nation (driven by followers) are unlikely to converge.

Finally, a brief discussion of the military is important due to the traditional role of this institution in nation-building. In the internal SPLM/A conflict, the two factions established, used and armed ethnic militias, which often lacked training, discipline and a clear command structure (Jok & Hutchinson 1999: 134). At the same time, the NIF had formalized and legalized the use of militias, such as the *Murahaliin* (in the south-west) and the *Rufa'a* (in the southern Blue Nile), through the Popular Defence Act of 1989 (Ayers 2010: 166–7; De Waal 1998: 138). Such armed forces are unlikely to produce the same unifying and socialization effect as a distinct military. In the end, it would lead to a proliferation of militias, interests, loyalties and conflicts that would become a severe challenge in the post-CPA and post-secession period.

## The disintegration of collective will and collective responsibility?

Despite the internal conflict in the south, followers across the divide held the same goals of fighting Khartoum (Jok & Hutchinson 1999: 130). According to Nyaba (2000: 5–6) fighting the north was more appealing and understandable amongst the southern population because '[Southerners could] still see the "Jelaba" controlling the market and exploiting them through unequal exchange'. However, this unity of purpose did little to ease the south's continued struggle with building and exercising collective will, action and loyalty. In fact, the allegiances of various militant groups were highly dynamic and shifting (Glickman 2000: 270). By the early 2000s the civil war, while still a political conflict between Khartoum and the south, was being fought largely by and amongst southerners (Martin 2002: 112). This was the product of internal rifts in the SPLM/A, the proliferation of various militia groups (often with an ethnic loyalty) and Khartoum's ability to practise a policy of 'divide and rule'. The Nasir faction itself also mutated, first forming SPLM-United with other SPLM/A-Mainstream defectors, and then splintering into the South Sudan Independence Movement (SSIM/A) led by Machar and the SPLM-United led by Akol (Rolandsen 2005: 37–8).

What this internal conflict did do was stimulate a discussion about the decision-making structures of southern Sudanese society (i.e. how the will of the people is determined). Since the defecting factions portrayed themselves as more democratic, the SPLM/A was forced to respond with more democratic practices in order to maintain the support of the southern intellectuals, soldiers and populace (Rolandsen 2005: 39). The competing factions subsequently engaged in a 'propaganda war' to win support of southerners, intellectuals and foreigners (Rolandsen 2005: 39). Akol, part of the Nasir faction at the time, characterized Garang's side as engaging in 'mud-slinging' and 'character assassination' (Akol 2003: 87). Yet, in some of their communications, the Nasir faction regularly referred to Garang as 'the Monster' (Akol 2003: 135, 137–9). While the Nasir faction had early support from intellectuals, this faded as they proved unable to implement their promises of a more democratic movement (Rolandsen 2005: 39). In general, therefore, a pattern appears to emerge in which elite interests trumped the need to foster a collective identity, build a responsive state and engender collective will and loyalty.

More evidence of this is seen when the Nasir faction, while it had separated from the SPLM/A on the basis of seeking a harder stance on self-determination, subsequently and paradoxically allied with Khartoum (Deng 1995: 20). Faction leaders were heavily criticized for this (Deng 1995: 20–1). Peter Adwok Nyaba (2000: 3–4), a member of the Nasir faction who later returned to the SPLM/A-Mainstream, argues that this collaboration with Khartoum was done in secret, without the knowledge or approval of other leaders in the faction. The decision to cooperate with Khartoum, however, was driven by logistical necessity. In particular, Machar lacked access to other neighbouring countries from which to import military supplies (Jok & Hutchinson 1999: 129). As a result, Khartoum became the primary source of support for Machar and Akol (Young 2019: 6). This culminated in the 1997 Khartoum Peace Agreement between Machar's faction and Khartoum, but its slow implementation led to many of Machar's followers returning to the SPLA (Young 2019: 6). This reiterates the centrality of personal ambitions in the SPLM/A rift.

Central to this discussion is the issue of leadership. As explained, the south/south war was not driven by the needs or grievances of society at large, nor were most civilians from either ethnic group interested in continuing this conflict (Jok & Hutchinson 1999: 127, 130–2; Nyaba 2000: 5). Pinaud (2021: 135–6) refers to Garang and Machar as 'ethnopolitical entrepreneurs' who pushed narratives glorifying their own groups and demonizing the 'enemy' groups for the sake of mobilizing sufficient numbers of soldiers. Furthermore, the collective desires of the people were overridden by elite interests and the military strength of combatant leaders (Jok & Hutchinson 1999: 127, 130). For example, communication and cooperation between Dinka and Nuer ethnic groups were reportedly suppressed by military leaders of both factions (Jok & Hutchinson 1999: 130). Yet, this narrative risks simplifying the situation into one of 'elite puppet-masters', and neglecting the agency of followers.

Laying the blame for the conflict solely at the feet of the SPLM/A leadership does not explain why ethnic identity interests (e.g. 'tribal wealth'), ethnic structures (e.g. ethnic militias) and ethnic loyalties were able to override the reportedly widespread enmity with the north and secessionist aims. This is further evidenced in the way inter-ethnic marriage between the Dinka and Nuer, previously part of the SPLM/A's strategy to maintain support, decreased during this period (Pinaud 2016: 247–8). Also, the use of pastoralist militant groups demonstrates the power smaller groups held over SPLA leaders. These groups would shift their loyalties based on the SPLA's ability to serve their needs or their existing inter-communal disputes (Wild et al. 2018: 6). The Toposa in Eastern Equatoria would fight for or against the SPLA based on who was providing weapons and food (Wild et al. 2018: 6).

In other words, it is interesting to note that soldiers' and community members' loyalty appears to have been determined by ethnicity rather than ideology – this despite most southerners supporting the Nasir faction's stated reason for rebelling – seeking a harder stance on self-determination than Garang was providing at the time (Young 2005: 539). The SPLM/A included a political arm in its 'Movement' component and was led by Garang, whom many characterized as an 'intellectual' (Johnson 2011b: 10; Young 2005: 544–5; Wöndu 2011: 171), but remained 'first and foremost an army which had developed little in the way of a practical social politics of a liberation' (De Waal 1998: 136).

Both the Marxist and Sudanism ideologies that rhetorically underpinned the SPLM/A were promoted for pragmatic reasons, and primarily an international audience, to garner sympathy and support. But an ideology that stemmed from and spoke to the values, experiences and visions of southern Sudanese was not carefully cultivated, beyond a non-negotiable desire for self-determination. In other words, the SPLM/A did not provide the ideology and social and political structures that long-standing ethnic identities did. These structures provide the norms and mechanisms for collective action as well as the protection and services that generate loyalty in return. It could be argued that this contributed to the domination of ethnicity as the guiding indicator for loyalty and action.

In the end, the SPLM/A-Mainstream emerged the more powerful party due to Garang's logistical advantage and not because followers supported his 'New

Sudan' vision (Young 2005: 539). This advantage included Garang's 'international credibility', while Machar and Akol were only able to get support from Khartoum (Young 2019: 6). Therefore, in this case, ideology appears to hold less loyalty than ethnic identity and outcomes were determined less by popular support and more by contextual factors. This indicates that despite the unity of purpose in opposing the north, southerners lacked the foundations and leadership to rally behind a collective ideology. As a result, by the late 1990s, both factions of the SPLM/A had splintered further, resulting in a proliferation of militia groups and a military stalemate (Jok & Hutchinson 1999: 135). While struggling to maintain a sense of unity in the south, the SPLM/A turned its efforts towards a broader movement encompassing the whole Sudan (Iyob & Khadiagala 2006: 102).

## Inner turmoil: Leadership, power and influence

The conflict arising from the 1991 split of the SPLM/A has been characterized as a 'war of the Southern educated elite', with Garang and Machar being referred to as 'the two doctors' (Jok & Hutchinson 1999: 125, 128). This would reflect a general rift in southern society between the formally educated/urban minorities and rural communities. As an example of the distaste held for the leaders during this conflict, Jok and Hutchinson (1999: 131) quote a Nuer chief as saying:

> They used to tell us that the reason why Nuer and Dinka fight each other was because we are ignorant. We don't know anything because we are not educated. But now look at all this killing! This war between the Nuer and Dinka is much worse than anything we experienced in the past. And it is the war of educated [elite] – it is not our war at all!

This was not a passing sentiment. Nyaba (2000: 5) narrates how during 'the Akobo conference of 1994, one elder asked why the wars instigated by the intellectuals don't seem to end'. The way in which Machar gained influence amongst the Nuer is also telling. He used a prophecy from an influential Nuer prophet, Ngundeng, about a battle led by a messiah-like figure matching Machar's description, to mobilize the Nuer youth who would participate in the

Bor massacre (Wild et al. 2018: 5). Machar had to piggy-back on the influence and referent power Ngundeng held to exchange influence with a population that he had little in common with. This is but one example of the ways traditional leadership and political leadership would intersect, sometimes in a symbiotic manner, and sometimes in a conflictual manner.

Nevertheless, leaders of both sides were accused of starting and fomenting this war solely for their personal political interests and rivalries (Deng 1995: 20; Jok & Hutchinson 1999: 136–7). Machar and Akol, who were members of the movement's high command, are accused of coopting the nascent 'agitation' for a more democratic SPLM/A only after they personally 'fell out' with Garang (Nyaba 2000: 1). In the end, this factional war had the effect of reducing followers' faith in both Garang's and Machar's leadership (Jok & Hutchinson 1999: 130).

As discussed, both Khartoum and southern leaders used existing, small-scale economic disputes such as cattle-raiding and grazing land disagreements to mobilize militias on their respective sides. One of the ways this was achieved was by undermining traditional leadership and authority. For example, the traditional hierarchical age-set system within the Dinka *Titweng* was erased in order to incorporate these 'cattle guards' into the SPLA (Wild et al. 2018: 5). Within his Nuer community, Machar introduced a difference between government/secular violence (*koor kume*) and traditional/homeland violence (*koor cieng*), the first of which was considered exempt from the traditional costs, responsibilities, rituals and justice mechanisms associated with killing (Wild et al. 2018: 4–5). The result would be severe, brutal and widespread violence against civilians (Wild et al. 2018: 4–5). In this way, the leadership process, driven by converging interests rather than shared goals and vision, resulted in the breaking down of societal norms rather than the building of them.

Military activity was driven less by a mutual goal between leaders and followers and a collective understanding of group identity than separate interests that momentarily converged. It is fairly evident that, while influence was exchanged in the short term, there was no mutuality of interests and needs, which forced leaders to resort to identity narratives to mobilize collective action. In the long term, this ran counter to leaders' stated goals by fragmenting society further. As a result, the leader/follower gap led to a disjuncture of goals and action, as action became driven by short-term situational factors that primarily affected leaders. The ease with which allegiances were shifted also implies limited commitment to the visions espoused by their respective leaders.

A discussion of Garang's leadership is also important at this time. The source and degree of Garang's legitimacy is difficult to determine. Understandably, no election or similar exercise was conducted during the conflict to gauge his popular support (Martin 2002: 121), though even post-independence he is viewed as a unifying figure (Interview D 2017). And while it could be said that Garang and the SPLM/A emerged as the dominant representative of the southern people, the discussion above illustrates that this was not a simple relationship. There appears to have been a certain acceptance of the SPLM/A amongst southerners as necessary to lead them to independence, but also a degree of contempt for the elite, particularly the educated, urban elite. It is possible that southerners held a similar regard for Garang. Nevertheless, Garang appeared adept at shifting tactics and building support when necessary. While this seemed evidence of a skilled politician at the time, it would result in long-term nation-building challenges. Young (2005: 539) says of Garang:

> His rule has been tough and high-handed, but many argue necessary in the difficult political environment of south Sudan. However, the costs of his leadership have been high. The SPLM/A has never developed an ideology that was coherent and acceptable to its followers because it always had to be subject to the dictates and needs of Garang. By calling for a united Sudan and at the same time giving support to southern self-determination, Garang has been able to be all things to all people. In the Arab world and for Northerners his rhetoric has been strongly in favour of a united and democratic Sudan, while in the South he presented himself as a true son of the soil.

While the above description may be reflective of a skilled politician and even charismatic leadership, when understood within the context of the leadership process it reveals several challenges. Garang likely used multiple sources of power, including referent, expert and legitimate power. Garang's referent power and charisma is hard to dispute. This is particularly evident in the spiritual myths he would come to embody – being likened to Moses leading his followers to the Promised Land (Frahm 2012: 38). Steven Wöndu, an SPLM/A member, recalls how he was 'impressed' by Garang's radio broadcasts before joining the movement (Wöndu 2011: 126). Garang's oratory skills are described by Hilde Johnson (2011b: 11):

> He was a master of crowds, mobilising thousands with speeches that could go on for hours. He spoke in the popular idiom, with analogies and stories the people knew. People would roar with laughter, and cheer in anticipation and appreciation, 'SPLM Oyeeee'. Even during his first visit to the Nuba Mountains, at Kauda, Dr. John got everyone's attention with his knowledge of Nuba history and use of old myths, proverbs and traditions. He was an entertainer of sorts.

The use of myths and stories that resonated with his audience demonstrates an understanding of his followership and a degree of mutuality. It also reflects referent power in that his followers were able to see themselves in him. His speeches likely also contributed to myth-building processes and an affirmation of southern identities that had historically been neglected. It therefore contributed to the continued process of identity construction found in nation-building.

However, Garang's use of coercive power to maintain his position and his vision indicates two things. First, his vision, and perhaps even his leadership, lacked the political and popular support needed to form the collective will and collective loyalty indicative of a nation. The following passage by Wöndu (2011: 171–2) is illustrative:

> That he was a sophisticated intellectual came out very clearly. I felt that Southern Sudan was blessed to have him at its hour of most need and that those Southerners who sought to bring him down were making a grievous mistake. Yet, I did not understand why this great thinker, strategist, tactician and fighter shared these heavy matters with me. Deep in my heart, I felt that John Garang was being charitable to the Arabs. To him, only a small minority clique of Arabs was responsible for the carnage in Sudan. In other words, the majority of Northerners were innocent or even victims of neglect and oppression by the minority clique. This was a new and strange line of thinking to me. My own experiences as a child did not corroborate Dr Garang's digression. My soul could not reconcile with the idea of peaceful coexistence with the Arabs … My reservations notwithstanding, John Garang's analysis of the Sudanese conflict made some sense.

In this passage we see the complexity of leadership and nation-building. Garang, with all his charisma, could not override the depth of feeling that lived experiences and historical narratives had instilled in Wöndu, even if that feeling had been created by constructed myths and identity formation. Yet, at the same time, he fulfilled a need within the southern population for a leader to provide guidance and manage meaning. This generated an almost contradictory leadership process, using referent power to pursue one direction and coercive and reward power to pursue another. This would result in a nation rife with contradictions.

As a result, leaders and followers failed to act as a collective even in the face of a common enemy, evidenced in the shifting alliances and inter-communal conflict characteristic of the 1990s. While Garang's coercive power may have managed some of these rifts, it did not mend them. And, since coercive power cannot transcend the leader's death, South Sudanese politics and society would fracture to a disastrous degree in the future.

Secondly, the use of coercive power is indicative of a lack of mutuality and, as a result, a failure to exchange influence beyond short-term goals. Garang may have provided the guidance necessary to confront Khartoum and mobilize support for this confrontation, but his espoused values and norms of unity, non-racialism, non-discrimination and respect for human rights were not reflected in those of his followers. Therefore, the leader/follower relationship appears almost transactional, despite his portrayal as a transformational leader.[2] Leadership in southern Sudan, however, appears to have a tradition of transactional leadership. Traditional leaders, for example, were historically chosen largely on the basis of their wealth, allowing them to provide for the community, and later on their status and education, permitting them to act as a mediator between state and people (Leonardi 2013: 162–3).

In this way, the case of John Garang illustrates that nation-building requires more than charismatic or transactional leadership. First, nations cannot be built through the use of coercive power where a mutual vision of the nation, espoused by both leader and led, is lacking. Secondly, where a mutuality of norms and values is lacking, the construction of a national identity and substantive ideology is very difficult. A national identity is necessary to promote cohesion. An ideology helps drive collective action and forms the basis of the state. While the 'costs' of Garang's leadership are not readily apparent at this stage, they would become critical in the post-CPA and post-secession phase.

## Conclusion

In this chapter, we see a fracturing of the leadership process, which leads to a fracturing of the developing South Sudanese nation. Garang's influence, driven by a mixture of charisma, coercion, chance and resources, generated the mirage of a cohesive society in pursuit of a common goal. The common goal – secession – was real, but cohesion, trust and a shared responsibility was lacking. Why? The SPLM/A elite dynamics during the rift illustrate a situation of inter-elite influence, bolstered by prototype leadership. Garang was able to court the international community, providing him with the logistical and material resources to exercise coercive and reward power over his commanders. Other leaders, such as Machar, made unsavoury deals to maintain relevance. Meanwhile, the citizens, who had surrendered the power to define reality, were rewarded with competing visions of this reality.[3] As a result, the societal dynamic fragmented, as predicted by Smircich and Morgan (2011: 20) in such situations, and the most evident, logical and pragmatic course was to turn to leaders who represented the reality southerners faced daily: their ethnic community.

## Notes

1   See Stewart 2008: 8.
2   See Burns 2012: 3–5 for a discussion on transformational and transactional leadership.
3   See Smircich & Morgan 2011: 20.

Part Three

# Independence and Civil War: Building a State, Forgetting a Nation (2002–15)

# 5

# Negotiating and Implementing Peace

## Introduction

In 2005, the Comprehensive Peace Agreement was signed, signalling a formal end to the war between Khartoum and southern Sudan. This is also when the state and the nation in South Sudan began to diverge. This divergence stemmed from the way in which the peace process was driven by elite interests, and popular needs and voices were neglected. Identity, a driving issue in the war and peace processes, lost its relevance in the interim period. At least, this was the case for elites bargaining at the national level. At the local level, governance dominated by traditional ethnic structures and violence stoked along communal lines reflected the reality of day-to-day life. But the negotiation for the future of the Sudanese and South Sudanese states was decided at the highest level, between elites and the international community.

This debate centred around the technical and institutional aspect of the state: distribution of state resources, elections, borders and government positions. All of this reflected the interests of elites. In this way, the conversations on the future of the state and the nation were separated between the leaders and the followers. As the elites fought over the state, the followers were confronted with the national questions of who belongs to 'us' and 'them', who could be trusted to provide protection, and who shared the same values. Without any national guidance or dialogue on this issue, citizens looked towards the local, and the nation-building and state-building processes diverged. While the South Sudanese state was being birthed, the South Sudanese nation was busy fragmenting into smaller and smaller fractals.

## Negotiating peace

Throughout the Second Civil War, the peace process experienced several stops and starts. Under Nigerian leadership, peace negotiations took place in Abuja in the early 1990s, with little success (Young 2012: 82). The Inter-Governmental Authority on Development (IGAD) stepped in to lead the peace process in 1993, with the 1994 Declaration of Principles being hailed as its first success (Rolandsen 2011: 553). Surprisingly, this declaration included an acknowledgement of the south's right to self-determination in the event that democracy and secularism failed in Khartoum, which led to its ultimate rejection by the Sudanese government (Young 2012: 84). The peace process faltered after this, with new actors becoming involved while others lost interest (Rolandsen 2011: 553). For example, a joint Libyan–Egyptian initiative was launched in response to, amongst other things, 'African domination of the peace process' (Young 2012: 86–7). But these efforts were seen to be competing with the IGAD process (Iyob & Khadiagala 2006: 101).

IGAD then reinvigorated its peace process in 2001 and 2002, due to a series of events and circumstances that presented a changing context more favourable for peace (Rolandsen 2011: 553). The resulting Machakos Protocol of 20 July 2002 would pave the way for the CPA of 2005 (Rolandsen 2011: 551). Hilde Johnson (2011: 1–3), a key mediator in the peace process, details how Vice-President Ali Osman Taha initiated direct talks with John Garang in 2003, which would make significant contributions to an eventual agreement. The final CPA included the Machakos Protocol (which provided for an interim period of six years and the southern Sudanese referendum), a power sharing agreement signed on 26 May 2004, a wealth sharing agreement signed on 7 January 2004, resolutions on the Abyei, Southern Kordofan and Blue Nile conflicts signed on 26 May 2004, and an agreement on security arrangements signed on 25 September 2003 (Comprehensive Peace Agreement 2005).

### The influence of identity narratives on the peace process

By the 1990s and 2000s, identity had become so entrenched in the Sudanese conflict that it began to bleed into the peace process. For example, the appointment of an ordained Episcopalian minister, Senator John Danforth, as the United States' special envoy was received with suspicion from Khartoum, which viewed it as a subtle signal of support for the south (Martin 2002: 124). However, the focus on the issue of religion and the north/south conflict would lead to a peace process that failed to understand the myriad identities at play.

The first of these is the urban/rural divide – an oft-overlooked identity marker that has consistently influenced peace and conflict processes in the background. A clear division between rural and urban populations and the less-educated and educated populations in southern Sudan meant that the 'educated elite' and their development initiatives were viewed with antagonism, 'resentment' and 'suspicion' by many rural southerners (Leonardi 2013: 161–2). At the same time, the educated urban population often looked to the rural dwellers with a paradoxical sentiment of both 'idealised [nostalgia]' and 'disdain' (Leonardi 2013: 162). These distinct identities are exemplified in the statement by an urban-dwelling southerner:

> It is not good for chiefs to be in town. If we mix things in the town, there will be no difference between outside people and town people – we need to differentiate; this is one of the most important things now. The town is supposed to be only for soldiers, students, the educated, traders, technical people and government.
>
> Quoted in Leonardi 2013: 162–3

His emphasis on the need to keep the urban and rural populations distinct from each other is telling. It also reaffirms the growing evidence that, despite the near universal opposition to the north and the dominant narratives of oppression and exploitation that united southerners, there were many competing identities in the region. A related divide can be found in class differences. The marriage market created by the SPLM/A during the war, with inflated bridewealth prices, served to install the SPLA military elite as the dominant class (Pinaud 2016: 251–4). All this reflects the distrust between the educated and less formally educated peoples of Sudan, which inevitably mirrored the leader/follower gap. This would make ensuring an inclusive peace process difficult. However, the exclusion of such a core identity group (the rural population) from a peace process that would determine the future identity of state and nation would pose significant challenges in the future.

With regard to religion, the Christian Church had grown substantially in southern Sudan by the 1990s and had played a significant role in south/south reconciliation. The New Sudan Council of Churches (NSCC) engaged local communities and leaders to promote Dinka–Nuer dialogue, and some have attributed the eventual reconciliation between Garang and Machar to the NSCC-led *Wunlit* process, which brought hundreds of representatives of the warring communities together to reach an agreement (Moro 2015: 6). However, the church, and in fact civil society in general, was excluded from the north/south peace process, which was largely an elite affair between the NCP and the SPLM/A (Moro 2015: 4).

In the matter of religion, the north/south peace process was primarily focused on the status of Islam. The conflict had brought to light and entrenched a multitude of tensions and contradictions across multiple identity markers. Yet, the peace process placed a spotlight on religion (Johnson 2011b: 46, 49; Machakos Protocol 2002: 3–4, 6, 8, 12–13). Specifically, it centred on the role of religion in the state. Once again, this reveals a leader/follower gap. Leaders' interest in identity would rise and fall based on how it would influence their access to power and the state structures they were a part of. However, their use of identity was founded on and contributed to the social reality of their followers. Identity difference and conflict in South Sudan reinforced each other. However, due to a lack of mutuality between leaders and followers, this dangerous cycle of identity construction was not addressed in the peace process.

## Statehood and nationhood: Laying the groundwork for the future state(s)

After nearly two decades of conflict in which both sides appeared immovable, international events rather than domestic circumstances are attributed with moving the peace process forward. The relationship between Khartoum and the United States was critical, particularly Sudan's effort to renegotiate its label as a sponsor of terrorism and increased interest in Sudan's oil reserves (Ayers 2010: 162; Martin 2002: 111–12, 115–16). The two key sticking points throughout these years were the role of religion in the state and self-determination for the south (Johnson 2011b: 42–50; Rolandsen 2011: 555).

The Declaration of Principles of 1994 affirmed the right to self-determination in the event that democracy and secularism failed, but also prioritized unity (Iyob & Khadiagala 2006: 105; Young 2012: 84). This declaration was eventually rejected by Khartoum (Young 2012: 85). Hilde Johnson (2011b: 42–54) describes how the final negotiations nearly failed because of these two points: the SPLM/A was unwilling to compromise on a referendum and wanted Sudan to be a secular state in the interim period, while Khartoum was unwilling to relinquish the Islamist agenda and *Sharia* law if the south was likely to secede in any case. A breakdown in negotiations was averted, however, and a breakthrough was achieved with the Machakos Protocol (Johnson 2011b: 49–55).

The Machakos Protocol, similar to the Declaration of Principles, made provision for a southern referendum with the condition that efforts would be made to maintain unity (Machakos Protocol 2002: 2, 12–13, 17). It also dedicated significant space to the issue of religion, highlighting Sudan's diversity and the need for freedom of religion, while also indicating that areas outside southern Sudan 'shall have as its source of legislation *Sharia* and the consensus of the people' (Machakos Protocol 2002: 3–4, 6, 8, 12–13). The question of religion and separation boiled down to whether and how the state would represent its citizenry. Those around the peace table had to determine what the relationship would be between the nation and the state. However, there was no consensus on what constituted the Sudanese nation(s), and the document primarily focused on religion rather than other aspects of Sudanese identities. In the end, the CPA would lay out the nature of the Sudanese state and not the nation.

An important change in the Second Civil War was the introduction of oil as a key interest. The discovery and extraction of oil in the south added an economic element to the conflict, within a wider context of an economy in turmoil. In an effort to 'depopulate' oil-rich regions, Khartoum began a 'scorched earth' policy in the 1980s that would continue throughout the war (Ayers 2010: 167). By the 1990s and 2000s, Khartoum intensified its efforts to achieve a military victory, at least in the oil-producing areas (Martin 2002: 119). Khartoum's unwillingness to compromise on the issue of self-determination has been attributed to its desire to hold the south's oil reserves (Martin 2002: 118–20; Rolandsen 2011: 555).

Yet it is important not to confuse oil as a complicating factor with oil as a cause for war. The First Civil War took place without this issue. When oil was discovered in the 1980s in southern Sudan it sparked debate about how this resource would be developed and shared (Mayen 1982: 7), which did contribute in part to the breakdown of the Addis Ababa Agreement (Nyaba 2000: 24). Sudan only began exporting oil in 1999 (Ayers 2010: 165). Any argument that the conflict is resource-driven negates the decades of federalist and separatist demands of the south that had been blocked since pre-independence by the Khartoum elite.

Meanwhile, in the south, the SPLM/A was competing for authority of the region. In its early days, the SPLM/A had an ambivalent or even antagonistic relationship with NGOs, civil society organizations and traditional institutions (Leonardi 2013: 1, Rolandsen 2005: 30; Young 2005: 540). Yet, the SPLM/A relied on traditional leaders and institutions, in the form of 'intimidated or coopted' chiefships and customary courts, to extract resources (taxes and troops) from the populace (Pinaud 2021: 98–9). The relationship of the SPLM/A and the central state with the people or nation would often occur through an intermediary of traditional systems. By the end of the Second Civil War, the SPLM/A was perceived by many southerners 'as the new *hakuma*'[1] (Leonardi 2013: 159). As the war progressed, the nature of the state and the perception of it amongst southerners began to change. Expectations of service delivery increased as the SPLM/A sought to include more of the population in its 'state' (Leonardi 2013: 160–1). However, some have noted that while expectations rose, there was not a corresponding increase of responsibility for the sustainability of the state, its institutions and its infrastructure amongst the population (Leonardi 2013: 160–1). This is indicative of a failure to generate collective responsibility. One of the reasons for this may be the way in which state or political leaders have tended to rely on the legitimacy of traditional institutions and leaders rather than their own legitimacy or state institutions.

In this way, the SPLM/A had to consider how to build a state in a war-torn society in preparation for peace. This intention was signalled in a statement signed by John Garang and released in 2003. The statement primarily blamed poor institutionalization on 'a lack of resources' (SPLM/SPLA 2003: 2). However, in the 1996 conference on 'Civil Society and the Organization of Civil Authority in the New Sudan', Lawrence Luay Akuey accused the SPLM/A of a 'lack of interest' in building a system of education (SPLM 1996: 3). Some southerners accused the SPLM/A of destroying historical 'relations of dependency and clientage' that had previously ensured the protection of vulnerable members of society, shifting the responsibility to the state (Leonardi 2013: 161).

Of course, within the context of conflict and with limited resources, the SPLM/A was unable, and perhaps unwilling, to fulfil its state-building task. The SPLM/A appeared to frame its vision of the state on a hybrid of traditional structures used by the colonial government and Western models of democratic states. In the late 1990s and 2000s, the SPLM/A began to acknowledge the role of traditional leadership, reversing its earlier antagonism to the system (Leonardi 2013: 1, 159). This is likely because traditional leadership was one of the few mechanisms through which the state had historically reached its citizens (Leonardi 2013: 9). One respondent indicated how 'power centres' could be found at the local level, as people resorted to the traditional institutions in the absence of functioning formal institutions (Interview C 2017). While urban dwellers viewed traditional leaders as separate and distinct from government, the system of traditional leadership was in fact an extension of the state and served as an intermediary between the state and the rural population (Leonardi 2013: 9, 162–3).

In short, with a peace agreement now imminent, the SPLM/A had to confront the many contradictions between nation and state in southern Sudan. However, the leader/follower gap made this a challenging endeavour. There was no extensive dialogue or consensus on what constituted the nation that the state was meant to represent and indeed what the purpose of the state would be. This followed nearly two decades of shifting SPLM/A ideologies and policies driven by external factors and elite interests rather than a mutual exchange of influence with the southern people. As a result, at independence South Sudanese leadership would lack a guiding ideology from which to move forward (Interview C 2017).

## Continued challenges of collective will and collective responsibility

Following the official reconciliation between the warring factions of the SPLM/A, the movement was able to present a more unified front at the negotiating table, while also negotiating on behalf of other Sudanese regions (Rolandsen 2011: 553). Yet, the final peace agreement indicates that the SPLM/A was negotiating primarily for the south, and even there, it may have been negotiating primarily for the southern elite. The SPLM/A had conducted the war on the basis of a 'New Sudan' in conjunction with other political forces and armed rebellions in the country. However, the peace agreement largely excluded these conflicts. For example, the questions of Abyei, the Blue Nile and Southern Kordofan were handled in separate chapters of the agreement and Darfur was excluded altogether (Comprehensive Peace Agreement 2005: 63–84). Similarly, many members of the NDA were opposed to various elements of the Machakos Protocol, requiring Garang to personally contact these members to explain the SPLM/A's signing of the agreement (Johnson 2011b: 56). While southern Sudan was able to act collectively with other regions and peoples of Sudan, this appeared superficial and did not signal the collective will of a nation.

In addition, the SPLM/A's leadership crisis was far from resolved. From 29 November to 1 December 2004, amidst growing opposition to Garang's leadership style and rumours that he was planning to remove and arrest Salva Kiir, SPLM/A leaders held a meeting in Rumbek to confront Garang regarding his leadership style (Young 2005: 541). Hilde Johnson (2011: 163–4) describes this as a very tense period, especially as negotiations were reaching a conclusion. She also argues that Salva Kiir was acting largely under pressure from other leaders (Johnson 2011b: 163–4). Yet Salva Kiir apparently 'accused Garang of carrying the SPLM/A in his briefcase' (Young 2005: 541). Garang's critics were silenced, as they often were in the past, by the argument that open dissent and disunity amongst leaders was counter-productive to the movement's goals – a theme that would be repeated in the succession battle after his death (AUCISS 2014: 29; Rolandsen 2015: 168; Young 2005: 541–2).

The peace process was an exclusive one. By bringing in the top leaders of both parties, mediators were able to end over a decade of gridlock in the negotiation process (Johnson 2011b: 1–2). At the same time, it prevented the inclusion of a range of voices which, arguably, may have had different demands. Civil society, for example, was excluded, and other political parties were sidelined in the agreement (Akol 2014: 3–4; Moro 2015: 4). It is also unclear whether the SPLM represented the interests of other southern elites who were excluded (Interview F 2017). Consultations, however, did take place (Interview F 2017). It is therefore difficult to gauge how well the interests of southerners were represented at the negotiating table.

As is well established by now, the one thing that seemed ubiquitous was the desire for secession. In this at least, 'the SPLM did represent the collective sentiment of the people of South Sudan' (Interview F 2017). Hilde Johnson (2011b: 49–50) describes how rural school children were taught and performed songs that promoted self-determination by portraying the Addis Ababa Agreement as a betrayal. She also discusses how early negotiations were jeopardized by this issue when not only leaders but commanders in the field began to suspect that Khartoum would not compromise on self-determination (Johnson 2011b: 47). In the end, when the process was reaching conclusion, Garang had to '[embark] on a highly successful three-week tour' to 'sell' the agreement to southerners (Johnson 2011b: 149).

It is fair to ask why, after decades of stalemate and continuous conflict, the two sides – or rather, the leaders of the two sides – were willing to enter a peace agreement. Proposed arguments include war fatigue, oil production and the heightened role of the United States (Rolandsen 2011: 551). Several scholars have pointed towards the determining role played by the international environment (Iyob & Khadiagala 2006: 101–2; Martin 2002: 112, 115–16, 118–20, 123–7; Rolandsen 2011: 552–5). The central role of international actors in pushing for peace begs the question of popular support and collective will amongst the population. In other words, if the international environment was a determining factor in the parties' willingness to pursue peace, it indicates that the influence being exchanged was more between national and international leaders rather than between Sudanese leaders and their followers.

In summary, while the signing of the CPA in 2005 could be seen as a success, a leadership analysis reveals some concerns. Specifically, the exclusion of other actors (i.e. civil society and other political parties), the suppression of internal dissent in the SPLM/A and the dominant role of the international context may be indicative of a lack of not only representation but an exchange of influence as well. In other words, to what degree did the southern population's interests and needs influence leaders' decisions at the negotiating table?

## Negotiating peace: Leadership or inter-elite exchange?

The motives of leaders during the peace process must be understood in order to assess the level of mutuality and influence exchange with their respective followers. Early efforts at negotiations were seen as disingenuous and 'public relations rhetoric' (Deng 1995: 16). The IGAD peace process was begun on the invitation of al-Bashir. His reasons for doing this were largely pragmatic, including a 'need to preempt foreign intervention' (Iyob & Khadiagala 2006: 103). This included not only a suspicion of UN-led mediation but also a fear of US military intervention (Young 2012: 83). Garang was accused by some of not being committed to the peace process since peace was not seen to be in his interests (Martin 2002: 121). In addition, when direct talks were first proposed, Garang was hesitant, claiming that the top leaders should only be brought in at the end of the negotiation process (Johnson 2011b: 1).

By the time peace was achieved, the peace agreement provided Garang with 'a virtual hegemonic position in the south and the holding of a strong vice presidency nationally' (Young 2005: 535). One can infer that how and when leaders engaged in the peace process was often driven by elite interests and situational factors. This further exemplifies the inability to develop a sense of collective purpose and, particularly in this case, a collective future. Yet, this does not mean that leaders acted without any influence from the population. The issues of secession for the south and *Sharia* for the north were problematic precisely because a compromise on these issues would lead to 'political suicide' for the respective parties (Johnson 2011b: 49).

Nevertheless, the peace process remained largely an elite affair. The negotiations leading to the signing of the Machakos Protocol on 20 July 2002 reveal the leadership dynamic in both Khartoum and the SPLM/A. The four delegates – Said al-Khatib and Yahia Husein Babikir for Khartoum and Deng Alor and Nhial Deng for the SPLM/A – were left alone to negotiate the text of the document (Johnson 2011b: 50). However, they appeared to spend more time making calls with their superiors rather than negotiating, leading some to conclude that they did not actually have the mandate to negotiate and make decisions (Johnson 2011b: 50–4). This reiterates the centralized nature of leadership in Sudan and southern Sudan. Combined with what has already been discussed regarding the leader/follower gap, it confirms that decisions, visions and narratives that would determine the nature of the Sudanese nation and state were driven by a select few whose interests did not necessarily align with society as a whole.

The role of the international context has already been discussed. This is important, because the increased international involvement interrupted the leader/follower exchange by compelling leaders to cater to international needs and interests, often neglecting those of their followers. It may even be argued that mutuality existed between leaders of Sudan and their regional and international counterparts rather than between leaders and followers. Nations require a collective choice and will amongst the people of the nation, which was not reflected in a peace process that would determine the fundamental character of that nation. The role of humanitarian aid is also important in understanding the leader/follower gap in southern Sudan. With services being provided by humanitarian agencies, some have argued that this allowed leaders to continue the war without having to take into account the costs (Martin 2002: 123). In fact, in the eyes of many southerners, NGOs, government organizations, SPLM institutions and the UN agencies formed a collective *hakuma* (Leonardi 2013: 160). This further allowed leaders to function and survive in a situation where they were not confronting the needs and narratives of the population. It also indicates that the desire for peace, and the nature of said peace, was driven by elite interests, rather than that of the population.

## Implementing peace (2005–11)

In July 2005, Sudan's interim constitution was signed and John Garang became first vice-president of Sudan. Garang was greeted in Khartoum by crowds of celebrating Sudanese (Johnson 2016: Ch. 1). He would die three weeks later in a helicopter crash (Johnson 2016: Ch. 1). The peace agreement would now have to be implemented without the charismatic leader who was so central to the struggle. While a document had been signed, much still had to be done to achieve sustainable peace. An immense peacebuilding and nation-building challenge now confronted the Sudanese people and their leaders.

As per the CPA agreement, southern Sudan was given regional autonomy (Comprehensive Peace Agreement 2005: 12–13, 32). What followed was the six-year interim period that was meant to further a democratic and social transformation in Sudan. At the end of this period, southern Sudan was to be given a referendum to decide whether the region would separate from Sudan (Comprehensive Peace Agreement 2005: 3–8). Despite multiple delays and the incomplete implementation of the agreement, often supported by both sides who delayed and renegotiated in accordance with partisan interests, this referendum was an immovable target (Arnold & Le Riche 2013: 117–21; Bereketeab 2014: 312). These actions would lay the foundation for future challenges in an independent South Sudan.

## Defining the nation(s) and reconciling conflicting identities

With reference to identity, the primary matter at hand during the interim period was reconciling the conflict-hardened identities of Sudan towards a national, unified Sudanese identity, or accepting that these identities were irreconcilable within a single political unit. Little effort was made to achieve the first, and a *prima facie* acceptance of the second led to the separation of the country without confronting the multiple contradictions in Sudanese and southern Sudanese identities. On paper, the CPA acknowledges Sudan's multicultural and diverse nature (Comprehensive Peace Agreement 2005: 5). Nevertheless, the peace process served to further foster a reductionist understanding of identity in Sudan, by highlighting the 'binary' identities of Arab/Muslim and African/Christian (Bereketeab 2014: 313). It failed to take into account the significant and multilayered diversity in the country (Medani 2011: 143).

In addition, the SPLM/A's northern allies viewed the movement's signing of the agreement as a 'sell-out' or abandonment of the Sudanism ideal (Young 2012: 155–6). The eventual secession would leave said allies 'facing an old enemy, [the NCP], on their own' (Arnold & Le Riche 2013: 133). While a few SPLM leaders continued to support unity, others chose to decrease pressure on the NCP for democratic transformation in exchange for pursuing independence (Arnold & Le Riche 2013: 117). Rather than trying to realize Garang's vision of a unified Sudanese identity, the NCP and the SPLM/A instead embedded the north/south divide during the interim period (Bereketeab 2014: 314).

By this time, identity had also become inextricably entwined with politics. A few examples serve to illustrate this point. When the SPLM selected Yasir Said Arman to run for the Sudanese presidency, concerns were raised that southerners would not be willing to vote for an Arab and northerners branded him as a 'racial traitor' (Young 2012: 151). Similarly, when Lam Akol decided to run against the SPLM in the south, his primary support base was his own ethnic group, the Shilluk (Young 2012: 162). Garang and Kiir's identities also influenced political relationships, as seen in this statement by an NCP leader: 'People looked upon Garang as a Sudanese, not a Southerner, like Salva' (Young 2012: 141). Finally, the 2008 census was rejected by the SPLM due to the belief that southerners had been under-counted, potentially affecting the referendum and the division of oil resources (Medani 2011: 143–4; Young 2012: 138). Identity became a tool in elite political competition. Elites were more concerned with ensuring official figures reflected favourably on their political goals than with understanding the actual social landscape of Sudan for the purpose of pursuing nation-building in a unified country.

Within southern Sudan itself, divisions in identity were also apparent. As the SPLA withdrew from certain regions, inter-communal conflict escalated (Pendle 2014: 236). This withdrawal left a weakened traditional authority system in charge of 'a militarised and armed population' (Awolich 2015: 11). In addition, ethnic militias continued to be sponsored by the NCP government through the Khartoum-sponsored South Sudan Defence Forces (SSDF) militia (Arnold & Le Riche 2013: 128). The Juba Declaration of 2006 had unified the SSDF and the SPLA, but splinter units continued their activities (Arnold & Le Riche 2013: 128; Young 2012: 13–14). Much of these conflicts formed along ethnic divisions and signalled an effort by groups to position themselves in power in preparation for an independent South Sudan. For example, in 2009, Dinka members, sanctioned by the SPLA, began systematic attacks against Shilluk members in the Upper Nile in order to take control of Malakal (Young 2012: 162). In addition, some leaders who failed to win seats at the 2010 elections used existing ethnic tensions to mobilize and respond with rebellion (Thomas 2015: Ch. 5).

At the same time, the dominant Dinka and Nuer ethnic groups manipulated the peace process and state-building process in order to ensure their supremacy in an independent South Sudan (Gerenge 2015: 94–5), indicating that ethnic or subnational identities were already starting to take a more predominant position than national identity. The peace process, which would determine the nature of the Sudanese and South Sudanese state, was dominated by the Nuer and Dinka-dominated SPLM, to the exclusion of almost all other voices (Gerenge 2015: 94–5; Moro 2015: 4). The way in which the state would be constructed would not only further their hold on power, but also crystallize and deepen ethnic divisions. As a result, state-building and identity construction would interact as these conflicts would continue into the independence era. The evidence, therefore, was clear that southern Sudan did not yet hold a national identity. The CPA process, and the leaders implementing it, did little to confront this reality, as attention was diverted to more elite interests.

## Statehood and nationhood: Unity or secession?

These elite interests tended to centre on the state, which is where most peacebuilding efforts were directed. However, this was a largely technical and unsuccessful affair that did little to reconcile nation and state. A key reason for this was the elite-centred nature of the process. The CPA provided the south with regional autonomy and southern politicians with access to the Khartoum government (Medani 2011: 142). A concerted state-building effort followed (Gerenge 2015: 87). The government of southern Sudan endeavoured to build the necessary administrative structures for a funcational state, but the result was often plagued by inefficiencies, corruption and SPLM domination (Panozzo 2011: 24). At the same time, aid agencies and NGOs filled the void that decades of civil war had created in state services (Ajak 2015: 8).

The result was a state composed of only poorly functioning institutions at independence (Ajak 2015: 4–5). As one respondent indicated, 'With the dawn of independence, Southerners were not ready because capable, functional institutions were not yet crafted' (Interview C 2017). In addition, the Sudanese pattern of a resource-concentrated centre and neglected peripheries was replicated in independent South Sudan (Thomas 2015: Ch. 5). The government adopted an approach of 'decentralised democracy', whereby oil revenues would be transferred to those states that produced little resources of their own (Thomas 2015: Ch. 5). Very little, however, was actually transferred to said states, a problem that would persist into the independence era (AUCISS 2014: 45; Thomas 2015: Ch. 5).

In response to this challenge, one respondent expressed frustration that this decentralized system that was meant to 'protect the interests of the citizens' was not being implemented (Interview B 2017). They argued that 'the state is not serving the interests of people' but 'serving personal interests' (Interview B 2017). In short, the reliance on humanitarian aid and the failure to distribute resources indicate that elites were less concerned with building a state for the people or the nation they claimed to liberate. It would, however, also result in a situation where leaders held little influence over followers and vice versa. This would lead to serious challenges in the post-independence era.

Regarding unity and secession, the stated – though perhaps not intended – purpose of the interim period was to form a Sudan in which southern voters would wish to remain (Arnold & Le Riche 2013: 115–16; Bereketeab 2014: 313–14). Rather than pursuing substantial reforms in Sudan as a whole, the primary goal appears to have been a smooth separation of northern and southern Sudan (Young 2012: 134–5). Although the CPA stated that efforts must be made to 'mak[e] the unity of Sudan attractive', many viewed this to be the responsibility of the NCP and not the SPLM/A (Comprehensive Peace Agreement 2005: 4; Deng 2010: 6). The 2010 elections were meant to signal a transition to democracy, in support of this bid to make unity appealing (Medani 2011: 136, 143). Instead, they served the purpose of entrenching the SPLM and NCP in power, while providing the apparent legitimacy of being democratically elected (Arnold & Le Riche 2013: 131; Young 2012: 134–5). This democratic legitimacy is often desired to please an international audience rather than building actual legitimacy with the population (Young 2012: 9–10).

In addition, it was general knowledge that the 'vast majority' of southerners preferred separation over unity (Deng 2010: 6–7, 9). In fact, it has been contended that this was the primary reason southerners voted for the SPLM in 2010, rather than a true sense of mutuality with the party (Young 2012: 174). After Garang's death, the SPLM all but abandoned the unity vision (Arnold & Le Riche 2013: 116). One respondent stated: 'Garang was a unionist … He passed away at the wrong time … And those who succeeded him [wanted secession]' (Interview A 2017). Then, when the head of the party, Kiir, deferred from running for the Sudanese presidency in 2010, it was seen as a signal that the SPLM was aiming for independence (Young 2012: 150). The same conclusion was drawn when the SPLM boycotted the Sudanese presidential elections and turned their focus solely on southern elections (Young 2012: 152–3, 156). In short, for the SPLM the elections were a means to ensure their hold on power in the soon-to-be-independent south rather than a way to overthrow the NCP to build a new Sudan (Arnold & Le Riche 2013: 130). However, the initial success of the SPLM candidate, Yasir Arman, is evidence that Garang's 'New Sudan' vision held sway in many people's minds (Young 2012: 156). This unity-versus-secession debate remained volatile and led to violent demonstrations in Khartoum in the run-up to the referendum (Medani 2011: 143).

Meanwhile, there were other state-building measures that would, or were meant to, impact nation-building. Overall, these efforts were uncoordinated and often contradicted each other, leading to a further fragmentation of society. The reason for this can be found in leadership again. Many of the policies or laws that were implemented or neglected received the respective attention based on elite interests. These interests were often divergent from those of followers because of the mutuality gap present in society. Consequently, the resulting state-building actions often ran counter to the nation-building ideal. One example of this is the politics of borders, which was often related to political competition. The most hotly contested issue – and one that dominated elite debate – was the demarcation of borders, because of its impact on 'power-sharing quotas, sharing oil wealth, undertaking force redeployment and preparing for the election and referendum' (Arnold & Le Riche 2013: 122–3). Border disputes were also seen as essential for each party to maintain its legitimacy. As a result, both sides were uncompromising on these issues (Arnold & Le Riche 2013: 125).

At the same time, in 2009 a Land Act was signed that permitted land rights to be determined by ethnic groups, sparking violent conflict over county borders in southern Sudan (Pendle 2014: 237). Here, the conflicts were often driven by a need to access resources for livelihoods (Pendle 2014: 238). Linking such an essential resource to ethnicity allows for the persistence of ethnic identity over national identity. While communities were fighting over land for reasons of livelihood, however, elites were doing so for political interests. The state and its borders thus remained a prize over which elites were competing rather than a form of political organization that would enable the nation to govern itself. Borders were being debated and drawn based on their ability to ensure elite access to the state and economic resources rather than to reflect social reality or ensure greater functioning of the state.

Other instances where state-building was unable to foster nation-building are more related to elite apathy. For example, as people began to return to southern Sudan, they were reliant on ethnic and kinship networks to settle and navigate the new space; government assistance was not forthcoming, with only 10 per cent of returnees being assisted between 2005 and 2008 (Thomas 2015: Ch. 5). This has contributed to the persistence of ethnic structures in society, as people often returned to their ethnic communities which provided the social and economic safety nets needed to re-settle (Thomas 2015: Ch. 5). As a result, subnational identity groups were providing many of the services of the state, which would likely foster loyalty to these identity groups rather than the state and the nation.

Similarly, in a non-committal attempt to begin the integration of the armed forces, Joint Integrated Units (JIUs) were created (Arnold & Le Riche 2013: 125–7). These units, however, were not a priority for either the NCP or the SPLM and the units proved ineffective (Arnold & Le Riche 2013: 125–7). Therefore, neither side was particularly committed to building a new Sudanese nation. This lack of commitment stems from a lack of leadership in the sense that Garang was no longer present to guide the vision of a unified Sudan, that leaders were pursuing their own interests, and that leaders were responding to the overwhelming support for secession in the south.

At the same time, the SPLA was tasked with southern nation-building through the formation of ethnically mixed units using an ethnic quota system (Thomas 2015: Ch. 5). But even developing a southern military unit that would represent the future South Sudanese state was difficult. Kiir and the SPLA's forces were outnumbered by other active militant groups, whose commanders he tried to co-opt with positions and oil money (De Waal 2015: 195). Local militant groups which had been used during the war and refused absorption, like the SSDF through the Juba Declaration, became the target of the SPLA's forceful disarmament campaigns (Young 2019: 18). The Nuer White Army was one of these groups, which resisted disarmament because of the insecure environment as well as a perception that other southern groups posed the greatest threat to their community (Young 2019: 17–18). There were a multitude of competing armed and political groups in southern Sudan, and the SPLM/A's approach to state-building and nation-building was to forcefully suppress the competing narratives and leaders available to southerners (discussed below).

As mentioned previously, the SPLM/A took a state-building approach that tried to merge traditional and formal state institutions borrowed from the West. But marrying traditional leadership and institutions with the formal state as conceived by the international community and experienced at the centre was not easy. One example of this can be found in the justice system. Traditional justice mechanisms and customary law varies across different groups in South Sudan (Pendle 2019: 32). It also differs from the formal justice system imposed at the nation-state level. One of the key differences between state law and traditional justice systems, as seen in Dinka customary law, is the emphasis placed on punishment in state law over the emphasis placed on restitution and societal peace in the Dinka system (Deng 2018: 334–8). Also, while judges in the state system are impartial and largely inaccessible to people, judges in the traditional system play an investigatory role and are easily accessible to hear complaints in person (Deng 2018: 338).

The differences in the system resulted in tensions between chiefs in the customary law system and judicial authorities in statutory courts, seeking to either maintain authority (chiefs) or capture authority (state authorities) (Pendle 2018: 44–6). This tension between and differing nature of customary and statutory leaders reflects the dichotomous nature of the state and leadership in South Sudan. The state, and the leaders attached to the formal state, are far removed from the people, and in many ways more closely associated with and responding to international actors. Meanwhile local leaders and local structures perform the functions of effective leadership and the state: exchanging influence, responding to needs and providing accessible justice. In such a situation, there is little incentive for high-level leaders to bring the state closer to the people, or for the people to take responsibility for or give loyalty to the wider nation state.

### Collective will and collective responsibility: A divergence of leader and follower interests?

While the previous chapters have indicated the limited ability to foster collective will and responsibility through conflict, peacebuilding also requires this through collective action, trust and decision-making. However, the peacebuilding process created little of this. The approach taken by Sudan has been characterized as liberal peacebuilding or state-building (AUCISS 2014: 37–8; Gerenge 2015: 87; Young 2012: Preface, 1, 4, 7, 9–10). As part of this liberal peacebuilding philosophy, the 'appearance of democratic accountability' was important, while the actual concern was that of stability (Young 2012: 135–6). Justice, a key demand amongst the people of southern Sudan, was also neglected for the sake of stability (AUCISS 2014: 29; Deng et al. 2015: 26–7, 37–9). Immense international aid was provided for state-building and humanitarian aid but failed to alleviate the daily challenges of southerners (Ajak 2015: 2–5; Gerenge 2015: 87).

The pattern here is that of neglecting the voice, views and needs of followers, respectively, indicating some weaknesses in the liberal peacebuilding model. The purpose in pursuing self-determination is to ensure that people have a say in the way they are governed (UNGA 1970), but this did not occur. Self-determination also presupposes that a collective will exists or can be formulated through collective dialogue and decision-making. This did not occur in Sudan and southern Sudan because leaders held more mutuality with each other than with their followers, and the primary pathways of influence were between leaders and the international community rather than between leaders and society. Liberal peacebuilding, which is primarily conducted by international actors, creates challenges by inserting other actors into the state/society social contract.

In this way, the elite-centred nature of the CPA led to several problems. First, the allocation of seats as stipulated in the CPA was determined by the two parties rather than through any systematic, objective or consultative process (Young 2012: 138). Also, despite the CPA's demands for significant national reforms, many of these were not implemented, as the SPLM was primarily interested in gaining South Sudanese independence (Medani 2011: 147–8). In addition, parties on both sides viewed the CPA less as a binding agreement and more as a guideline for ongoing negotiations (Arnold & Le Riche 2013: 120). After the CPA, the SPLM directed its efforts towards building the consensus needed to gain independence (Pendle 2014: 228). In fact, despite the many prescribed milestones of the CPA, the primary – and, for some, only – concern was the referendum (Arnold & Le Riche 2013: 122). There was little collective desire or will to pursue a social and democratic transformation in Sudan, at least amongst the elites of the two key parties.

As a result, much of the focus in the post-CPA era was on reconciling the north/south differences to prepare the country for secession. Contentious issues included borders, oil and security (Arnold & Le Riche 2013: 119). Since the conflict had been framed as a north/south conflict, this is where attention appears to have been diverted. Little attention was given to building a cohesive South Sudanese nation beyond ensuring a vote for independence. In addition, the CPA neglected reconciliation in favour of security and negative peace (Medani 2011: 144). Forty per cent of the budget in southern Sudan was allocated to security institutions (Ajak 2015: 3). Peacebuilding initiatives, on the other hand, were 'ad hoc' and 'reactive' (Ajak 2015: 4; Kisiangani 2015: 9). Also, much of the development and peacebuilding plans initiated by international actors were 'transplanted' from established practices rather than tailored to the local context (Ajak 2015: 5).

At the same time, despite the collective goal of independence, the south remained divided as it had throughout the liberation struggle. Inter-communal violence continued, much of which was part of a continued strategy of proxy war by Khartoum (Arnold & Le Riche 2013: 128). During the 2010 elections, 357 SPLM members chose to run as independent candidates (Young 2012: 148). This was in response to the poor party procedures in selecting candidates, the widespread maladministration in the region and inter-communal disputes (Young 2012: 147–50). These disagreements amongst elites were not indicative of differing visions or ideology (Young 2012: 150). The political process, then, was not conducive to forming a sense of collective will but rather an arena for elite disputes to be resolved.

While the interim period was tense, a return to north/south war did not occur. Some may perceive this as a success and this achievement should not be negated. However, the establishment of negative peace[2] between north and south did not mean peace had been achieved in the south. It also represents a disproportionate focus on the reductionist understanding of the conflict as a north/south issue. Violence continued in southern Sudan in the form of smaller rebellions and violent cattle raiding (Frahm 2015: 260; Panozzo 2011: 25). Jonglei state was one arena in which conflict would often resurge during the interim period and well into independence (Johnson 2016: Prologue;

Thomas 2015: Part Two). For example, prior to the 2010 elections a former SPLA general, George Athor, rebelled against the SPLM/A and was subsequently convinced to sign a ceasefire until after the referendum, at which point he rebelled again (Panozzo 2011: 24–5). Inter-communal conflicts also occurred at sub-ethnic levels, and gradually escalated after the CPA (Pendle 2014: 236). While not all group members engaged in or approved of conflict, it has been argued that these conflicts represent collective action on the part of ethnic groups who engage in 'collective decision-making' and benefit from the spoils of the conflict (Pendle 2014: 234). As such, it appears evident that southern Sudanese were unable to maintain a sense of collective will when not faced with a crisis in the form of a clear and well-defined enemy. Without this enemy, elite interests began to divert from that of followers, leading to a fragmentation of southern society.

## Implementing peace: Leadership in a new context

The peace agreement signalled a significant change in situation in Sudan and southern Sudan. With the cessation of north/south hostilities and a working plan to resolve the north/south conflict, the situation now demanded leadership that would confront the immense economic, humanitarian and social challenges in society. Elite attention, however, was directed towards the building of state institutions and ensuring a hold on said institutions, while these challenges were outsourced to international actors (Ajak 2015: 1–4). Southern identity, which had been used to mobilize the south against the north, now seemed a secondary concern. Such influence over the population was no longer needed as the competition for power became a negotiation between two elite parties with an international referee. As the primary exchange of influence drifted more towards other elites and the international community, identity as a mobilization tool lost its utility, to be called upon primarily for the referendum. Nevertheless, the identities that had been constructed during the conflict remained essential to the daily lives of followers. Competition for state institutions that served elite interests also eroded collective will and collective loyalty, while state functions were provided by external actors. In the end, the nation-building conversation between leaders and followers that should have determined Sudan's future became a dialogue and negotiation between two leaders. This stemmed from a flawed leader/follower relationship that lacked mutuality and the ability of followers to influence their leaders.

As pointed out previously, the CPA was an elite pact between the SPLM/A and the NCP. In an effort to make the process more inclusive after the fact, meetings were held with the NDA in Cairo after the signing of the agreement, but the CPA had already distributed power primarily to the NCP and SPLM (Johnson 2011b: 177). In the end, the NDA failed (Bereketeab 2014: 313). Similarly, following a law passed in 2007, only parties that supported the CPA were permitted to compete in the national elections, precluding any further negotiation of the peace agreement (Young 2012: 137). Also, the NCP and SPLM, both being undemocratic, did not necessarily represent the interests of their respective followers in the peace process (Medani 2011: 136). The events that would unfold after the CPA signing would confirm this. The SPLM/A has been accused of 'mov[ing] expeditiously to ... manipulate the transition and interim constitution-making process and entrench itself in power' (Kisiangani 2015: 4). In this way, despite decades of conflict, the NCP and SPLM entered into an alliance to ensure their respective goals of maintaining NCP power in Khartoum and seceding from the north through referendum (Arnold & Le Riche 2013: 117; Medani 2011: 144). The fact that elites shared more in common with each other than their respective constituencies allowed such an alliance to occur. It acts as another illustration of the lack of mutuality between leaders and followers in Sudan.

The 2010 elections, in particular, illustrated this. These elections were repeatedly delayed because elites were concerned about their success at the polls (Young 2012: 136). The SPLM went so far as to claim that, as a liberation movement, it did not need its legitimacy confirmed through a democratic mandate (Young 2012: 136). In addition, there is evidence that the SPLM and the NCP colluded to influence the outcome of the election (Young 2012: 151–3). The elections in the end were rife with irregularities that were set aside for the sake of maintaining peace, even by the international community (Medani 2011: 136, 143; Young 2012: 134–77). These irregularities were instigated by both parties and included, *inter alia*, arrests, intimidation and problematic voter registration (Arnold & Le Riche 2013: 130–1; Young 2012: 134–77). One respondent recounted how they witnessed and experienced intimidation against non-SPLM/A campaigners from other political parties, including imprisonment (Interview B 2017). In the end, both the NCP and SPLM/A won the elections with significant margins (Johnson 2016: Ch. 1). This should not be seen as resounding evidence of their support.

As a result of the SPLA's dominant presence in rural areas during the civil war, the SPLM held a significant advantage by being the most, and sometimes only, familiar political actor or party (Young 2012: 159). But the SPLM/A was not the only organization with political legitimacy. This can be seen in the Unity State rebellion. Kiir's appointed governor of Unity State, Taban Deng, had turned on, attacked and marginalized the more legitimate 'strong man' Paulino Matiep (Young 2019: 15). Resentment of these actions and the 2010 election led to an armed insurgency under Peter Gadet and the South Sudan Liberation Army's (SSLA) Mayoum Declaration, which challenged the SPLM/A's coercive tactics to silence opposition voices and sideline traditional leaders (Young 2019: 16). The emergence of the SPLM/A and its members as leaders for the new state required the continued suppression of alternative leaders (such as Paulino Matiep) and leadership institutions (such as traditional leadership). The ability to do this was to a large extent driven by the SPLM/A's relationship with external actors rather than the southern Sudanese population.

The elections then served to entrench and confirm the SPLM/A and NCP in power rather than promote democratic transformation or provide the people of Sudan with a voice in the country's future (Young 2012: 9–10, 134–77). After the elections, Kiir tried to appease opposition parties by bringing twenty-four parties together under the Political Parties Leadership Forum to make plans for an independent South Sudan's constitution, but this forum was quickly sidelined and shut down once independence had been achieved (Young 2019: 13–14). In addition, the division amongst southern elites was overcome with the help of oil revenues (Pendle 2014: 228). This indicates a lack of representation of followers and their needs by these elites, and consequently a lack of mutuality. While there are some legitimate reasons not to rush into elections following a peace agreement, the more important point here is that leaders were conscious of their limited support amongst the population. Rather than confronting this legitimacy crisis, elites sought ways to manipulate the system in their favour. In this way, the focus on institution-building after a conflict can fail when there is no contract between followers and leaders to uphold the institutions and influence leaders to maintain the integrity of the process.

Following the CPA, Garang became vice-president of Sudan and president of southern Sudan. For this reason, the peace agreement is also seen as a tool to enhance Garang's hold on power (Young 2005: 535). In addition, Garang's popularity across Sudan made him a threat to al-Bashir's presidency in any election (Deng 2010: 10). A strategy to push out al-Bashir with Garang as the new Sudanese president was supported by the US government (Young 2012: 142). However, his death sparked riots in Khartoum and Juba, which quickly devolved into Arab–African racial violence (Medani 2011: 143). Some have argued that unity and democratic transformation would have been possible had Garang lived (Interview A 2017; Deng 2010: 10). He was seen as the only one able to reconcile the competing unity and secession visions (Arnold & Le Riche 2013: 116). In addition, without Garang the SPLM/A lost its 'unity of purpose' (Ajak 2015: 5). This again illustrates a lack of mutuality between Garang and his followers. If his vision and purpose had been based on a mutual understanding of the challenge and how to face it, his death, while it may have hindered the SPLM/A vision, should not have derailed it.

After his death, Garang was immediately succeeded by Salva Kiir in order to prevent a succession crisis (Johnson 2016: Ch. 1). Yet, the divisions in the SPLM came to a head in its 2008 national convention where Riek Machar and Nihal Deng were prevented from challenging Kiir's leadership in an effort to maintain a public face of unity (Young 2012: 141–2). At the same time, Kiir's attempt to centralize control and reduce the number of deputies was blocked (Young 2012: 141–2). In the end, politicians agreed to set these divisions aside, along with the concurrent nation-building and reconciliation challenges in southern Sudan, in favour of 'deal[ing] with the enemy first' (AUCISS 2014: 29). As a result, a fragile consensus had emerged amongst the southern elite to focus attention on independence, which was possible with Garang's death (Arnold & Le Riche 2013: 119). These problems, however, remained unresolved and would re-emerge after independence, demonstrating a reliance on a common enemy for unity to prevail and an inability to form a cohesive 'us' without 'them'.

The six-year interim period was by no means sufficient time to deal with the nation-building challenges created by centuries of 'othering' processes, state formation and societal fragmentation. Yet, it did provide a space to set in motion a more concerted nation-building process. But Sudan-wide nation-building was a non-starter. After Kiir took control of the helm, he diverted his attention primarily to southern issues (Arnold & Le Riche 2013: 118). Even so, despite the opportunity the interim period presented, leaders failed to use it to prepare for life after independence (Johnson 2016: Prologue). Rather than confronting the many social and economic challenges facing the country, the SPLM focused its efforts on disputes over borders and government positions (Thomas 2015: Ch. 5). In other words, it turned its attention to the state because this was the entity that would serve its own interests, rather than ensuring the state served the interests of the nation.

Further evidence of elite interests trumping those of the population includes the majority of the security budget for southern Sudan being directed towards 'highly inflated salaries', while doing little to actually improve security (Ajak 2015: 3). This pattern was also replicated at lower levels. General Athor's rebellion, for example, was driven by his own interests and disagreements with other leaders rather than any attempt to fight for his followers' interests (Thomas 2015: Ch. 5). Similarly, the 'most significant crisis' of the CPA was sparked when the SPLM abandoned the Government of National Unity (GoNU) on 11 October 2007, following disputes over oil revenues (Arnold & Le Riche 2013: 127). The SPLM returned to the GoNU due to international pressure and NCP compromise on oil, troop deployment and borders (Arnold & Le Riche 2013: 127).

The fact that it was oil revenues that proved so contentious is telling. The issue of religion, so central to the peace negotiations, hardly signified in their implementation. As explained previously, the impact of oil on the north/south conflict has been exaggerated. Also, in hindsight, it is evident that southern elites primarily sought oil revenues to enrich themselves rather than to ensure southern economic development, as seen in the post-independence era. One can presume, therefore, that southern leaders were no longer as concerned with the identity issues they had used to mobilize the southern masses during the conflict. Now that mobilization was less needed, elites abandoned the original narratives in favour of pursuing personal interests.

The GoNU walk-out and return once again raises the issue of international influence. While international involvement diverted influence from leaders and followers to leaders and the international community, it also created a pathway of influence between followers and the international community.

In short, international involvement in various aspects of peacebuilding interrupted the exchange of influence between leaders and followers. For example, the political implementation of the CPA was handled primarily by the NCP and SPLM, while issues of security, development and humanitarian aid were relegated to the international community (Johnson 2011b: 177). In this way, leaders were permitted to continue the pattern of seeing to their own needs and interests with little concern for the wider needs of society. A continuation of this pattern post-independence would result in a flawed relationship between state and society. In short, dissociating the political from the social in this way prevents the development of mutuality. This hinders nation-building, as leaders are driven to frame identity and nationhood in terms that suit their political goals while negating the broader needs and realities of society.

## Conclusion

After this peace process, as South Sudan entered its next phase as an independent state, much remained unresolved. It is, of course, not possible to resolve all the causes and complications of war in a single document such as the Comprehensive Peace Agreement. But the peacebuilding process here suffered from a more fundamental flaw: a broken social contract stemming from a flawed leadership process. The divergence of societal and elite interests is ever-present in any analysis of this period. But the context and the mutuality gap did not permit new leaders to emerge who would be better placed to address the challenges of the new situation. As a result, the nation-building process could not move forward, but rather splintered as the leadership process of the previous years replicated itself at smaller levels. The superficial South Sudanese nation was the product of said leadership process, and its dismantling would be too.

## Note

1   An Arabic term used to denote the government and state structures (Leonardi 2007: 394).

2   For a discussion of positive and negative peace see Galtung 1969.

# 6

# Freedom, Fragility and Fragmentation[1]

## Introduction

For decades, the nation-building endeavour in southern Sudan was set aside in favour of pursuing statehood. From brushing over factionalism and societal divisions in favour of unity for the referendum, to pursuing a state-building agenda in the peace process while setting aside issues of reconciliation, the realization of a *de jure* Westphalian state was prioritized. The cost of this prioritization would come to a head in 2013, when a political dispute sparked the brewing antagonism, discontentment and hurt in South Sudan. After months of political tension and manoeuvring in Juba in 2013, and while these tensions were reaching their peak at the December National Liberation Council meeting, fighting broke out within the presidential guard and quickly spread across the capital and the country. Former Vice President Riek Machar emerged as the leader of an insurgency named the SPLM-In Opposition (SPLM-IO). Juba appeared ready to fall until Uganda intervened (Rolandsen 2015: 166), and the nation, which only two-and-a-half years earlier rejoiced in its unity, fractured.

In South Sudan's post-secession period, the interests of leaders and followers diverged even more, further widening the gap between state and citizen. The new South Sudanese state was not built or managed to serve the interests of the people (or nation), but to serve the interests of the elite. The people then turned to the local and the traditional for security, services and community. Meanwhile, a third player – the international – interrupted the exchange of influence between state and citizen, leader and follower, in the way they managed peace processes and service delivery. As a result, when leaders were required to mobilize popular support, they relied on coercive and reward power, or the fanning of ethnic flames.

## 'Us' without 'them': In search of a national identity

While the conflict with Khartoum was far from fully resolved after secession, South Sudan's independence resulted in a significant shift in conflict dynamics. Most importantly, the decades-old, perhaps centuries-old, common enemy of northern Sudan was no longer as immediate a threat. Identity is more easily perceived in the face of 'the other'.[2] Southern Sudanese identity was founded on opposition to the north (Deng 1995: 61–90). The desire to have English as an official language, despite Arabic being more widely spoken, and to maintain a Christian identity, albeit a foreign religion as much as Islam is, was arguably founded more on attempting to distinguish southerners from northerners than to build a uniquely southern identity. Now that that distinction had led to complete separation from the north, southern cohesion and nationhood required a stronger foundation to move forward.

So, the situation had changed from fighting a clear and distinct enemy to facing the multitude of complex internal contradictions and challenges of South Sudanese society – from advocating and fighting for an independent nation state to building and governing said nation state. This change required a different leadership process from that needed in war. It required a shift in framing and mobilization techniques. The narratives used to mobilize a society for war are different from those needed to mobilize for peace. But the SPLM/A did not change. Rather, as with many liberation movements, it remained consistent in its manner of mobilizing and engaging the populace, and in ensuring coherence and compliance. The effect: instead of building a cohesive nation, society fragmented further.

The most obvious reason for this is the loss of a common enemy after independence. While the SPLM/A tried to keep this memory of northern oppression alive, more pressing and immediately felt challenges would take precedence. On a macro level, one of these was the nation-building challenge, of which leaders were not ignorant (Copnall 2014: 25–6). But this nation-building challenge could not be addressed by focusing on the north, or even the historical struggle against the north. It can be argued that the shared history of oppression and struggle, a shared Christian religion and the shared Arabic language provided some foundation for nationhood (Thomas 2015: Ch. 5). Shared history, shared values and shared language are all important elements in nation-building (Deutsch 2010; Eley & Suny 1996: 8; Guibernau 2007: 14; Smith 1998: 196; Weber 1994: 22), but do not guarantee nationhood in themselves (Weber 1994).

Nationhood is more than a common identity. Rather, a common identity, whatever the attribute, serves as the foundation for how the nation governs itself through norms, values and institutions, ensuring 'predictability' and collective will and responsibility (Hopf 1998: 74). The mere presence of these shared attributes of history, religion and language are not what is important, but rather how they are framed, experienced and perceived. In this way, the collective desire to secede from the north is insufficient as an indicator of national unity and identity (Frahm 2015: 253). In this case, it illustrates more a sense of difference from the north than cohesiveness amongst South Sudanese.

But the SPLM/A relied on this narrative throughout southern Sudanese history and into independence. Exclusively using a struggle narrative to build nationhood is problematic on several levels. First, while the struggle is a unifying narrative, it has been used in a divisive way in South Sudan, by attaching membership value to participation in the struggle (discussed below). Second, the struggle narrative is often used by leaders for personal gain, rather than a nation-building purpose or to reconcile a nation's past with its future. Examples provided below of patronage, identity-based electioneering and disputes over access to peace dividends are evidence of this. Third, relying on a struggle narrative continues a destructive practice of 'othering' in framing political debates. The cause of Sudan's civil war with the south was not a fundamental difference of identity, as the narrative often espoused (see Chapters 2–4), but an endemic practice of 'othering' that sustains politics. In other words, a sense of 'us' and 'them' was created between northerners and southerners in an effort to both make sense of political and economic conflicts and mobilize support in these conflicts. It was not the incompatibility of northern and southern identity that caused the civil war.

Regarding the use of the struggle for division, while a narrative of oppression and struggle was used during the war with Sudan to mobilize southerners, the same narrative was used after secession for exclusionary purposes. For example, those outside South Sudan during the Sudanese wars are seen as 'second-class citizens' who did not participate sufficiently in the liberation movement, and are thought to have adopted external cultures from northern Sudan or East

Africa (Frahm 2015: 254). Similarly, regarding the second point, ethnic groups that dominated the liberation movement (such as the Dinka and the Nuer) have been accused of claiming a right to greater benefits because of this role (Gerenge 2015: 85, 87). Members of such groups have used their respective roles in the struggle to justify greater access to peace dividends, particularly government positions (Gerenge 2015: 85, 87; Thomas 2015: Ch. 5). In the words of one respondent: 'They say "we are the ones who liberated and fought for freedom", so they are treated like first-class citizens' (Interview G 2017). Elites in particular justified their entitlement to state resources based on their leadership during the struggle (Johnson 2016: Ch. 2). As aptly described by Johnson, it was their 'turn to eat' (Johnson 2016: Ch. 2). Because of patronage networks, this entitlement translated into an ethnic entitlement.

This practice of 'othering' is persistent in South Sudan because of the flawed leader/follower relationship, which relies on identity rather than mutuality to build legitimacy and raise support for leaders. Hogg theorizes that prototypical leadership can be effective because it reduces the need to exercise power, but it also runs the risk of 'increasing status-based differentiation between leader and followers' in the long run, which counteracts the influence provided by the shared identity (Hogg 2001: 194). This may lead to the 'pitfalls' of prototype leadership, including the abuse of power in an effort to maintain leadership and the reliance on prototypicality rather than the needed skills and abilities for the situation when identifying leaders (Hogg 2001: 195). Both these trends have been seen in South Sudan. The SPLM/A elite have been driven to using reward and coercive power to maintain influence (see below) and reports indicate that despite a lack of interest in the political conflict, ordinary South Sudanese are being compelled to choose sides, often because of their ethnic identity (Hutchinson & Pendle 2015: 427; De Vries & Schomerus 2017: 337). The presence of an external threat may be useful in reducing these trends as it enhances the group identification processes that support prototypical leadership (Hogg 2001: 194). Since the external threat has diminished in South Sudan, it is indicative that the situation calls for a new process of leadership emergence that does not rely on prototypicality.

From this, and related to the third reason struggle narratives are problematic, narratives of ethnic supremacy have emerged (Gerenge 2015). Using the same logic of superior and inferior identities that Khartoum used to exclude southerners, these narratives have hindered cross-ethnic identity formation in the form of norms and cooperative mechanisms (Gerenge 2015), and continue the practice of endemic 'othering'. As captured by one respondent: 'You don't have the security of being South Sudanese if you are not a Dinka' (Interview D 2017). Participation in a previous war cannot be a prerequisite for membership of a nation and the subsequent rights of citizenship. If this were the case, no nation would survive past the first generation of said war.

So, particular concerns were raised about Dinka dominance in post-CPA southern Sudan (Bereketeab 2014: 312; Medani 2011: 143). There was a clear perception of favouritism being given to Dinka members in the allocation of government positions in the new state (Frahm 2012: 29). This perception was driven by symbolism as well. For example, during independence celebrations in Upper Nile, where the Dinka and Shilluk had been fighting for dominance, the preference given to Dinka dance performances was seen as politically significant (Thomas 2015: Ch. 5). Also, some southerners in Khartoum were hesitant to return or move to South Sudan because of the domination of the Dinka (Schultz 2014: 316). This ethnic favouritism is important because of the link between ethnicity and the state, discussed further in the next section. In short, just as Khartoum did, the South Sudanese central government organized its relationship with the peripheries, and the way in which resources are allocated, using ethnicity (Thomas 2015: Ch. 5).

This perceived domination of the Dinka and Nuer ethnic groups has raised fears of exclusion or extermination amongst other groups such as the Equatorians and the Murle (Frahm 2015: 260). In particular, Equatorian communities have a history of 'marginalisation' and 'land dispossession' under the SPLM/A (Medani 2011: 143). In this example, it is important to note that Equatoria is a regional identity rather than an ethnic one. While the alliances of Equatorian communities often shifted, the recent perception of domination by larger ethnic groups has prompted these smaller groups to find common interests and experiences to forge a regional identity and a separate rebellion. One respondent indicated that the 'small tribes feel vulnerable' (Interview D 2017). Another stated that in Equatoria, 'People are told if you don't support Dinka, you are supporting the Nuer or vice versa ... so people took [up] arms' (Interview G 2017).

While mutuality between leaders and followers during the war was founded on a shared sense of oppression and opposition to the north, mutuality in an independent South Sudan had to be founded on a shared sense of belonging, interests and vision for the future. While leaders could influence followers during the war by appealing to narratives of identity difference with the 'enemy', such a narrative is not of use when the enemy is 'defeated' and the current challenge stems from internal sources. Instead, such tactics are likely to increase fragmentation and division. Not only did the leadership process fail to adapt to the situation, the leader/follower relationship retained the same inherent flaws and gaps that had hindered nation-building in the past. In particular, the lack of mutuality between leaders and followers became ever more evident as the most shared experience, that of northern oppression and exclusion, no longer carried the same relevance. With this, the ability of leaders, particularly those at the centre, to influence followers decreased, and followers' ability to influence leaders remained low. Efforts to use reward and coercive power had their limits. Expert and legitimate power were in short supply. And referent power was driven by narrow forms of ethnic identification rather than the charisma and shared values shown by the leader. As a result, leader emergence or selection was determined by prototypes,[3] resulting in leaders vying for power through patronage and ethnic mobilization.

At the same time, little was done to promote social cohesion. As explained in the previous chapter, peacebuilding efforts reflected a shift towards state-building over nation-building as leader interests lied more in the apparatus of the state. This trend continued after independence. Little was done to address the societal rifts caused by war (Johnson 2016: Ch. 2). Even more, efforts to reconfigure South Sudanese identity towards a more cohesive nation were non-existent beyond shallow rhetoric and symbolism. There were multiple attempts by civil society and political leaders to urge national unity after independence (Frahm 2012: 28–9). For example, President Kiir said in his independence speech:

> Let all the citizens of this new nation be equal before the law and have equal access to opportunities and equal responsibilities to serve the motherland. We are all South Sudanese. We may be Zande, Kakwa, Nuer, Toposa, Dinka, Lotuko, Anyuak, Bari and Shilluk, but remember you are South Sudanese first!
>
> Gurtong 2011

But leaders are not able to manipulate the population solely through rhetoric. An exchange of influence must be engendered whereby followers accept the leaders framing of reality (Pierce & Newstrom 2011: 25). This became more difficult as mutuality between elites in Juba and the South Sudanese populace deteriorated. Such statements of unity were not able to overcome the social reality of ethnic divisions, and they ring hollow in the face of Kiir's future actions. Similarly, attempts at unification by leaders were not completely lacking, but struggled in the face of other contradictions.

Rather, the public discourse on identity and nation-building that followed independence was dominated by issues surrounding subnational rivalries and loyalties, remembrance of the struggle, 'language politics' and religion (Frahm 2012: 21). Nevertheless, despite surveys indicating that people identify as 'South Sudanese first', the dominant identity attribute that drives debate and determines collective responsibility is ethnicity (Frahm 2015: 253). One respondent noted how in social interactions, the 'first thing people ask is which tribe you are from' (Interview D 2017). Another reiterated this, stating that if you say you are South Sudanese, you are asked: 'South Sudanese from where?' (Interview B 2017). This is not surprising, as ethnicity is the primary foundation for social and political structure. It provides people with key social networks, capital and safety nets (Thomas 2015: Ch. 5). While ethnicity dominates social and political life in rural areas, it also plays an important role in urban society, where ethnic associations are used to navigate urban life and urban spatial organization often mirrors ethnic groupings (Thomas 2015: Ch. 5). It also influences the ability to find employment, as ethnicity becomes a factor in the hiring process (Interview D 2017; Interview G 2017). Finally, ethnicity remains the primary means and structure through which South Sudanese identify their representatives (Interview B 2017; Interview C 2017; Interview D 2017; Thomas 2015: Ch. 5).

As a result, people retreated to and gave influence to the leaders who served their post-conflict needs and resembled their community prototype. This tended to be ethnic and sub-ethnic communities. For example, in Nuer communities, key prophets such as Gatdeang, Nyachol and Dak Kueth Deng have, in differing ways, exercised significant influence in their communities by providing safe spaces (Gatdeang) or mobilizing and blessing militant action in response to an insecure environment (Nyachol and Dak Kueth Deng) (Johnson

2016: Chs 4 & 6; Hutchinson & Pendle 2015). Their influence, founded on prototypical norms and referent power, often rivalled that of the state and state leaders (whose power rested in official positions that only provide legitimate power if the position itself is considered legitimate) (French and Raven 2011: 138–9). Hutchinson and Pendle (2015) document two instances where this occurred with Gatdeang and Nyachol, in which President Kiir made a personal visit to Gatdeang following a Dinka cattle raid and where Nyachol was able to avoid arrest due to fears of a violent response from her followers.

The liberation struggle, therefore, failed to mould a supra-ethnic identity that would supersede these ethnic ties. Influence was determined primarily on a destructive form of referent power and prototype leadership that is dependent on identification with leaders, and the institutions they represent, through ethnicity. So, while leaders were concerned with the workings and apparatus of the central state in Juba, people were surviving and governing themselves through ethnicity-based systems and leadership processes.

This reliance on ethnic structures was cemented by a struggle narrative espousing Africanism, aimed at preserving African customs, to distinguish the south from the north. (Pendle 2019: 43; Thomas 2015: Ch. 5). As will be discussed below and as illustrated in previous chapters, these structures inspire complex perspectives and responses and therefore should not be viewed as an inherently 'good' or 'bad' form of governance. Nevertheless, such traditional governance structures have contributed to the persistence and predominance of ethnicity as the guiding framework for societal interaction and relationships. As a result, when the situation again shifted towards conflict, the 'default' tool for framing and understanding the conflict was that of ethnicity. The choosing of sides in a political conflict between elites was determined largely by identity. Trust, responsibility and respect of another's rights was influenced by identity perceptions. Disagreement over access to state or natural resources was framed as a threat towards an ethnic group.[4] And the prevalent leadership process reinforced rather than challenged this norm.

So, when fighting broke out in December 2013, due to a political disagreement between Machar and Kiir for leadership of the SPLM/A, it did not take long to spiral into an ethnically framed conflict. As rumours spread that Nuer members were being attacked in the capital, retaliatory attacks occurred in other regions (Gerenge 2015: 96; ICG 2015a: 10–11). During the ensuing conflict, rebel and government forces 'deliberately targeted' people of opposing ethnic groups (Frahm 2015: 259). At the same time, Machar's and Kiir's supporters were formed primarily of their respective ethnic groups (AUCISS 2014: 26; Kisiangani 2015: 6–7). As a result, some commentators characterized the ensuing conflict as an ethnic one (Pendle 2014: 227). Others were quick to minimize the role of ethnicity and caution against labelling the conflict as such (Kisiangani 2015: 7; Rolandsen 2015: 163). These commentators perceive identity primarily as a mobilization tool in a political conflict (Kisiangani 2015: 7). This caution is justified because the complex structural and economic issues in the conflict cannot be ignored. But these issues overlap with identity issues. The polarization of society and its effects remain something that must be addressed. While leaders may only be using ethnicity as a mobilization tool, the role of ethnicity in the lives of citizens is very real.

One respondent explained this process by arguing that leaders had to make the conflict appear to be about the people, because political battles are not fought in 'an isolated boxing arena' (Interview F 2017). To explain how this occurs, one respondent said that leaders make claims about other ethnic groups 'taking our position[s]' and 'killing our people', which go unquestioned (Interview D 2017). But the use of identity to mobilize followers resulted in a severe brutality and human rights violations (Gerenge 2015: 95–6). By using identity in war, one shifts the narrative from a conflict over economic or political resources towards a person's very right to be, raising the stakes. In April 2014, a UN protection camp in Bor was attacked in which Nuer were targeted specifically (Patinkin 2014; UNMISS 2015: 18–22). Other reports of violence recount how people were identified and killed based on their ethnicity during violent attacks (Arensen 2016: 14; Interview D 2017; UNMISS 2017: 3; UN 2016: 1, 3–5). This included, for example, identifying Nuer based on their facial scarring (Johnson 2016: Ch. 6). One respondent recounted how, in their attempt to flee a violent region, the ability to speak Dinka, despite not being Dinka, was important. They said: 'if you don't speak Dinka you are gone' (Interview D 2017). The AU and the UN have released multiple reports detailing the violence and violations committed by both sides, which include rape, forced cannibalism and mass murders (AUCISS 2014; Human Rights Council 2016; UNMISS 2017).

The new civil war mirrored that of the 1990s (Kisiangani 2015: 6). This is not a coincidence. The efficacy of ethnic mobilization was demonstrated in the south/south conflict and the experiences of said conflict remain in the minds of citizens (Kisiangani 2015: 6–7). The human rights violations of the 1990s were still strong in social memory and had gone unaddressed (AUCISS 2014: 29). As a result, memories of this conflict were called upon for mobilization (Interview D 2017; Kisiangani 2015: 6–7). Such mobilization and memory would contribute to further human rights violations in the 2013 civil war as a form of retribution (Interview C 2017; Interview D 2017). As one respondent summarized: 'The killing occurs because people want you to suffer what others have suffered ... There is a hatred there' (Interview G 2017).

This likely produced a cycle of entrenching ethnic differences. Both the Dinka and Nuer groups have developed 'victim-liberator narrative[s]' that are used to avert blame, ignite fears and mobilize ethnic militias (Interview B 2017; Interview D 2017; Gerenge 2015: 96–7). Politicians have used narratives of 'ethnic demotion' to build and mobilize their follower base (Thomas 2015: Ch. 5). These narratives, in turn, produce different perceptions of the conflict. For example, one interviewee characterized the current conflict as political and the 1990s conflict as ethnic due to the Bor massacre of Dinka in 1991 (Interview B 2017). Another placed more emphasis on the targeting of Nuer in the current conflict while minimizing the importance of the Bor massacre (Interview D 2017). In the process, ethnic identities have been further solidified while eroding the limited cross-ethnic norms and trust that were present (Interview B 2017; Interview D 2017; Deng et al. 2015: 33–4; Gerenge 2015: 98).

As a result, perceptions of identity in general also differ and produce contradictions. One interviewee argued that identity has not changed and has remained consistently ethnic, while later acknowledging that in 2011 people momentarily viewed themselves as South Sudanese (Interview B 2017). Another claimed their South Sudanese identity and discontentment with the ubiquitous need to identify one's regional or ethnic heritage (Interview G 2017). In short, perceptions differ on whether ethnic, geographical or regional (including north/south) identities are reflective of traditional and antiquated social realities or constructed through and for political processes. Identity markers have fluctuated in their dominance both to fuel conflict and in response to it. Currently, the dramatization is leaning towards ethnic difference, which, considering the irreconcilability of the north/south identities following decades of conflict, presents a danger of becoming irreversible.

Also, as in the previous war, violence has been outsourced to ethnic militias (Fleischner 2015: 16–18; Reeve 2012: 41–3, 64). This serves to further fragment society. It is also one of the likely reasons why the liberation movement failed to build a collective identity as the armed forces were not formed of a single, cohesive guerrilla army. This use of ethnic militias and local grievances also allows leaders to minimize the costs of war to themselves. However, it also leads to the proliferation of goals and motives as ever more actors become involved. Leaders often lose control of the conflict narrative and collective goals as a result. For example, non-Dinka and non-Nuer militant groups became involved in the conflict through a 'widening circle of reprisal and revenge' (Gerenge 2015: 96). As the conflict progressed, ethnic groups not connected to the original dispute began to take part in violence to express their own grievances at being excluded (Interview D 2017; Foltyn 2015). At the same time, other inter-communal disputes unrelated to the broader conflict and driven by local political and resource competition also persist in the background (Gerenge 2015: 101). In the end, South Sudan finds itself in a state of deep, violent and apparently irreconcilable identity differences that have been constructed over decades of 'othering' through political and armed conflict.

In this way, an identity premised on a narrative of oppression proves problematic on several levels. For one, it is too relational. It remains dependent on the presence of a common enemy and fails to bind a nation when the context changes. As one respondent stated: '[After independence] the enemy changed face from what was external to the community to what was reconstructed from within' (Interview C 2017). Similarly, struggle narratives can easily be used to exclude certain group members on the basis of their actions during this oppression, which may be used to deny said members certain privileges and even rights. Finally, while it indicates a shared history, it does not necessarily provide the values and beliefs that frame the future vision of the nation and drive future collective action. It is predominantly backward-looking rather than future-looking.

# Building a state for whom? The demarcation, contestation and limitation of the South Sudanese state

Becoming an independent state is no small endeavour. Despite the half-century of struggle for this outcome, building a new, independent state was a dramatic change in situation for South Sudan. Technical and political challenges abounded. From the highly political process of demarcating borders to the technical and controversial job of drafting a constitution, South Sudanese leaders and people faced an uphill battle. Most importantly, the time had come for politicians and citizens alike to take responsibility for South Sudan's future. As Kiir said in his independence speech:

> From today on, we shall have no excuses or scapegoats to blame. It is our responsibility to protect ourselves, our land and our resources. It shall be the duty of this government to prepare and equip the next generation with the necessary skills. The challenges are great but we must begin the task of facing up to them today. While the pillars of a house are important, its foundation is even more critical. We must build a strong foundation for our new nation.
>
> Gurtong 2011

But South Sudan was not a blank slate. Decades of war and centuries of identity formation provided the half-filled canvas on which South Sudan had to paint its future.

One of the most immediate concerns, seemingly, was that of concretizing boundaries, both with Sudan and within South Sudan. This is one of the most fundamental elements of statehood, as conventionally understood. Second was the issue of ensuring security, traditionally the primary responsibility of the state. This includes the physical security of the state and citizens but can also refer to issues of human security – such as providing essential services related to health and education and jump-starting a stagnant economy. Third was that of institutionalizing the state and government through a functioning bureaucracy and political structure. All of these issues were formed and influenced by previous wars and leadership processes. With this situation, it was necessary for leaders to emerge who were suited to these specific challenges. This did not occur. The lack of mutuality between political leaders and followers became ever more evident in the boundary-making process and the lack of security. The exchange of influence needed to build a functioning and relevant state was not present.

The demarcation of the state remained a highly contested issue after secession, both internally and externally with Sudan. The latter dominated international and national interest at first, but in the end it would be internal borders that would prove the most contentious and disastrous. Abyei, an oil-rich region used and inhabited by both Dinka and Arab Messiria, on the border between Sudan and South Sudan, was the primary source of conflict between the two states. The fate of Abyei was a source of disagreement during the interim period, and meant to be decided through a referendum that never happened (Arnold & Le Riche 2013: 123; Medani 2011: 145). To the Dinka and the nomadic Messiria, Abyei's future was inextricably tied up in their own futures and livelihoods, either placing the Dinka, who had fought for independence with the SPLM/A, under the authority of Sudan, or depriving the Messiria of important grazing lands (Johnson 2007; Medani 2011: 146). For the political leaders, the problem centred on Abyei's oil reserves (Arnold & LeRiche 2013: 125; Frahm 2015: 257).

An area of less than 11,000 square kilometres thus bears immense significance. Abyei represents (1) the problem of equating statehood with identity and (2) the dangers of using identity as unifying mechanism amongst leaders and followers with different interests. A state requires territory; territory is immovable. Identity is bound up in people; people move. The decades of conflict and state-building, and the leadership process this entailed, had entwined the concepts of identity and statehood in a way that was too inflexible for the reality of the context. Ethnic, racial and religious groups cannot be separated as easily as drawing lines on a map. But narrow interpretations of identity allowed elites to pursue their particular interests during the conflict to mobilize support and, after the conflict, to pursue their oil interests. As the situation changed, mutual interests between leaders and followers were less clear. And these interests drove leaders to pursue state-focused solutions to a complex identity challenge that would give them access to material gains while neglecting the needs of those who abide in and rely on this region.

Not only was Abyei important to South Sudanese politicians for its oil wealth, but also for its symbolic potential. With independence, elites now had to face immense challenges with a less obvious mobilization tool than fighting an oppressive 'other' in the north. Focusing on border disputes with Sudan kept this tool viable by sustaining nationalist sentiment amidst a dire service delivery challenge (Frahm 2015: 256–7). Securing the South Sudanese territorial state became a tool for the SPLM/A to maintain its own legitimacy in a changing situation (Arnold & LeRiche 2013: 125; Frahm 2015: 255). This was one of several ways in which the leadership co-opted the state-building endeavour for the purposes of elite survival and prosperity rather than the security and service of the citizens.

But it was not only external boundaries that came into play; internal administrative boundaries were highly contested. A debate about the structure of the South Sudanese state echoes that of the Sudanese state at independence, specifically the argument for federalism. The case for federalism was partly raised in fear of Dinka domination, similar to the fear of Arab domination after Sudanese independence (Bereketeab 2014: 312). In theory, federalism would maintain ethnic identity while also promoting a national identity (Frahm 2012: 31), but the fluidity of identity complicated this endeavour. The drawing of administrative boundaries became intertwined with ethnic difference, which became more or less pronounced when confronted with a perceived threat, such as encroaching on a boundary thought to belong to the group (see below). Once again, the dominant approach to dealing with a perceived identity difference was to reconfigure the state. And, as in the Sudanese civil war, this became an elite concern.

The federalism route was already adopted after the CPA with an increase in administrative units as part of a decentralization strategy meant to increase rural development, urbanization and service delivery (AUCISS 2014: 48–52; Pendle 2014: 237; Thomas 2015: Ch. 5). These states, counties and *payams* usually ran parallel to ethnic groups, leading to an equation of ethnic and geographical boundaries (Pendle 2014: 237; Thomas: Ch. 5). But the simplification of complex identity groups that instil a sense of belonging, generate norms and provide safety nets, into administrative territorial units is not straightforward, as Cormack explains regarding efforts to translate the Dinka *wuɔt* (cattle-camp) system into government administrations (Cormack 2016: 508–12).

Ethnic identities have thus been validated by the creation of internal states and counties, hindering cross-ethnic nation-building (Frahm 2015: 261). As a result, instead of resolving the tension between nation and state, the creation of a new state enhanced competition over territory as smaller ethnic and regional groups sought to 'assert their claims to territory, status and recognition' (Frahm 2015: 260–1). Elites encouraged this competition in their own pursuit of state access (Thomas 2015: Ch. 5). In the process, old disputes from previous generations were added to the mix (Thomas 2015: Ch. 5). The state thus became a source of destabilization rather than the arbiter of societal relationships.

This is further evidenced by the patronage system in state institutions. Access to the state and bureaucratic positions provide a leader and their followers (largely determined by kinship) access to state resources, particularly oil profits (Awolich 2015: 4; Gerenge 2015: 98–9; Rolandsen 2015: 165). As a result, debates surrounding administrative borders spark conflict because of their impact on state access (Frahm 2015: 261; Thomas 2015: Ch. 5). For example, a dispute between the Monyjooc and Ajak sections of two different Dinka 'sub-tribes' around ownership of the Maŋar settlement and boundary was 'related not to competition over shared natural resources but to obtaining a place in a new administration' and 'symbols of the state' such as letters, signs and flags were used to assert authority (Cormack 2016: 522). The state, then, became a source of contestation. In addition, the basis for prototype leadership (referent and legitimate power) became enmeshed with reward power. As a result, the norms that would foster the exchange of influence between leaders and followers would have to compete with pathways of influence that relied on the provision of concrete rewards generated through state access.

In this process, we see the interaction between the more concrete and abstract value of land. Land serves as provider, organizer and home to the people of South Sudan. It is the primary source of sustenance through agriculture and grazing ground, in a largely subsistence economy (Rolandsen 2015: 165). It structures social and political life by bounding groups and their authorities. And it both grounds and feeds the imagination of the community by standing as the perceived homeland. However, due to a history of migration and displacement, fuelled by war and economic needs, it becomes ever harder to reconcile the concrete with the abstract, borders with communities, and the state with the nation. The most evident example of this can be found in the repatriation challenge of southern Sudanese in Khartoum after secession, whose belonging was linked to their place of origin rather than the place they had made home amidst a challenging environment (Schultz 2014: 305–7). Homelands remain linked to ethnic or clan identity rather than national identity, to the convenience of elites. The usefulness of the narrative of 'southern Sudan as the home of all Southerners' (Schultz 2014: 306–7) was wearing thin without the northern threat.

Therefore, while some feel that federalism would reduce identity-related conflict by separating groups into their respective administrative units (Interview B 2017), 'federalism can't be the cure for nationhood' (Interview E 2017). In fact, bringing ethnicity into the federalism debate appears to have complicated matters. While federal discussions should be centred on questions of viability and territory, they have been incorporated into what are described as 'historical conflicts' between various identity groups (Interview E 2017). One respondent argued that defining borders should be the final concern of the debate and focus should rather be placed on defining the functions and character of the unitary and federal states (Interview F 2017). He also argued that conflating federal states with ethnic communities is dangerous, as 'homogenous units are an inherent danger to national unity' since they are more likely to fuel irredentist and separatist agendas than heterogenous units (Interview F 2017). In order to avoid a situation of unity at the centre and fragmentation at the periphery, the respondent contends that diverse administrative units would 'administer diversity from the source ... [by bringing] groups together and giv[ing] them power' (Interview F 2017).

Part and parcel of the border conflicts discussed above is inter-communal conflict and cattle raiding. Both continued with little intervention from the state (Pendle 2014: 228). Following decades and generations of insecurity, security of person is a key need for South Sudanese. For example, in Jonglei, one of the most volatile regions post-secession, survey evidence indicates that security was the primary concern for citizens (Maxwell et al. 2014: vii, 8–9, 16, 20–2). Unfortunately, one of the primary causes of insecurity, cattle raiding, had been exacerbated by the state-building process. The acquisition of deadly weapons from the state and the erosion of traditional authorities that historically governed cattle raiding has resulted in a severe escalation of this type of violence (Wild et al. 2018: 1–2, 6). At the same time, high-level leaders who have mobilized and armed cattle-raiding militant groups and exempted them from traditional authority, while only loosely integrating them into state authority, have very little control over these actors (Wild et al. 2018: 4–6).

State security institutions, despite immense funding relative to other budgets, did little to increase security (Ajak 2015: 3–4; Maxwell et al. 2014: vii, 8–9, 16, 20–2). Positions in the SPLA were used in Salva Kiir's 'Big Tent' strategy to buy peace (AUCISS 2014: 38, 252). Kiir lacked the influence and mutuality to ensure unity without reward power. Again, the state became the commodity through which these rewards were handed out. But state resources relied heavily on oil revenues, which significantly reduced as a result of dropping oil prices and transit fee disputes with Khartoum (Young 2019: 14–15). At the same time, the SPLA remained inextricably intertwined with the SPLM (AUCISS 2014: 24), making the military loyal to the party and party factions over the state and the state's citizens. As one respondent indicated: 'There is no distinction between the military and the political' and 'the gun-class determines what the country should look like' (Interview C 2017). The combined result was a security architecture that failed to provide security and, at times, created insecurity (Maxwell et al. 2014: 16). In 2013, this led to disaster as the struggle over control of the SPLM equated to a struggle over the state (Kisiangani 2015: 5-6).

The other significant concern for South Sudanese was the provision of basic services. With the main budgetary and political focus being directed towards security institutions, however, responsibility for service delivery was relegated primarily to NGOs. Estimates indicate that 80 per cent of services in rural areas were provided by these organizations (Kisiangani 2015: 3). In addition, development and aid projects were largely supply-driven with limited community input (Ajak 2015: 5). Because of this, Ajak characterizes South Sudanese communities as 'idle consumers of donor aid' (Ajak 2015: 5). The rationale for the state based on the notion of the social contract, however, requires not only provision of services from the state but responsibility on the part of citizens as well. A reliance on NGOs, and especially international NGOs, thus limits the ability of the state to create a sense of collective loyalty and responsibility.

In addition, the predominance of international actors in the service delivery field results in an interrupted exchange of influence between state and society and leaders and followers. Leaders are known to cater to external needs, perspectives and ideas (Ajak 2015: 6), while followers have been seen to conflate government, military, party and international NGOs in a single *Hakuma,* or government (Leonardi 2007: 394; 2013: 160). In fact, research even indicates that some South Sudanese would lay blame on the international community rather than the state for failed service delivery (Reeve 2012: 51). As a result, the relationship between state and society is interrupted, hampering meaningful nation-building.

The final key component of state-building is that of institutionalizing the state bureaucracy, which is closely linked with the above. Borders determine how a bureaucracy is divided and functions, and the working of the bureaucracy determines the delivery of key services including security. A federal arrangement is meant to bring the state closer to the people (Interview B 2017; AUCISS 2014: 44–8, 51), but can also lead to a proliferation of conflicts over ever smaller boundaries (Frahm 2012: 31; 2015: 261; Thomas 2015: Ch. 5). In South Sudan, this led to a tension between the two key elements of statehood: boundaries and institutions. Many have attributed the continued conflict in the country to the weakness of state institutions (Interview C 2017; Pendle 2014: 228). As a result, most attention was dedicated to state-building efforts (Gerenge 2015: 87; Pendle 2014: 228). But state-building has also played a role in destabilizing the country, by shifting power dynamics between groups through the creation of 'administrative units' and 'judicial initiatives' (Pendle 2014: 242). This occurs because of the patronage networks that dominate the new system.

Exchanges of influence in the state bureaucracy were structured along kinship and ethnic lines. As the state was a key source of income and monetary resources, political positions and the state bureaucracy became an arena for ethnic competition. For example, leaders in the SPLA would often choose the location of a barracks as their home areas, which provided the local community with economic resources (Thomas 2015: Ch. 5). Also, by using an ethnic quota system, leaders are forced to mobilize support using ethnicity (Thomas 2015: Ch. 5). This has proved disastrous in the current conflict, where leaders used the threat of communities losing government positions to mobilize along ethnic lines (Interview D 2017). The state has thus become a highly pursued commodity rather than an entity that exists to protect and serve the people it houses.

The state should, in theory, provide leaders with legitimate power through their positions in political and administrative office. It is important, however, to qualify this with the foundations or preconditions of legitimate power identified by French and Raven, namely cultural values, an 'acceptance of the social structure . . . as right', and/or appointment by another legitimate authority (French & Raven 2011: 138–9). Legitimate power is dependent on the values of the followers, not on the personal power or abilities of the leader (French & Raven 2011: 138–9). Many of these preconditions are absent in the South Sudanese state, and there are competing authorities with overlapping or greater authority. For example, survey evidence suggests that the vast majority (90 per cent) of people rely on traditional leaders to provide security, followed by neighbours and religious leaders, and lastly state security institutions (Wild et al. 2018: 7).

The greater legitimacy of prophets amongst the Nuer has already been commented on, but this can also be seen in land governance. For example, in Yei Town and its surroundings, traditional authorities such as the *monye menu* (land 'custodians') and *monye kuro* (clan elders), the chiefs (who occupy a position in between traditional and state authority) and the *Payam* (administrative authority appointed by the state) compete for authority over land governance, with their influence being determined by differing groups' perception of the legitimacy of the traditional or state structures (often guided by whether the community originated from the area or had migrated there during the war) (Van Leeuwen et al. 2018). Nevertheless, competition for state access remains high, not for the legitimate power it should embody but for the reward and coercive power it provides access to.

Another example of competing authorities can be found in local militant groups, which hold a complex relationship with state authority and local communities. The *titweng* (Dinka-armed cattle-keepers) for example, have been at times incorporated into the state, at other times competed with the state, and yet other times been relied on by state officials for protection of their own cattle (Pendle 2015). Their legitimacy and influence stems from legitimate and reward power through the cultural norms that place high value on *titweng* membership and their ability to protect their communities.[5] This and examples of recruitment and leadership through established 'historical practice' in Equatorian militant groups during the recent civil war have been used to demonstrate the blurred lines between state/formal and community/informal uses of violence (Kindersley & Rolandsen 2017; Pendle 2015). Contrary to the Weberian understanding of the state as the 'monopol[y of] the legitimate use of force' (Weber 2014: 8), the South Sudanese state appears to rely on the legitimacy afforded to communal uses of violence both to fulfill the role of protector of citizens and to defend against opposition.[6]

In the end, the state often served to unbalance inter-group power relations (Pendle 2014: 227). As the state is captured by the elite, converting administrative units into 'tribal fiefdoms' and promoting inter-ethnic conflict, the societal structures and norms that managed conflict in the past have been eroded (Gerenge 2015: 97–8). As a result, state-building in the South Sudanese case actually led to an erosion of cross-ethnic ties and nation-building foundations, while further fragmenting society (Gerenge 2015: 100). Meanwhile, the current conflict has emerged in part because of this identity-based patronage system. The political conflict between Kiir and Machar threatened their respective ethnic groups' access to the state (Awolich 2015: 4). With ethnicity as the primary pathway to influence leaders and gain access to state resources, the stakes of ethnic representation are high.

Outside of the state bureaucracy, traditional authority persists as the dominant structure governing social relations (Frahm 2012: 27–8). It is the more present and legitimate authority to many South Sudanese (AUCISS 2014: 270). One respondent indicated that the average person will 'always bring [an issue] to the traditional chief' (Interview D 2017). Another noted how 'MPs will just be [in Juba] and will not go back to consult with their communities' (Interview C 2017). Traditional leadership, though, is not uncontroversial nor universally accepted (Deng et al. 2015: 28, 37–40; Maxwell et al. 2014: 26). As one respondent indicated, the process became politicized as chiefs were appointed by government, sometimes against the community's wishes and fuelling fears that the appointed leaders would act as spies (Interview D 2017).

In this way, the interplay between traditional authority and the state has complicated matters. The state further legitimized traditional authority in its 2005 and 2011 constitutions, which use traditional authority as the framework for rural administration, thereby 'deepen[ing] the linkage between ethnicity and administration' (Thomas 2015: Ch. 5). Traditional authority is largely based on ethnicity and has historically embedded ethnic divisions. By using traditional authority as the primary form of governance, cross-ethnic nation-building becomes limited as social and political life continues to orbit around ethnic identity rather than national identity.

The return to conflict is also evidence that the state-building and institution-building approach promoted by the international community and embraced by the SPLM has failed to account for the needs and grievances of the ordinary South Sudanese. Many policies and laws that are meant to address the challenges of service delivery and good governance are not adhered to. The local government act, which is meant to link the central state to local communities, is one such example (Interview B 2017). As a result, local administrative leaders are being appointed rather than elected, failing to bridge the gap between leaders and followers (Interview B 2017). Parliamentary oversight is often circumvented by the executive (Interview B 2017). Leaders are accused of preventing the passage of laws that may pose challenges to their interests in the future, such as the Human Rights Bill (Interview B 2017).

Some have pointed out that building social capital that furthers inter-group cooperation is more the product of a shared identity and outside the purview of the state (Gerenge 2015: 103). This is not necessarily true. As discussed in Chapter 2, certain state institutions, such as education and the military, can be instrumental in building a collective identity. Also, if a state serves the needs of its citizens, it is likely to foster a sense of loyalty and responsibility. However, this is not a one-way street. State-building also requires a degree of loyalty and responsibility on the part of citizens, and institutions must reflect accepted norms and values to avoid imposing an identity. This is therefore a delicate balance that requires a leadership process which fosters collective decision-making – a leadership process that was not present in South Sudan. The key goal for South Sudanese people was a state that ensures their security and livelihoods. The primary goal for leaders was to ensure access to political resources and cement their place in the new state. The intersection of interests – the only element of mutuality – in these two diverging endeavours was that of using ethnicity and identity to secure their portion of the state. The state was now a commodity and ethnicity the currency.

# Collective will and collective responsibility without the collective threat

With a fracturing national identity and a commodified state, South Sudan found little in the way of social bonds or institutionalized rules to engender collective decision-making, ensure societal trust and build a sense of collective responsibility for the nation's future. While the staggering majority (98 per cent) with which the people of South Sudan voted for independence may give the impression of collective will, this was an illusion. Collective will came easier during the struggle. Collective action was driven by the liberation goal (Interview F 2017). But the situation had changed. The primary goal now, in theory, was peacebuilding and development – a true test of collective will. When faced with a collective enemy, the nation is framed primarily as 'other than': 'We are not them, and they are not us.' Mutuality is manufactured by simplifying collective needs to the elimination of the perceived threat. But without this enemy, and with a multitude of wicked problems[7] to address, a more nuanced understanding of nationhood is needed. The identity that would engender loyalty, the rules that would govern societal interaction, the laws that would ensure stability and the structures that would permit collective decision-making and action must all be negotiated upon a shared understanding of the nation – of 'who we are'. This shared understanding requires, first and foremost, mutuality.

While the illusion of unity faded, so did the dreams of a new country. Independence was meant to liberate South Sudan from the uneven development felt under Khartoum and usher in a 'new era of peace and prosperity' (Kisiangani 2015: 3). Southern Sudan's challenges and justification for war had been framed partly on problems of uneven development. But life after independence did not improve as expected (AUCISS 2014: 27–8; Kisiangani 2015: 3). Of course, it takes more than three years to undo the effects of decades of conquest, colonialism and oppression. Also, simplifying South Sudan's challenges to the actions of the perceived oppressor created unmeetable expectations of life after independence, in the same way that reducing identity to 'other than' Arab/Muslim created unrealistic perceptions of unity. In fact, the leadership and governance patterns of Khartoum seemed to replicate themselves in independent South Sudan, indicating a deeper problem than differing identities and uneven state development.

Instead of prosperity, or even the seeds of prosperity, independent South Sudan suffered more of the same. Oil profits, while no longer directed solely to Khartoum, were directed to the new centre in Juba (Thomas 2015: Ch. 5) and the 'pockets of individuals' (Interview B 2017). Service delivery remained slow, inconsistent or non-existent (Ajak 2015: 1–4; Rolandsen 2015: 165). Plans for development were not realized. And cattle raiding continued to increase in scope and violence, causing hundreds of deaths annually and hampering economic activity (Frahm 2015: 260; Pendle 2014: 228). Elation and euphoria gave way to frustration and anger (Gerenge 2015: 96; Johnson 2016). The life of the ordinary South Sudanese did not change. But the life of the liberator, the rebel leader, the politician? This did change.

Many believe that elites used their new-found power to enhance their own wealth through plundering the country's oil profits, rather than using these revenues and the nation's long-hoped-for sovereignty to further economic and social development (Johnson 2016: Prologue; Kisiangani 2015: 5). One respondent lamented the dire economic situation – how, for many, it is 'better to go to a refugee camp' while 'leaders don't talk about it' (Interview D 2017). Another said that the state 'is not serving the interests of people', but is rather 'serving personal interests' (Interview B 2017). The mounting evidence of corruption during the interim period and after secession supports this view (Johnson 2016). Elites were now feasting at the table. The people, once again, were not invited.

Another hindrance to collective decision-making and action was the societal rifts that had crystallized through war, history and economic competition. Globally, the two most common approaches to this peacebuilding challenge have been to (1) design state structures (constitutions, electoral law, federal arrangements) according to the key identity issues, and (2) pursue reconciliation and justice through a variety of truth commissions and/or tribunals.[8] In South Sudan, the first approach led to the federalism debate, but the second was lacking. Peace and stability was favoured over punitive justice. Reconciliation was pursued in an ad hoc manner through peace conferences for inter-communal conflicts and co-option into the SPLM/A of opposition leaders who posed a threat (Ajak 2015: 3; AUCISS 2014: 38; Awolich 2015: 9; Frahm 2015: 260; Reeve 2012: 56; Wilson 2014: 3, 5–7). In a way, these two different tracks for reconciliation symbolize the diverging path of leaders and followers post-secession. While people were faced with reconciling differences that continued to have an impact on their daily lives and livelihoods, elite interests shifted towards political manoeuvring. In such a case, the collective suffers in its ability to determine its will, as the situations faced by the majority and those speaking for the majority are vastly different.

At the same time, peace conferences were an insufficient tool to confront the complex layers of loyalty, identity and division in society. These meetings, ranging in size and number of actors, are used to promote dialogue aimed at resolving potential or existing conflicts between communities (Wilson 2014: 5). South Sudanese and observers, however, have become sceptical of these conferences' efficacy, partly because of a failure to include the relevant communities and actors and because of disingenuous participation (Reeve 2012: 53, 56–8; Wilson 2014: 6–7). Such a reactionary, incomplete and ad hoc approach may address instances of tension and division but not create collective will and responsibility. This requires the building of relationships and trust to ensure an interconnectedness that promotes loyalty and collective action.

Collective action, then, becomes dependent on the pathways of influence between leaders and followers and the mobilization tools used by said leaders. Throughout South Sudanese – and indeed global – history, the most effective mobilization technique is the invocation of a common enemy (Frahm 2015: 254). But in South Sudan, this went beyond collective action for a transitory goal to moulding collective will and identity. What united southerners was being located in the south rather than the north, which is 'why [they] are called South Sudanese' (Interview F 2017). The sense of belonging to the geographical entity of South Sudan, which drove the collective will to secede, was founded on a narrative of 'discrimination and marginalization' (Schultz 2014: 314). Belonging is also integral to collective will and responsibility. If one does not feel 'a part of' a community or nation, one is less likely to participate in collective decision-making and action or feel a sense of responsibility and loyalty to the collective's future and its other members. The question then is this: Was the liberation struggle a case of an existing collective fighting a common threat, or 'the enemy of my enemy is my friend'? The truth may be somewhere in the middle, but the speed with which collective responsibility broke down in 2013 tempts one towards the latter interpretation.

In this way, the political culture of South Sudanese elites suggests a reliance on 'othering' that is troubling. If 'othering' is the best – and possibly only – tool available for leaders to mobilize followers, then a lack of mutuality is evident. This forces leaders to manufacture mutuality by using 'the other', creating a temporary sense of affinity with the leader. Such affinity may result in collective action but is often superficial and temporary, while also creating divisions that further conflict. In addition, the experience of South Sudan suggests that as this becomes an entrenched practice it tends to fragment society at ever smaller levels. The absence of an external collective enemy forces leaders to look for internal enemies to raise support. Leadership founded on mutuality, on the other hand, is likely to be more effective in building collective will and collective responsibility without fragmenting society, since leaders are forced to respond to the actual challenges and situations facing a society.

Aside from a lack of mutuality, another key problem in the building of collective will is the inability of leaders and followers to exchange influence. One of the fundamental requirements for this to occur is the ability to dialogue and hold national conversations. Perhaps the most pertinent example of this is the stalled constitution-making process immediately after independence. As one respondent noted, constitutions emerge as part of a 'bargaining between the population that got themselves trapped in that geographical entity and elites pursuing their own interests' (Interview F 2017). This 'bargaining' process, however, got off to a false start. The drafting of South Sudan's new constitution was delayed and did not follow the public consultation process outlined in the transitional constitution (AUCISS 2014: 41–4). South Sudan has, to date, failed to collaboratively design and bring into force a national constitution, indicating a fundamental lack of collective will.

The problems in the constitution-making process were multiple. The National Constitutional Review Commission (NCRC) was formed predominantly of SPLM members (Republic of South Sudan 2012: 2–3). In addition, rather than appointing technical experts, Kiir largely appointed representatives from political parties (forty-four out of fifty-five members), which turned the commission 'into an economically and politically accommodating venture' (Akol 2013: 4). Only nine of the fifty-five seats were given to civil society members (Akol 2013: 4). In fact, when it became clear that the government was not going to fulfil its obligations to hold widespread public consultations, it fell to civil society leaders to take up this role, under the leadership of the South Sudanese Law Society and Justice Africa (AUCISS 2014: 42–3). In some of these consultations, held at the University of Juba, a participant is quoted as saying: 'My mother will not come to Juba; she is waiting where she is – *but she is waiting for you*' (Tier et al. 2013: 16). At the same session, the audience expressed a resounding feeling of not having been consulted (Tier et al. 2013: 16).

All this indicates and has bred a problem in terms of collective will and collective responsibility. While this problem was evident in the previous civil war, the perceived sense of nationhood at independence and the nationalist rhetoric created the impression that South Sudanese viewed each other as equal members in a new society. This illusion was quickly shattered. As elites sought to consolidate or expand their hold on power without a common enemy, they shifted towards a system of reward and coercive power. Loyalty in the military, for example, was maintained through patronage. While this promoted a cohesive SPLM/A for a while, it proved unsustainable (Gerenge 2015: 99). Collective loyalty was thus fostered primarily through reward power. Once these rewards were depleted or in dispute, the façade of unity quickly faded. Had loyalty been built on other bases of power and mutual values and experiences, the results may have been different.

Perhaps the best indication of the lack of collective loyalty in South Sudan is the speed with which violence spread across the country in 2013. The conflict had reached the eastern provinces within ten days (Pendle 2014: 227). The high instance of human rights violations is also a clear indication that cross-ethnic collective responsibility, which assumes all members of a group hold certain rights, is nearly non-existent. The sources of this lack of collective will, loyalty and responsibility can be seen in the leadership process.

The primary problem rests in a lack of mutuality. Militias mobilized for war but, as in the previous war, these soldiers' motives for violence were often separate from those of national leaders. In fact, the Nuer White Army had already mobilized due to ongoing conflicts against the Murle prior to the political dispute (Johnson 2016). Militants are often driven by resource related grievances, economic gains, ongoing inter-communal conflicts and community self-defence (AUCISS 2014: 28; Fleischner 2015: 16–18; Reeve 2012: 41–3, 64, 69). Such interests are far removed from and little served by the power struggle that sparked the conflict. But unlike the previous civil war against Khartoum, there is no collective goal of self-determination to bind these disparate interests. This makes peace even more elusive, especially as peacemaking approaches are constrained by the need to negotiate amongst elites, leaving many of these issues unresolved.

At the same time, few South Sudanese support the ongoing conflict (AUCISS 2014: 27; Fleischner 2015: 9; Maxwell et al. 2014: 16). According to one respondent: 'Those who have experienced it don't want war' (Interview B 2017). In other words, just as in the 1990s, this conflict is perceived as an elite affair where those pursuing the conflict are assumed to be little affected by it, and in some cases profiting. One respondent lamented that the home regions of politicians seemed less affected by violence, saying: 'Maybe if there is fighting in Bahr-al-Gazhl we will find that they don't want war' (Interview B 2017). Yet the people of South Sudan are unable, for various reasons, to influence their leaders or build cross-ethnic ties to challenge the narratives being instrumentalized to their own detriment. The result is a situation in which people feel no ownership in the national project and no sense of future in the country, which makes building collective will and collective responsibility near impossible. As one respondent states: 'Many people do things on the idea that tomorrow "I will go to another country"' (Interview B 2017).

Even more evidence of the poor sense of collectivity is the ease with which factions began to fragment. In fact, many of the political relationships that upheld Machar and Kiir were driven by hardliners in the background and held together by shared ethnic identity (Johnson 2016). For example, key leaders driving Nuer mobilization and early military mobilization were not Machar, but included SPLA defector Peter Gadet and White Army leaders Bor Doang and Dak Kueth (Johnson 2016). Peter Gadet, who had a troubled relationship with Machar (Johnson 2016), would later defect from the SPLM-IO (ISS 2015). Kiir's actions have also been restricted and guided by hardliners (Johnson 2016), including the Jieng Council of Elders (Fleischner 2015: 11–14). At the same time, other politicians discontented with Kiir's rule did not join Machar as he expected but formed their own non-militant camp – the Former Detainees (Johnson 2016; ICG 2015b: 1; Rolandsen 2015: 164). While this demonstrates the severe fragmentation of interests and factions, it more importantly implies an interrupted exchange of influence where elite factions fight over elite interests, with little evidence that these leaders have engaged in a process of collective decision-making with their targeted followers.

All this complicated any peace efforts. While the CPA had emerged from years of dialogue and 'thrashing out the issues' (Interview F 2017), this process felt more rushed. Civil society and South Sudanese in general, despite efforts to the contrary, were once again left out of the conversation (Moro 2015: 1; Akol 2014: 3, 5–13; Deng et al. 2015: 21–2). Again, influence exchange was found amongst elites and between politicians and foreign actors. The 2015 agreement, which failed, was perceived as an external imposition, and presented this way by leaders (Interview E 2017; Interview F 2017). The more recent agreement, led by Sudan, appears to be another elite pact, with many new government positions being formed, continuing the tradition of buying peace. Yet, this agreement has been marketed as internally driven and thus more likely to be successful. With the fundamental leadership process unchanged, I remain cautious in my analysis.

## Secession and the descent into civil war: The recurrent leadership gap

One of the key underlying issues not discussed in the dynamics above is that of power. In South Sudan, the primary means of exerting influence appears to be through coercive or reward power. Such power is not conducive to producing collective will and loyalty because people act out of personal interest or coercion rather than a fundamental agreement of the problem, solution and goals. The power influenced by prototype leaders is also superficial if not based on mutual experiences, needs and values. Prototype leaders have historically used their power, founded on their identity attributes, to fragment South Sudanese society by dramatizing certain identity attributes. The state became an increasingly ethnicized commodity. The collectivity of South Sudan disintegrated. While the elites at the top may be blamed for this, the cyclical and fractal nature of this at all levels indicates a problem in the leadership process.

Many have criticized elites for how they have governed the new country and for the ongoing conflict (Interview B 2017; Interview C 2017; Interview D

2017; Kisiangani 2015: 3). In particular, one can point to the persistent military nature of the ruling party, undemocratic tendencies and extensive corruption (Interview C 2017; Frahm 2015: 259; Johnson 2016: Ch. 2; Kisiangani 2015: 2, 4). Much of this is typical of liberation movements-turned-government (Johnson 2016: Ch. 2). The SPLM's claim to rule rests on its role in liberating the country (Frahm 2015: 256). This has bred a sense of entitlement not only to power but the country's resources, of which the South Sudanese elite had been deprived under Khartoum (Johnson 2016: Ch. 2).

But a situational understanding of leadership indicates that this is an insufficient claim to lead. Leadership is based on a leader's ability to respond to a situation. As a result, elites have largely lost their influence amongst the population. In one case, a respondent indicated that people have 'lost trust' in the political leadership, that 'people are confused' and that they have no 'clear idea' of who to choose as their leader (Interview G 2017). In another example, one person indicated that the 'President is there for the Dinka so people are not interested' (Interview D 2017). Another explained how difficult the peace process is simply because it is so hard to identify the different stakeholders and the people who represent their interests (Interview F 2017). Currently, the government or the official opposition's legitimacy to speak on behalf of the people at the negotiating table is questioned (De Vries & Schomerus 2017). While the SPLM/A may have been best suited to respond to a situation of oppression and conflict, this does not necessarily mean it is best suited to a peacebuilding situation. In addition, oppression and conflict permits leadership to be founded on the narrative of 'the other', as discussed above. This is not the ideal form of creating legitimacy and mutuality in a peacebuilding situation. In order to lead the country, a change is necessary.

The use of reward power is a key example of this. This approach created a dual problem of overstretching the resources of the state (to keep up with the 'rewards') and entrenching a pattern of leadership emergence that relies on coercion rather than mutuality. The SPLM's chief strategy for dealing with rebellion was its 'Big Tent' approach whereby rebel leaders and warlords were provided with amnesty and co-opted into government (Ajak 2015: 3; AUCISS 2014: 38; Awolich 2015: 9; Frahm 2015: 260). This made violence and rebellion a realistic means of accessing power and government office (Awolich 2015: 9) by 'rewarding rebellion' (Interview E 2017). Consequently, South Sudan has an inflated security sector; the SPLA houses the second-highest number of generals in the world (Ajak 2015: 3). Other services suffered as a result (Ajak 2015: 3–8). The purpose of South Sudan's security institutions, then, was to 'buy peace' rather than ensure the safety of the population (Ajak 2015: 3). This indicates a preference on the part of elites to employ a strategy that would ensure their continued hold on power rather than dealing with the root causes of discontent and conflict. It also illustrates the limitations of state-building without understanding the leadership dynamics.

Access to leadership positions and employment is also driven by kinship and personal networks. Promotions, jobs and access to state patronage became enmeshed with the marriage market and bridewealth prices (Pinaud 2016: 253). One respondent indicated that when applying for jobs, people are asked questions like 'Who is your father?' 'Where are you from?' and 'Which tribe are you from?' (Interview G 2017). This is the case even at the highest levels of politico-military leadership. Paul Malong was known to be a close friend of President Salva Kiir, 'even offer[ing] . . . to pay for the bridewealth of [Kiir's] second wife – which was particularly telling to which of the two of them really had power' (Pinaud 2016: 253). In the SPLM-IO, Machar's second-in-command, Taban Deng Gai, was raised in Machar's wife's household, while the *de facto* third-in-command was Machar's wife, Angelina (Young 2019: 97–8). This is a further indication of an inter-elite exchange of influence rather than a leader/follower exchange.

Another form of accessing power is through the drawing of borders and boundaries. Gerrymandering along ethnic lines becomes an issue as leaders, whose political prospects were more limited at the centre and larger administrative units, promote smaller units in which they will 'be the king' (Interview E 2017). The debates surrounding borders often occur amongst elites with little to no dialogue with followers (Thomas 2015: Ch. 5). So, while decentralization and federalism is portrayed as a way to protect the interests of minorities, it has been used as a tool for the enhancement of elite interests. The state-building and institution-building process then becomes co-opted by elites whose interests do not lie in nation-building. State-building as peacebuilding regularly faces these challenges when a flawed leadership process is present. At the same time, the role of the state has been passed off to civil society organizations, who are welcomed by elites in this regard but not when criticizing the government (Ajak 2015; Moro 2015: 3). In other words, leaders have accepted civil society as long as this has permitted them to escape their responsibility to serve the needs of their followers.

How, then, do leaders engage with their followers? The way in which influence is exchanged is telling for a nation. In a unified nation, where collective will exists, followers across the nation should be able to influence leaders and vice versa. However, the channels for communication between leaders and followers are almost non-existent in South Sudan. Elites communicate with their rural constituents primarily through subnational ethnic organizations and associations, and rarely travel to said areas personally (Interview B 2017; Thomas 2015: Ch. 5). Similarly, followers engage their leaders through traditional processes. For example, during the South Sudanese Civil War when the relationship between Machar and his generals grew tense, it was the Nuer community that demanded leadership disputes be resolved to preserve 'tribal unity' (Young 2019: 92). Of course, this was done in a context where the community faced an 'existential threat' (Young 2019: 92). The exchange of influence between the highest levels of leadership and followers is therefore identity-based and highly situational.

This serves the dual purpose of continuing the ethnicization of politics by limiting influence exchange to leaders within one's ethnic group, and preventing the development of mutuality between leaders and broader society. Rather, mutuality is manufactured when it is in the interest of leaders to do so, through gerrymandering, for example. Such a system creates a similar problem to that of the liberation struggle. While a mutual goal is evident (independence or a new administrative boundary), it is not founded on mutual interests and needs. As a result, when said goal is achieved, leaders are not compelled to continue serving the interests of followers. Consequently, collective will becomes a volatile and elusive goal when mutuality is lacking.

As South Sudan continued to descend into an intractable civil war, the hopes of sustainable peace seemed ever more elusive. How did a country that less than three years earlier appeared so full of hope, fragment so quickly? The leadership process trends provide some indication. In particular, the lack of mutuality between leaders and followers, the limited pathways of influence between leaders and followers, and the reliance on coercive and reward power contributed to a failure of the leadership process when the situation changed from war to peace.

The actions of leaders just before and during conflict present some of the clearest evidence of elite interests overruling those of their followers. Prior to the conflict, accusations had emerged characterizing Kiir's leadership as authoritarian (AUCISS 2014: 21–7). These were not unfounded. To date, no post-independence elections have been held in South Sudan. Considering the severe irregularities in the 2010 elections, it is difficult to argue that the SPLM holds a democratic mandate. It is also difficult to determine whom leaders represent and whether they reflect the aspirations of their claimed followers (Interview C 2017).

Kiir's removal of Machar and other leaders, such as Pagan Amum, from their positions was attributed to their bid to run against Kiir for president of the SPLM (Kisiangani 2015: 6). The president's response to accusations of authoritarianism and criticism is encapsulated in his opening speech at the NLC meeting, in which he chose to call up memories of the 1991 south/south conflict and the inter-ethnic violence that followed:

> I must warn that this behaviour is tantamount to indiscipline which will take us back to the days of the 1991 split. We all know where the split took us from that time. This could jeopardise the unity and the independence of our country and we must guard against such things, my dear comrades. I am not prepared to let this happen again.
>
> Quoted in Johnson 2016: Ch. 5

After violence broke out, Hilde Johnson describes her efforts to try and get both Machar and Kiir to renounce the violence; both avoided or obfuscated (Johnson 2016: Ch. 6). Machar considered releasing a statement only if Kiir did the same, while Kiir responded with a statement claiming that the security situation was being handled, failing to address the serious threat to civilian lives that had emerged (Johnson 2016: Ch. 6). He did so in full military uniform (Johnson 2016: Ch. 6). Neither Machar nor Kiir were willing to come out strongly against ethnic targeting or the killing of civilians (Johnson 2016: Ch. 6). In this situation, both leaders were responding based on their personal interests, while citizens suffered.

This attitude appears to become more evident as the war progresses and the massive cost of war to civilians continues to grow, while elites continue to focus attention on factional battles. By 2016, reports indicate that 50,000 people had lost their lives and 3.5 million people had been displaced (OCHA 2016; Reuters 2016). Having lost the hope brought on by secession, it now appears many South Sudanese are choosing to leave the country (Interview B 2017). The widely publicized *Sentry* report uncovers the extensive wealth that South Sudanese elites have accumulated through the formalization of their power in the post-CPA era and the 'kleptocratic' networks that have thrived in the conflict (The Sentry 2016). In addition, most of the country's oil revenues have been redirected to fighting the conflict, squandering much of the nation's wealth on a war that is not being fought for the nation's interests (ICG 2015a: 20).

Meanwhile, the gap between political leadership and those being mobilized to fight is evident. In fact, the mobilization of troops is primarily driven by traditional institutions. Wild et al. (2018) detail how cattle-raiding groups have been militarized by a dual processes of capitalizing on traditional institutions and norms, while simultaneously undermining them. But political leaders' control over these groups is minimal at best, or non-existent at worst, with no real shared ideology (Wild et al. 2018). In the case of the White Army, those who do have control and exercise leadership are local commanders whose legitimacy stems from their traditional backgrounds and community leadership (Young 2019: 91). Machar, on the other hand, is seen to be too Western and not Nuer enough (Young 2019: 92, 103). The instrumental, and at times contradictory, relationship between the politico-military elite and traditional leadership is evident. Its effect on the formation of a nation state is also clear. The 'national' leadership at the state level exchanges influence with the wider population through an inherently parochial intermediary: the traditional leadership. But this only occurs when interests converge, rather than through a concerted effort to form a collective community, and the moments of cooperation are also complicated by ongoing competition for authority between the state and the traditional.

Justice also remains elusive. While the 2015 agreement made provisions for justice mechanisms, including a Commission for Truth, Reconciliation and Healing (CTRH), a Hybrid Court for South Sudan (HCSS) and a Compensation and Reparation Authority (CRA), these were never implemented. Leaders took an ambivalent and pragmatic approach to this agreement (Interview E 2017), which later failed. Despite survey evidence suggesting the majority of

South Sudanese desire justice (Deng et al. 2015: 37–57), it has been slow to manifest. In January 2021, the South Sudanese government finally announced that it was beginning processes to establish the Hybrid Court (UN News 2021).

Similarly, Kiir unilaterally decided to create twenty-eight new states after signing the 2015 peace agreement (UN News Centre 2016). This disrupted the power-sharing arrangements in the agreement (Associated Press 2015). It was justified as a fulfilment of the federalism desire, though this is debatable (Sudan Tribune 2015). Machar, originally a staunch supporter of federalism, was now against this move (Associated Press 2015; SSNA 2016; Thomas 2015: Ch. 5). Once again, elite positions proved highly flexible based on situational changes. However, the situations that changed their positions were those that affected their interests rather than those of their followers. Therefore, nations cannot be easily formed through a specific constitutional and institutional framework when said institutions are only framed in a certain way to suit leaders' interests. This would be less likely if mutuality exists between leaders and followers.

The decades of conflict have severely depleted societal trust in South Sudan. The failure to build mutuality founded on trust has aggravated this. Leadership is essential in maintaining societal trust. The actions described above indicate that trust will not be forthcoming as elites continue to pursue their own interests and the mutuality gap widens. The sources of power and pathways of influence between leaders and followers are eroding at alarming rates. As a result, society continues to fragment as individuals turn to ever smaller communities where trust, mutuality and influence is evident and is likely to protect them in a dangerous environment. If this continues, the limited foundations for a cross-ethnic identity and collectivity may disappear altogether.

## Conclusion

It is easy to see the intense societal fragmentation, proliferation of conflict parties and prolific violence, and label South Sudan a 'failed state', or 'failed nation'. But the apparent chaos in South Sudan is actually reflective of a continuous pattern replicated from Sudan, to South Sudan, down to the local communities. One can see patterns and similarities that hearken back to the war between Khartoum and the south. The systemic causes of the war in the centre/periphery divide, politicization of identity and elite capture of the state, among others, are not just cyclical, but fractal. They repeat at ever smaller ratios, creating the appearance of chaos, but are actually the product of a repeating pattern. This pattern is the leadership process. From the local to the national, leadership in South Sudan has relied on an influence process driven by coercion, rewards and identity, rather than mutuality. This promotes a fractal and violent nation-building process as collective action, responsibility and loyalty become transitory and contingent on situational factors.

# Notes

1  Parts of this chapter have been previously published in an article on www.tandfonline.com: Sonja Theron (2020) Power and influence in post-secession South Sudan: A leadership perspective on nation-building, African Security Review, 29:1, 58–81, DOI: 10.1080/10246029.2020.1748672

2  See the discussion in Chapter 1 on the relational nature of identity.

3  Prototype leaders are those that are seen to embody the prototypical characteristics of the social identity group. (Hogg, Michael A. 2001. 'A Social Identity Theory of Leadership', *Personality and Social Psychology Review*, 5(3), pp. 184–200).

4  See the discussion that follows in this and the next two sections for examples of these trends.

5  See Pendle 2015 for an explanation of the cultural norms that legitimize the *titweng* and their role as protectors.

6  See Pendle 2015 and Kindersley & Rolandsen 2017 for examples of this occurring.

7  See Rittel & Webber 1973 for an explanation of 'wicked' versus 'tame' problems.

8  For examples, see Colson 2000; David 2017; Horowitz 2008; Mani 2002; Reilly 2012 and Wolff 2012.

# Conclusion

## Introduction

On 12 September 2018, parties to the South Sudanese conflict signed the Revitalized Agreement on the Resolution of the Conflict in the Republic of South Sudan (R-ARCSS), but the situation remains unstable. The creation of a new state, in this case South Sudan, did not lead to peace nor did it address the root causes of the conflict, as they were far more complex and dynamic than a political and identity difference between northern and southern Sudan. This book set out to investigate the reasons South Sudan has been unable to build a nation that sustains peace. As explained in the Introduction, nation-building is formed of three key processes: identity construction, state-building, and the formation of collective will and collective responsibility, which constructs (or deconstructs) the five components of nationhood (a national identity, a designated territory, a functional political organization, collective will and collective responsibility). As the South Sudanese case has shown, when there are tensions or contradictions between the three nation-building processes, conflict is likely to emerge. For example, when state formation and state-building efforts are in direct contradiction with the dominant perceptions and trends of social identity, groups may reject or revolt against the state (as seen in the Arabization and Islamization policies of Sudan). When collective responsibility is determined by narrow identities, peacebuilding and state-building efforts suffer because loyalty and collective action is driven by sub-state identity markers (as seen by the ethnicization of politics in post-secession South Sudan). It is important, then, to understand how these processes unfold and emerge. In particular, it is important to understand, in a situation where institutions are still being formed and debated, how leadership influences these processes.

From South Sudan's experience, it is evident that identity is formed, constructed and reconstructed through the relationship between leaders and followers, in response to a variety of contextual and situational factors. The nature of the relationship, the nature of the influence exchange between leaders and followers, can impact how identities are dramatized to fuel both leaders' interests and followers' needs. When these interests and needs are not in line with each other, this dramatization can often be destructive. With regard to the second aspect of nationhood, the state and territoriality, it is important to distinguish between statehood and nationhood, while understanding their relationship. Consistencies and inconsistencies between the two must be acknowledged and understood within a given context. A leadership gap, in the case of South Sudan, has resulted in some of these inconsistencies, as the state has become the prize for leaders to pursue individual interests and a distant, often distrusted entity for followers. The nation, on the other hand, has become a tool for leaders in their pursuit of the state, while representing an unstable and fluctuating reality for followers. Finally, social consciousness and action that promotes peace or conflict is determined by a complex array of societal relationships. These relationships include those between leaders and followers, different leaders, institutions and people, and amongst groups. A few final words on the lessons learned from South Sudan in understanding the role of leadership in nation-building is needed.

## How is identity constructed through leadership and what is the relationship between identity construction and peace and conflict?

The trajectory of identity construction in South Sudan reflects many of the complexities addressed in debates around identity construction. Identities are clearly constructed through complex processes of social, political and economic change. However, identities are also rooted in certain historical narratives. Similarly, while elites have clearly manipulated and utilized identity narratives, the populace would often reject elite narratives of identity, illustrating the agency of both elites and masses in constructing social identities. Finally, while many identity attributes (such as religion, race and ethnicity) are perceived as objective and immovable, history and changing circumstances have shown that they are in fact very fluid. Using the leadership process as a theoretical framework to understand these complexities and contradictions has shed some light on this process of identity construction.

While the nature of identity construction in South Sudan is fluid and dynamic, these identities are perceived as real and have very real consequences. This includes the impact they have on conflict processes. The most evident example is the Arab/African binary created through centuries of conquest and exploitation. Chapter 1 and 2 discussed how the Arab/African divide had been created through a specific historical process rather than an objective racial distinction (Gray 1963: 1; Sawant 1998: 345). This distinction became more embedded after Sudan's independence, though it fluctuated between a racial and a religious distinction due to changing contexts and leader actions. This perceived difference was used to justify and legitimize both oppression and violent conflict. So, while identity was not the sole cause of the conflict, its interaction with political and economic processes did influence the conflict trajectory in a way that is indicative of more than a simple mobilization tool.

The situational understanding of leadership explains these changes and fluctuations in identity. The way in which identity narratives oscillated between racial, religious, ethnic and clan markers throughout South Sudan's history was generally determined by situational factors. However, identity is not simply a dependent variable that changes in a unilateral way when the situation changes. A key component of this was the way in which leaders chose to respond to those situational factors, and whether this response and the identity markers being dramatized responded to the realities facing followers. For example, in times of crisis, southern leaders relied on the narrative of a common enemy to mobilize support. This reflected the reality of southerners who held the experience of oppression and slavery in their collective memory. Garang's vision of unity and Sudanism, on the other hand, did not do this. As identity is relational, this use of 'the other' was key in crystallizing the northern and southern identities.

At the same time, the situational factors driving this use of the common enemy were often experienced differently by leaders and followers. The motivations for leaders often centred on political and state access, while followers were largely concerned with an improvement in daily life. The way in which the oppression narrative was used did not bridge this divide of interests. Thus, when situations changed, it often became evident that a broader collective identity did not exist. This is particularly evident in the periods following the Addis Ababa and CPA agreements, when formerly competing elites became allies and their followers' interests became a secondary concern (see Chapters 2 and 5). The ethnicization of politics in South Sudan reflects a similar pattern. Followers accepted the narratives of ethnic domination and fear because it reflected their realities in local resource competitions (see Chapter 6).

However, leaders were primarily pursuing elite interests. This process results in fluid and highly volatile identity boundaries. In other words, certain situations may lend themselves to influencing identity narratives. Leaders and followers respond to these situations based on their individual experience of said situation. Leaders may choose to frame identity a certain way or institute certain actions that are aimed at reframing identity boundaries. Followers may choose to accept or reject such actions and narratives. This leads to the perpetuation of certain identity markers, a deepening of their divisions, or the emergence of a more dominant identity marker. From this, as shown in a situational understanding of leadership (Murphy 1941: 677), a new situation emerges that will impact future processes of identity construction. Because of this, identity cannot be reframed at random but is dependent on the results of previous experiences of this cycle. This also helps explain why the reframing of identity after conflict is so challenging.

More importantly, however, the dominance of narrow identity markers in the identification of political allegiance and organization has entrenched certain identities and complicated peacebuilding efforts by normalizing the use of identity in political and social structures. In particular, politics became driven by narratives of a common enemy. While identity is relational (Eley & Suny 1996: 32; Guibernau 2007: 10), this heavy reliance on 'the other' proved destructive in South Sudan. By centring societal attention on a common enemy, South Sudanese society failed to form an understanding of what would bind members together. This would make unity dependent on the presence of an enemy, which led to the fragmentation of society after secession (Martin 2002: 122; Young 2003: 423). In addition, it created a political culture and leadership process that is dependent on 'othering'. Combined with the continuous cycles of conflict and violence, this proved highly destructive to social cohesion and nation-building.

Another important issue in leadership and nation-building is the role of power in identity construction. The South Sudanese experience shows that the success or failure of a certain identity narrative is often less dependent on the substance of said narrative than on the way it is transferred from leaders to followers. Multiple sources of power can be used to influence the nation-building process. Some are more successful than others and it is likely that various sources of power are necessary. The use of coercive power to impose an identity, as most clearly evidenced in the Arabization and Islamization programmes of Khartoum (see Chapter 2), are likely to be rejected by the population. This is especially true when the promoted identity is already linked to a history of oppression. The use of reward power, as seen in Kiir's 'Big Tent' strategy (see Chapter 6), has the ability to create the illusion of unity but does not foster a sense of collective identity. Followers and leaders only cooperate on a transactional basis and not on the basis of an identity that stems from shared experiences, values, norms and visions.

Referent power, on the other hand, often fosters a deepening of identity borders when leaders are chosen because of their identity characteristics. As often happened throughout Sudan's and South Sudan's history, leaders were chosen and identified based on a similarity of identity. In other words, prototype leaders emerged. These leaders, however, struggled to gain a cross-sectional following of multiple identity groups (with the exception of key leaders like John Garang who used other sources of power). As a result, the formation of a widespread Sudanese or South Sudanese identity was difficult since leaders served either their individual interests or those of their respective followers. Charismatic power also plays a role in identity construction, as seen in the example of John Garang. However, charismatic power, while useful in myth-building and mobilization, does not necessarily build deeper norms and ideologies that are needed in a national identity. This is perhaps where expert power is required in the form of intellectuals, philosophers and artists. South Sudan was lacking in this regard. In addition, the mutuality gap between the educated and less educated, and between the rural and urban (see Chapter 5), makes it difficult for such 'experts' to influence the population.

This leads to perhaps the most significant issue in the role of leadership in nation-building: the concept of mutuality. Throughout this study, the importance of the mutuality gap in South Sudan's nation-building failure has been explained. In short, South Sudan's experience illustrates the limitations of narrow and inflexible identity attributes (e.g. ethnicity, language, religion) in building mutuality. Such similarities between leaders and followers often create the illusion of mutuality, but it is not necessarily founded on shared experiences, needs, values and norms. Yet, in the absence of such a depth of mutuality, leaders and followers are often forced to identify and influence each other based on narrow identity markers. This mutuality rarely extends beyond early mobilization for conflict to more complex and systematic action for peacebuilding. Because of the emotive power of identity in conflict, especially where identity groups are central to social interaction and structuring, this process serves to further entrench narrow identity divisions (Kauffman 1996: 137). Thus, the process of identity construction continues. However, as shown in Chapter 6, because of the lack of mutuality, this process fragments and continues at ever smaller levels rather than a broader, national identity construction process. This occurs as leaders are forced to resort to narratives that are reliant on a common enemy rather than mutuality, building identity on notions of difference rather than unity. Yet, in current peacebuilding practice, which is elite-centred, the common enemy often becomes an ally. This is often to the detriment of followers when mutuality is lacking to ensure elites maintain a focus on follower interests. As a result, the lack of mutuality leads to a dependency on 'common enemy' narratives and fosters contradictions in vision when situations change, both of which contribute to conflict rather than peace.

The nature of mutuality between leaders and followers determines the way in which they influence each other. This is important in the nation-building process to understand how identity is constructed through an exchange of influence between elites and followers rather than being an exclusively top-down or bottom-up process. Where mutuality exists, leaders and followers are likely to exchange influence in such a way as to ensure the formation of a sense of collective identity that reflects common experiences, values and norms of both followers and elites. This would develop a shared understanding of what and who the nation is. Where it is absent, however, the nation-building process is likely to be fragmented and interrupted by other influences and actors.

The various efforts at nation-building from the top down in South Sudan have illustrated the importance of follower acceptance in nation-building. This is seen in the rejection of the Arab/Islamic state vision and Garang's Sudanism vision (see Chapters 2 and 3). The growth of the church (De Waal 1998: 143; Rolandsen 2005: 75–6) and the rapid ethnicization of politics in South Sudan (Frahm 2015; Gerenge 2015) show that a key determinant of follower acceptance of identity narratives is the degree to which the proposed identity marker responds to followers' needs and daily experiences. Again, this returns the notion of mutuality. Where mutuality is not present, leaders are unlikely to articulate a vision of identity that reflects the shared experience of followers. The vision is then likely to be rejected by followers. However, the use of identity as a mobilization tool does reflect the power that leaders do hold to influence followers and therefore the identity construction process. Yet, this influence can often be destructive when formed from a superficial or manufactured mutuality.

## How does the relationship between the nation and the state build and sustain peace or conflict?

This book has also highlighted the constant tension found between the nation and the state in Sudan and South Sudan. In large part, the decades of war in Sudan and South Sudan represent an effort to resolve this tension and the contradictions between statehood and nationhood. One thing that has made this particularly challenging in the case of South Sudan is the general animosity felt towards the state, from early opposition to the state to the more recent tension between urban and rural in modern South Sudan (see Chapters 1 and 5). At the same time, conflict has often arisen as a result of exclusion from the state, a consequence of the failure to correlate the state and the nation. The north/south civil wars were driven in part by the exclusion of southerners from the political and economic centre in Khartoum (Thomas 2015), while the current civil war in South Sudan was sparked by a disagreement over access to state benefits (Awolich 2015: 4; Rolandsen 2015: 164–5). As these lines of exclusion and inclusion were often framed by identity markers (Deng 1995; Frahm 2015: 260; Gerenge 2015; SPLM 1994a: 14; Young 2012: 3), it represents a failure to incorporate the whole nation into the state, or to define the nation and state clearly. The post-secession experience, however, illustrates the complexities of aligning statehood and nationhood. Self-determination clearly entails more than the creation of a *de jure* state to represent a perceived nation. It requires a clear and collective understanding and imagination of the nation.

An important distinction between a nation and other forms of identity is its link to the state or some claim to political autonomy (Breuilly 1993: 2; Smith 1998: 122). This is why one of the definitions for nation-building involves ensuring 'the boundaries of the state and the nation coincide' (Mylonas 2012: xx). Doing this, however, involves more than redrawing state borders, as the South Sudanese case illustrates. It requires a dialogue and exchange of influence between state and society to ensure the state is structured and functions in such a way as to represent the will of the nation – the ultimate goal of self-determination (UNGA 1970). This book has shown that correlating the state and nation cannot be achieved where a leader/follower gap is present, which hinders an exchange of influence between leaders, who represent and control the state, and followers, who make up the nation. Despite various attempts at renegotiating the state structure through policy and constitutional adjustments, South Sudan continually failed at nation-building and state-building due to this leader/follower gap. In short, as the negotiation of the state shifted from one between leaders and followers to one amongst leaders, the ability to ensure congruency between state and nation decreased significantly. This contributed to conflict, as key sections of society were excluded from the state-building and nation-building process.

Another important aspect of the state in nation-building is the way in which the state is used for a nation-building purpose. Indeed, the state holds several key institutions that can play a part in nation-building, such as education, the civil service and the military (Hearn 2006: 82–3). However, the way in which these institutions are used is essential to understanding their ability to direct the nation-building trajectory of a society. The leadership process provides some insight into this with its understanding of power. In particular, the use of coercive power by the state to impose a nation-building narrative is likely to lead to a rejection of the state and, as seen in South Sudan, a violent division of said state. The state can also be used for reward power, as seen in the way leaders were often co-opted into the state to quell rebellion (see Chapter 6). This proved effective only in the short term, as compliance with and loyalty to the state became dependent on the availability of rewards, not an ideological or emotional connection to the state. Therefore, the state-centred aspect of nation-building should not be an exercise in power but rather one of influence exchange. In order for this to occur, the state must be influenced by followers as much as leaders, which requires a move away from inter-elite dialogue and negotiations.

To achieve this, mutuality is needed. Without mutuality, the state may be used for elite interests. We see this in South Sudan, where the military was used to 'buy peace' rather than ensure the security of the nation and its people (Ajak 2015: 3). The federalism debate throughout southern Sudan's history has also been used to ensure elite access to the state rather than state access to the people (see Chapter 6). The failure of state-building efforts has been a recurring challenge in global peacebuilding. This case study illustrates one of the reasons for this challenge. When mutuality is not present between leader and follower, well-intentioned and well-planned state-building efforts are likely to fail because those tasked with building the state seek to form one that serves their interests rather than those of the nation as a whole. In this way, the pathways of influence are critical in reconciling the tension between nation and state in the peacebuilding process. If followers are excluded from the state-building conversation or if external actors interrupt said conversation, then it is difficult to ensure a state that reflects the nation. As this is the key purpose of self-determination and nationalist conflicts, a failure of the state to reflect the nation may lead to further conflict.

## How does collective will and collective responsibility form to promote either peace or conflict?

In the Introduction, it was argued that forming a nation requires the coordination of a collective identity, political organization, territory, collective will and collective responsibility. It was also proposed that the last two of these are likely the most challenging. South Sudan appears to reflect this. While there were periods of unity and foundations for collective identity, and the state was eventually divided to reflect perceptions of identity, the consistent problems appear to have been those of collective will and collective responsibility. The contradictions between all five elements, as a result, proved irreconcilable. But it is in these last two elements, collective will and collective responsibility, that the pitfalls of leadership in nation-building become most evident.

It has been shown that collective will in South Sudan was most present during times of conflict and in response to northern oppression. However, evidence also suggests that this is superficial, as even during conflict, South Sudan struggled with disunity and fragmentation of its liberation movements (see Chapters 2 and 4). In addition, the rapid fragmentation of South Sudanese society during the interim periods after the signing of the Addis Ababa Agreement and the CPA and the post-secession period illustrate that this collective will was almost wholly dependent on the presence of 'the other' as a threat. Similarly, the significant human rights violations and intermittent inter-communal and inter-ethnic violence (see Chapters 4 and 6) demonstrate a low degree of collective loyalty and responsibility. In this way, Sudan and South Sudan's struggle to form a collective identity, reconcile state and nation and develop the means to build collective will and loyalty have resulted in the inability to forge a nation that sustains peace.

The situational approach to leadership serves as a measure of collective will. While most societies will have moments of collective action, this does not necessarily reflect collective will. Collective will, or the ability to reach a collective decision (Weilenmann 2010: 43), needs to outlast a situation in order to be demonstrative of a nation. For example, the ability to mobilize for secession in South Sudan was a moment of collective action driven by leaders who were able to respond to a specific situation. However, because of the limited mutuality driving this action, the ability for leaders to continue the formation of collective will did not live beyond the moment of secession. The same can be seen in the Mahdist revolution's loss of southern support post-revolution (Collins 1962: 23, 29–30) and the rapid loss of legitimacy by southern leaders after the Addis Ababa Agreement (Johnson 2013: 107–8, 404). Peaceful nation-building, therefore, requires more than individual leaders who respond to specific crises. It needs a leadership process that is founded on a functioning relationship between leaders and followers, which allows for the appropriate leaders to emerge at the right time to represent the collective desires and visions of followers.

Another important aspect of leadership is the role of power in producing collective will and ensuring collective responsibility. Collective will ensures that society is able to determine and take a collective action (Weilenmann 2010: 43). Collective responsibility ensures that members of the nation are loyal to the state and fellow members in times of crisis and that fellow members are seen to hold equal rights and responsibilities in the nation (Deutsch 2010: 11–12; Miller 2000: 27; Smith 1998: 196). Neither of these can be achieved through coercive or reward power. The persistent rebellion by the south to external rule and the state in general is evidence of the limits of coercive power.

Similarly, Kiir's 'Big Tent' approach was an effort to prevent rebellion by providing leaders with access to the state (Ajak 2015: 3; Awolich 2015: 9; Frahm 2015: 260). In other words, he sought to build collective will and loyalty through reward power. This failed for two reasons. First, he was unable to maintain the rewards indefinitely. Second, this strategy excluded the multitude of followers who did not benefit from their leaders' access to the state. Influence based on this type of transactional leadership is not conducive to nation-building, especially if it becomes the norm for collective action. Referent power, as seen in John Garang and the various leaders who emerged through ethnic identification, appears to be more effective at building collective will and loyalty. However, it suffers from the problems of sustainability when situations change, as discussed above. More importantly, it perpetuates a system of prototype leadership that encourages the emergence of leaders for ever smaller identity groups, and results in the further fragmentation of society. It is possible that a combination of expert, legitimate and referent power can be used to form collective will and collective loyalty, but there is little use of this power in South Sudan and therefore more research would need to be conducted in another context to determine this.

Finally, mutuality is critical in the formation of collective will and collective responsibility. The ability to form a collective will requires some collective understanding of the key challenges and needs of the nation and how to address them. The secession solution appeared a straightforward one, but it was founded on a collective understanding of the common enemy and not of the nation and its needs. This stems from a rebellion that was driven by leaders whose needs and interests were far removed from those of their followers. Collective will, therefore, is relatively easy in the face of a clear, external enemy, which allows for mobilization that creates the illusion of a nation. In the face of more complex challenges such as economic stagnation and low-intensity inter-communal conflict, it is more difficult, particularly when these challenges do not impact leaders and followers in the same way or to the same degree. This is because leaders are important in guiding collective action but rarely succeed when there is no mutuality present, which is further complicated when external actors interrupt the relationship between leader and follower, as occurred in South Sudan. Such a situation allows leaders to escape the demands of followers and for external actors to determine the direction of collective will. Therefore, a collectivity needs to be founded on a vision that addresses the reality and needs of everyone within it.

# Conclusion

This book set out to better understand the tumultuous nation-building journey in South Sudan. It sought to illuminate the fault lines in Sudanese and South Sudanese societies and their complexities. It examined the role of leadership in a conflict that is often written off as elite-driven. And it identified patterns throughout South Sudan's history of conflict that illustrate the recurring, systemic and structured nature of these processes. The gap between leaders and followers in South Sudan may appear obvious and a natural consequence of politics in any country. Yet, the nature of this gap, driven by a lack of mutuality and a flawed exchange of influence and power, has resulted in the reproduction of a violent, fragmenting nation-building process.

It begins at the national level in colonial Sudan, where elites influenced and were influenced by external powers, leaving the population to seek leadership in their immediate communities and reject the encroachment of the state and its representation of conquest. It continues in independent Sudan, where elite competition for access to the new state prompted the formation of southern Sudan as a social and political entity, by manufacturing a transient and transactional sense of mutuality between southerners and southern leaders. And it ends almost where it began, with elites in a new state, influenced by external powers and each other, forging a new state with little engagement with or consideration for the nation within that state, driving your everyday South Sudanese to seek security, structure and services from their own narrow but present communities and leaders. As this pattern continues to repeat itself in ever smaller geographical units, the locus of leadership will continue to diversify, the 'nation' will continue to fracture, and communities of collective will and responsibility will grow more numerous and divergent.

# Bibliography

Abbas, Philip. 1973. 'Growth of Black Political Consciousness in Northern Sudan', *Africa Today,* (20)3, pp. 29–43.

The Addis Ababa Agreement on the Problem of South Sudan. 1972. Available online: https://peacemaker.un.org/sites/peacemaker.un.org/files/SD_720312_Addis%20 Ababa%20Agreement%20on%20the%20Problem%20of%20South%20Sudan.pdf. Access: 29 March 2021.

African Union Commission of Inquiry on South Sudan (AUCISS). 2014. *Final Report of the African Union Commission of Inquiry on South Sudan* (Addis Ababa, Ethiopia, 15 October). Available Online: http://www.peaceau.org/uploads/auciss. final.report.pdf. Access: 24 June 2018.

Ajak, Peter Biar. 2015. 'State Formation, Humanitarianism, and Institutional Capabilities in South Sudan', *Issue Brief,* International Peace Institute. Available Online: State Formation, Humanitarianism, and Institutional Capabilities in South Sudan. Accessed: 24 June 2018.

Akol, Lam. 2003. *SPLM/SPLA: The Nasir Declaration.* New York, London, Shanghai: iUniverse.inc.

Akol, Zacharia D. 2013. 'A Nation in Transition: South Sudan's Constitutional Review Process', Policy Brief, SUDD Institute. Available Online: https://www.suddinstitute. org/assets/Publications/572b7eb594fe6_ANationInTransitionSouthSudans Constitutional_Full.pdf. Access: 24 June 2018.

Akol, Zacharia D. 2014. 'Inclusivity: A Challenge to the IGAD-Led South Sudanese Peace Process', *Policy Brief, SUDD Institute.* Available Online: https://www. suddinstitute.org/publications/show/inclusivity-a-challenge-to-the-igad-led- south-sudanese-peace-process. Access: 24 June 2018.

Anderson, Benedict. 2006. *Imagined Communities: Reflections on the Origin and Spread of Nationalism, Revised Edition.* London & New York: Verso.

Arensen, Michael. 2016. *If We Leave We Are Killed: Lessons Learned from South Sudan Protection of Civilian Sites 2013–2016.* International Organization for Migration. Available Online: https://publications.iom.int/system/files/pdf/if_we_leave_0.pdf. Access: 24 June 2018.

Arnold, Matthew & Matthew LeRiche. 2013. *South Sudan: From Revolution to Independence.* Oxford, New York: Oxford University Press. E-book edition.

Available online: https://play.google.com/books/reader?id=eQEqBgAAQBAJ& printsec=frontcover&pg=GBS.PA50. Access: 30 June 2018.

Associated Press, 2015. 'South Sudan: Creation of New States Draws Opposition Protests', *The New York Times,* Available online: http://www.nytimes. com/2015/12/26/world/africa/south-sudan-creation-of-new-states-draws-opposition-protests.html?_r=0. Access: 17 February 2016.

Awolich, Abraham A. 2015. 'South Sudan's National Identity Challenge: The Interplay between Fragmented Social Structure and Elite's Negative Role', *Policy Brief, SUDD Institute,* March 1. Available Online: https://suddinstitute.org/publications/show/ south-sudan-s-national-identity-challenge-the-interplay-between-fragmented-social-structure-and-elit/. Access: 24 June 2018.

Ayers, Alison J. 2010. 'Sudan's uncivil war: the global–historical constitution of political violence', *Review of African Political Economy,* 37(124), pp. 153–71.

Bass, Bernard M. with Ruth Bass. 2008. *The Bass Handbook of Leadership: Theory, Research and Managerial Applications.* New York: Free Press. Kindle Edition. Available online: https://www.amazon.co.uk/gp/product/B003YCQ0IM/ref=oh_ aui_d_detailpage_o02_?ie=UTF8&psc=1. Access: 2 October 2015.

*BBC News.* 2013. 'South Sudan President Salva Kiir in profile', 23 December. Available online: http://www.bbc.com/news/world-africa-12107760. Access: 31 January 2016.

Bereketeab, Redie. 2014. 'Redefining National Identity and Nation-building in Post-secession Sudans: Civic and Ethnic Models', *Studies in Ethnicity and Nationalism,* 14(2), pp. 302–18.

Beshir, Mohamed Omer. 1968. *The Southern Sudan: Background to Conflict.* London: C. Hurst & Co.

Breuilly, John. 1993. *Nationalism and the State,* Manchester: Manchester University Press.

Brubaker, Rogers & David D. Laitin. 1998. 'Ethnic and Nationalist Violence', *Annual Review of Sociology,* 24, pp. 423–52.

Burns, James McGregor. 2012. *Leadership.* New York: Harper & Row. Kindle e-book. Available online: https://www.amazon.co.uk/gp/product/B007MFECFU/ref=oh_ aui_d_detailpage_o06_?ie=UTF8&psc=1. Access: 31 July 2015.

Collins, Robert O. 1962. *The Southern Sudan, 1883–1898: A Struggle for Control.* New Haven & London: Yale University Press.

Colson, Aurélien J. 2000. 'The Logic of Peace and the Logic of Justice', *International Relations,* 15(1), pp. 51–62.

Comprehensive Peace Agreement (CPA). 2005. *The Comprehensive Peace Agreement Between The Government of The Republic of The Sudan and The Sudan People's*

*Liberation Movement/Sudan People's Liberation Army.* Available online: https://
peaceaccords.nd.edu/sites/default/files/accords/SudanCPA.pdf. Access: 24 June
2018.

Copnall, James. 2014. *A Poisonous Thorn in Our Hearts: Sudan and South Sudan's
Bitter and Incomplete Divorce,* London: C. Hurst & Co., Kindle e-book edition.
Available online: https://www.amazon.co.uk/gp/product/B00N2WMCCW/
ref=oh_aui_d_detailpage_o01_?ie=UTF8&psc=1. Access: 2 October 2015.

Cormack, Zoe. 2016. 'Borders are galaxies: Interpreting contestations over local
administrative boundaries in South Sudan', *Africa: The Journal of the International
African Institute,* 86(3), pp. 504–27.

David, Roman. 2017. 'What We Know About Transitional Justice: Survey and
Experimental Evidence', *Advances in Political Psychology,* 38(1), pp. 151–77.

deGarang, E. M. 1971. 'The Return of Nimeri — Implications and South-Sudan
Reactions', Southern Sudan Liberation Movement Official Statement No. 1. *Grass
Curtain.* 4 August. Retrieved from Sudan Open Archive: https://sudanarchive.net/
cgi-bin/pagessoa?e=01off---v----100125--1-0-SectionLevel-0-0-1-1&a=d&cl=
CL1.7.1.1&d=Dpdrgd22_3. Access: 28 November 2016.

Dekmejian, Richard H. & Margaret J. Wyszomirski. 1972. 'Charismatic Leadership in
Islam: the Mahdi of the Sudan', *Comparative Studies in Society and History,* 14(20),
pp. 193–214.

Deng, Daniel Sorur Pharim. 1974. *An Early Manuscript on the Dinka Written by
Member of This Tribe,* ed. and trans. by Fr. E.V. Toniolo. Khartoum: Tamaddon
Printing Press. Retrieved from Sudan Open Archive: https://sudanarchive.net/
cgi-bin/pagessoa?e=01off---v----100125--1-0-SectionLevel-0-0-1-1&a=d&cl=CL1
.5.1.1&d=Djbrg54_1. Access: 28 November 2016.

Deng, Francis. 1995. *War of Visions: Conflict of Identities in the Sudan.* Washington,
DC: The Brookings Institution. E-book edition. Available online: https://play.
google.com/books/reader?id=_g2TSlsi_G4C&pg=GBS.PA17.w.1.2.0. Access:
30 June 2018.

Deng, Francis M. 2006. 'Sudan: A Nation in Turbulent Search of Itself', *The Annals of
the American Academy of Political and Social Science,* 603, pp. 155–62.

Deng, Francis. 2010. *Sudan at the Brink.* New York: Fordham University Press. E-book
edition. Available online: http://muse.jhu.edu/books/9780823249282/. Access: 1
October 2015.

Deng, David K.; Belays Lopez, Matthew Pritchard & Lauren C. Ng, 2015. *Search for a
New Beginning: Perceptions of Truth, Justice, Reconciliation and Healing in South
Sudan,* UNDP, (June 2015). Available online: http://www.ss.undp.org/content/
dam/southsudan/library/Rule%20of%20Law/Perception%20Survey%20

Report%20Transitional%20Justice%20Reconciliation%20and%20Healing%20-. pdf. Access: 24 June 2018.

Deng, J. B. B. 2018. 'Traditional Justice Methods and Their Possible Impact on Transitional Justice Models in South Sudan', *Max Planck Yearbook of United Nations Law Online*, 21(1), pp. 331–52.

Deng, Francis M. & M. W. Daly. 1989. '*Bonds of Silk*': *The Human Factor in the British Administration of the Sudan.* East Lansing, Michigan: Michigan State University Press.

Deutsch, Karl W. 2010. 'Nation-Building and National Development: Some Issues for Political Research', in *Nation Building in Comparative Contexts,* Karl W. Deutsch & William J. Fotz (eds). New Brunswick, New Jersey: Transaction Publishers.

De Vries, Lotje & Mareike Schomerus. 2017. 'South Sudan's Civil War Will Not End with a Peace Deal', *Peace Review*, 29(3), pp. 333–340.

De Waal, Alex. 1998. 'Exploiting Slavery: Human Rights and Political Agendas in Sudan', *New Left Review,* I/227, 135–46.

De Waal, Alex. 2015. 'The Price of South Sudan's Independence', *Current History,* 114(772), pp. 194–6.

Eley, Geoff & Ronald Grigor Suny. 1996. *Becoming National: A Reader.* New York & Oxford: Oxford University Press.

Fleischner, Justine. 2015. *Deadly Enterprise: Dismantling South Sudan's War Economy and Countering Potential Spoilers,* The Enough Project: The Political Economy of African Wars, 3, December. Available online: https://enoughproject.org/reports/ deadly-enterprise-dismantling-south-sudans-war-economy-and-countering-potential-spoilers. Access: 24 June 2018.

Foltyn, Simona. 2015. 'Conflict persists despite South Sudan peace deal', *Al Jazeera,* 21 November. Available online: http://www.aljazeera.com/news/2015/11/conflict-persists-south-sudan-peace-deal-151120033514547.html. Access: 8 February 2016.

Frahm, Ole. 2012. 'Defining a Nation: National Identity in South Sudanese Media Discourse', *Africa Spectrum,* 47(1), pp. 21–49.

Frahm, Ole. 2015. Making borders and identities in South Sudan, *Journal of Contemporary African Studies*, 33(2), pp. 251–67.

French, John R. P. & Bertram Raven. 2011. 'The Bases of Social Power', in *Leaders and the Leadership Process: Readings, Self-Assessments and Applications,* Pierce, Jon L. & John W. Newstrom (eds). New York: McGraw Hill.

Galtung, Johan. 1969. 'Violence, Peace and Peace Research', *Journal of Peace Research,* 6(3), pp. 167–191.

Garang, John. Ed. and intro. by Mansour Khalid. 1992. *The Call for Democracy in Sudan.* London & New York: Kegan Paul International.

Gellner, Ernest. 1983. *Nations and Nationalism*, Oxford: Basil Blackwell.

Gerenge, Robert. 2015. 'South Sudan's December 2013 conflict: Bolting state-building fault lines with social capital', *African Journal on Conflict Resolution*, 15(3), pp. 85–109.

Gilley, Bruce. 2004. 'Against the concept of ethnic conflict', *Third World Quarterly*, 25(6), pp. 1155–66.

Glickman, Harvey. 2000. Islamism in Sudan's Civil War. *Orbis*, Spring 200, 267–81.

Gosnell, Harold F. 1958. The 1958 Elections in the Sudan. *Middle East Journal*, 12(4), pp. 409–17.

Graen, George B. & Mary Uhl-Bien. 1995. 'Relationship-based approach to leadership: Development of Leader-Member Exchange (LMX) Theory of leadership over 25 years: Applying a multi-level multi-domain perspective', *Leadership Quarterly*, 6(2), pp. 219–47.

Gray, Richard. 1963. 'Introduction', in *The Problem of the Southern Sudan*, Joseph Oduho & William Deng. London, Karachi, Nairobi: Oxford University Press.

Gray, Richard. 1971. 'Some aspects of Islam in the Southern Sudan during the Turkiya', Symposium on Islamic Northern Africa, 14 September. London: African Studies Association of the United Kingdom.

Guarak, Mawut Achiecque Mach. 2011. *Integration and Fragmentation of the Sudan: An African Renaissance*. Bloomington, IN: AuthorHouse.

Guibernau, Montserrat. 2007. *The Identity of Nations*. Cambridge & Malden, MA: Polity Press.

Gurtong, 2011. 'President Kiir's Independence Speech in Full: H.E Genral Slava Kiir Mayadit,President of the Republic of South Sudan's Maiden speech. On the occasion of the proclamation of Independence in JUBA, 9th July 2011', 14 July. Available online: http://www.gurtong.net/ECM/Editorial/tabid/124/ctl/ ArticleView/mid/519/articleId/5440/categoryId/121/President-Kiirs-Independence-Speech-In-Full.aspx. Access: 15 May 2017.

Hearn, Jonathan. 2006. *Rethinking Nationalism: A Critical Introduction*. Houndmills, Basingstoke; New York: Palgrave Macmillan.

Hogg, Michael A. 2001. A Social Identity Theory of Leadership. *Personality and Social Psychology Review*, 5(3), pp. 184–200.

Holt, P. M. & M. W. Daly. 2000. *A history of the Sudan: From the coming of Islam to the present day*. Fifth edition. Essex, England: Pearson Education Limited.

Hollander, Edwin P. & James W. Julian. 2011. 'Contemporary Trends in the Analysis of Leadership Processes', in *Leaders and the Leadership Process: Readings, Self-Assessments and Applications*, Jon L. Pierce & John W. Newstrom (eds). New York: McGraw Hill.

Hopf, Ted. 1998. 'The Promise of Constructivism in International Relations Theory', *International Security,* 23(1), pp. 171–200.

Horowitz, Donald L. 2001. *Ethnic Groups in Conflict.* Berkeley, CA: University of California Press. Kindle e-book edition. Available online: https://www.amazon.co. uk/gp/product/B004FPHBVW/ref=oh_aui_d_detailpage_o01_?ie=UTF8&psc=1. Access: 12 August 2013.

Horowitz, Donald L. 2008. 'Conciliatory Institutions and Constitutional Processes in Post-Conflict States', *William and Mary Law Review,* 49(4), pp. 1213–48.

Howell, John. 1973. 'Politics in the Southern Sudan', *African Affairs,* 72(287), pp. 163–78.

Hroch, Miroslav. 1996. 'From National Movement to the Fully-Formed Nation: The Nation-Building Process in Europe', in *Becoming National: A Reader,* Geoff Eley & Ronald Grigor Suny. New York & Oxford: Oxford University Press.

Human Rights Council. 2016. *Assessment Mission by the Office of the United Nations High Commissioner for Human Rights to improve human rights, accountability, reconciliation and capacity in South Sudan* (10 March 2016). Report of the United Nations High Commissioner for Human Rights, Advance unedited version, A/ HRC/31/49. Available online: https://reliefweb.int/report/south-sudan/report-high-commissioner-human-rights-assessment-mission-office-united-nations. Access: 24 June 2018.

Hutchinson, John & Smith, Anthony D. 1994. *Nationalism.* Oxford: Oxford University Press.

Hutchinson, Sharon. 2001. 'A Curse from God? Religious and political dimensions of the post-1991 rise of ethnic violence in South Sudan', *The Journal of Modern African Studies,* 39(2), pp. 307–31.

Hutchinson, Sharon & Naomi Pendle. 2015. 'Violence, legitimacy, and prophecy: Nuer struggles with uncertainty in South Sudan', *American Ethnologist,* 42(3), pp. 415–30.

International Crisis Group (ICG). 2015a. 'Sudan and South Sudan's Merging Conflicts', *Africa Report No. 223.* Available online: https://www.crisisgroup.org/ africa/horn-africa/south-sudan/sudan-and-south-sudan-s-merging-conflicts. Access: 24 June 2018.

International Crisis Group (ICG). 2015b. 'South Sudan: Keeping Faith with the IGAD Peace Process', *Africa Report No. 228.* Available online: South Sudan: Keeping Faith with the IGAD Peace Process. Access: 24 June 2018.

Idris, Amir. 2005. *Conflict and Politics of Identity in Sudan.* New York, Hampshire: Palgrave Macmillan.

Idris, Amir. 2013. *Identity, Citizenship, and Violence in Two Sudans: Reimagining a Common Future.* New York: Palgrave Macmillan.

Interview A. 2017. Interview with S. Theron on 23 June. Juba, South Sudan.

Interview B. 2017. Interview with S. Theron on 22 June. Juba, South Sudan.

Interview C. 2017. Interview with S. Theron on 22 June. Juba, South Sudan.

Interview D. 2017. Interview with S. Theron on 21 June. Juba, South Sudan.

Interview E. 2017. Interview with S. Theron on 22 June. Juba, South Sudan.

Interview F. 2017. Interview with S. Theron on 26 June. Nairobi, Kenya.

Interview G. 2017. Interview with S. Theron on 24 June. Juba, South Sudan.

Institute for Security Studies (ISS). 2015. 'Deal or no Deal in South Sudan?', *News,* 26 August. Available online: https://www.issafrica.org/pscreport/addis-insights/ deal-or-no-deal-in-south-sudan. Access: 28 December 2015.

Iyob, Ruth & Gilbert M. Khadiagala. 2006. *Sudan: The Elusive Quest for Peace.* Boulder, London: Lynne Rienner Publishers.

Johnson, Douglas. 2007. 'Why Abyei Matters: The Breaking Point of Sudan's Comprehensive Peace Agreement?', *African Affairs,* 107(426), pp. 1–19.

Johnson, Douglas H. 2011a. *The Root Causes of Sudan's Civil Wars: Peace or Truce,* Revised Edition. Suffolk, UK & Rochester, NY: James Currey.

Johnson, Douglas H. 2013. *The Root Causes of Sudan's Civil Wars: Peace or Truce,* Revised Edition. Suffolk, UK & Rochester, NY: James Currey. E-book version. Available online: http://kcl.eblib.com/patron/FullRecord.aspx?p=1163179. Access: 29 June 2018.

Johnson, Hilde. 2011b. *Waging Peace in Sudan: The Inside Story of the Negotiations That Ended Africa's Longest Civil War.* Brighton, Portland, Toronto: Sussex Academic Press.

Johnson, Hilde. 2016. *South Sudan: The Untold Story from Independence to Civil War.* London & New York: IB Tauris. Kindle e-Book. Available online: https://www. amazon.co.uk/gp/product/B01I45QOWA/ref=oh_aui_d_detailpage_o07_?ie= UTF8&psc=1. Access: 12 May 2017.

Jok, Madut Jok & Sharon Elaine Hutchinson. 1999. 'Sudan's Prolonged Second Civil War and the Militarisation of Nuer and Dinka Ethnic Identities', *African Studies Review,* 42(2), pp. 125–45.

Justin, Peter Hakim & Lotje De Vries 2019. Governing Unclear Lines: Local Boundaries as a (Re)source of Conflict in South Sudan. In *The Struggle for South Sudan: Challenges of Security and State Formation,* Luka Biong Deng Kuol & Sarah Logan (eds). London & New York: IB Tauris. Kindle Edition. Available online: https://www.amazon.co.uk/Struggle-South-Sudan-Challenges-International/ dp/1788315189/ref=sr_1_1?dchild=1&keywords=struggle+for+south+sudan&qid =1616871050&sr=8-1. Access: 1 February 2021.

Kaufmann, Chaim. 1996. 'Possible and Impossible Solutions to Ethnic Civil Wars', *International Security,* 20(4), pp. 136–75.

Khalid, Mansour. 2003. *War and Peace in Sudan: A Tale of Two Countries.* London & New York, Bahrain: Kegan Paul.

Kindersley, Nicki & Oystein H. Rolandsen. 2017. Civil War on a Shoestring: Rebellion in South Sudan's Equatoria Region, *Civil Wars,* 19(3), pp. 308–24.

Kisiangani, Emmanuel. 2015. 'Reviewing options for peace in South Sudan', *East Africa Report,* Institute for Security Studies, 1 (March). Available online: https://issafrica.s3.amazonaws.com/site/uploads/E_AfricaReport2.pdf. Access: 24 June 2018.

Laitin, David D. 2007. *Nations, States, and Violence.* Oxford: Oxford University Press.

Leonardi, Cherry. 2007. '"Liberation" or capture: Youth in between "Hakuma" and "Home" during civil war and its aftermath in Southern Sudan', *African Affairs,* 106(424), pp. 391–412.

Leonardi, Cherry. 2013. *Dealing with Government in South Sudan: Histories of Chiefship, Community and State.* Woodbridge, Suffolk & Rochester, NY: James Currey.

*Machakos Protocol.* 2002. Secretariat on Peace in the Sudan. 20 July. Available online: https://peacemaker.un.org/sites/peacemaker.un.org/files/SD_020710_MachakosProtocol.pdf. Access: 25 March 2017.

Mahmud, Ushari Ahmed & Suleyman Ali Baldo. 1987. *The Dhein Massacre: Slavery in the Sudan.* London: Sudan Relief and Rehabilitation Association. Retrieved from Sudan Open Archive: https://sudanarchive.net/cgi-bin/pagessoa?e=01off---vand-TX-dhein+massacre--100125-%5bdhein+%5d%3aTX+%5bmassacre%5d%3aTX+-21-0-SectionLevel-0-0-1-1&a=d&cl=&d=Dslpd67.1.1. Access: 28 November 2016.

Mani, Rama. 2002. *Beyond Retribution: Seeking Justice in the Shadows of War.* Cambridge & Malden, Mass: Polity Press & Blackwell.

Mann, Michael. 1995. *A Political Theory of Nationalism and Its Excesses.* In *Notions of Nationalism,* Sukumar Periwal (ed.). Budapest, London, New York: Central European University Press.

Mann, Michael. 2001. 'Explaining Murderous Ethnic Cleansing: the Macro-level', in *Understanding Nationalism,* Montserrat Guibernau & John Hutchinson (eds). Cambridge: Polity Press.

Martin, Randolph. 2002. 'Sudan's Perfect War', *Foreign affairs,* 81(2), pp. 111–27.

Maxwell, Daniel; Martina Santschi, Rachel Gordon, Phillip Dau & Leben Moro. 2014. *Livelihoods, access to services and perceptions of governance in South Sudan: An analysis of Uror and Nyirol counties, South Sudan,* London: Secure Livelihoods Research Consortium, Overseas Development Institute. Available online: https://assets.publishing.service.gov.uk/media/57a089b9ed915d3cfd0003ca/

Livelihoods__access_to_services_and_perceptions_of_governance_in_South_
Sudan.pdf. Access: 28 January 2016.

Mayen, Gordon Muortat. 1982. *The Addis Ababa Agreement on South Sudan is Being Scrapped.* Retrieved from Sudan Open Archive: https://sudanarchive.net/cgi-bin/pagessoa?e=01off---v----100125--1-0-SectionLevel-0-0-1-1&a=d&cl=CL1.4.1.1&d=Dnbd6. Access: 28 November 2016.

Mazrui, Ali A. & Michael Tidy. 1984. *Nationalism and New States in Africa.* London, Ibadan, Nairobi: Heinemann Educational Books.

Medani, Khalid Mustafa. 2011. 'Strife and Secession in Sudan', *Journal of Democracy,* 22(3), pp. 135–49.

Miller, David. 2000. *Citizenship and National Identity.* Malden, MA: Polity Press, p. 127.

Moro, Leben Nelson. 2015. 'CSOs/CBOs and faith-based organizations-led peace reconciliation efforts' *Policy Brief,* December 12. The Sudd Institute. Available online: https://www.suddinstitute.org/publications/show/csos-cbos-and-faith-based-organizations-led-peace-and-reconciliation-efforts. Access: 18 December 2015.

Murphy, Albert J. 1941. 'A Study of the Leadership Process', *American Sociological Review,* 6(5), pp. 674–87.

Mylonas, Harris. 2012. *The Politics of Nation-Building: Making Co-Nationals, Refugees, and Minorities.* New York: Cambridge University Press, pp. xx

Nasong'o, Shadrack Wanjala & Godwin Rapando Murunga. 2005. 'Lack of Consensus on Constitutive Fundamentals: Roots of the Sudanese Civil War and Prospects for Settlement', *African and Asian Studies,* 4(1–2), p. 59.

Natsios, Andrew S. 2012. *Sudan, South Sudan, and Darfur: What Everyone Needs to Know.* Oxford, New York: Oxford University Press. E-book edition. Available online: http://kcl.eblib.com/patron/FullRecord.aspx?p=886569. Access: 29 June 2018.

Norman, Wayne. 2006. 'Thinking through Nationalism', *Negotiating Nationalism: Nation-Building, Federalism, and Secession in the Multinational State,* Oxford Scholarship Online. E-book edition. Available online: http://dx.doi.org/10.1093/0198293356.001.0001. Access: 29 June 2018.

Northouse, Peter G. 2016. *Leadership: Theory & Practice,* Seventh Edition. London: SAGE Publications.

Novicki, Margaret A. 1989. 'Interview: John Garang: A New Sudan', *Africa Report,* July–August, 43–7. Retrieved from Sudan Open Archive: https://sudanarchive.net/cgi-bin/pagessoa?e=01off---v----100125--1-0-SectionLevel-0-0-1-1&a=d&cl=CL1.7.1.1&d=Djbrg27_2. Access: 28 November 2016.

Nyaba, P.A. 2000. *The Politics of Liberation in South Sudan: An Insider's View.* Kampala: Fountain Publishers.

*The Observer.* 1965. 'South Sudan massacres reported', 17 October 1965. Retrieved from Sudan Open Archive: https://sudanarchive.net/cgi-bin/pagessoa?e=01off---v----100125--1-0-SectionLevel-0-0-1-1&a=d&cl=CL1.4.1.1&d=DwmrgdN10_3. Access: 28 November 2016.

Oc, Burak & Michael R. Bashshur. 2013. 'Followership, leadership and social influence', *The Leadership Quarterly,* 24, pp. 919–34.

OCHA. 2016. 'South Sudan: Crisis Overview.' Available Online: http://www.unocha. org/south-sudan. Access: 15 May 2017.

Oduho, Joseph & William Deng. 1963. *The Problem of the Southern Sudan.* London, Karachi, Nairobi: Oxford University Press.

Olonisakin, Funmi; Alagaw Ababu Kifle & Alfred Muteru. 2021. Shifting ideas of sustainable peace towards conversation in state-building, *Conflict, Security & Development.* DOI: 10.1080/14678802.2020.1862495.

Panozzo, Irene. 2011. 'Sudan's Separation: An Uneven Path Ahead for Two Unstable Countries', *The International Spectator: Italian Journal of International Affairs,* 46(2), pp. 23–8.

Patinkin, Jason. 2014. 'Why a pro-government militia attacked a UN compound in South Sudan', *The Christian Science Monitor,* 18 April, Available online: http://www. csmonitor.com/World/2014/0418/Why-a-pro-government-militia-attacked-UN-compound-in-South-Sudan. Access: 15 February 2016.

Pendle, Naomi. 2014. 'Interrupting the balance: reconsidering the complexities of conflict in South Sudan', *Disasters,* 38(2), pp. 227–48.

Pendle, Naomi. 2015. '"They Are Now Community Police': Negotiating the Boundaries and Nature of theGovernment in South Sudan through the Identity of Militarised Cattle-keepers', *International Journal on Minority and Group Rights,* 22(3), pp. 410–34

Pendle, Naomi. 2018. 'Learning from Customary Law: Forgin Ethnic and National Identities in South Sudan', in *The Struggle for South Sudan: Challenges of Security and State Formation,* Luka Biong Deng Kuol & Sarah Logan (eds). London & New York: IB Tauris. Kindle Edition. Available online: https://www.amazon.co.uk/ Struggle-South-Sudan-Challenges-International/dp/1788315189/ref=sr_1_1?dchil d=1&keywords=struggle+for+south+sudan&qid=1616871050&sr=8-1. Access: 1 February 2021.

Pendle, Naomi. 2019. Learning from Customary Law: Forging Ethnic and National Identities in South Sudan. In *The Struggle for South Sudan: Challenges of Security and State Formation,* Luka Biong Deng Kuol & Sarah Logan (eds). London & New York: IB Tauris. Kindle Edition. Available online: https://www.amazon.co.uk/ Struggle-South-Sudan-Challenges-International/dp/1788315189/ref=sr_1_1?dchil d=1&keywords=struggle+for+south+sudan&qid=1616871050&sr=8-1. Access: 1 February 2021.

Pierce, Jon L. & John W. Newstrom 2011. *Leaders and the Leadership Process: Readings, Self-Assessments and Applications.* New York: McGraw Hill.

Pinaud, Clémence. 2016. 'Military Kinship, Inc.: patronage, inter-ethnic marriages and social classes in South Sudan', *Review of African Political Economy*, 43(148), pp. 243–59.

Pinaud, Clémence. 2021. *War and Genocide in South Sudan.* Ithaca & London: Cornell University Press. Kindle E-book version: https://www.amazon.co.uk/Genocide-South-Sudan-Cl%C3%A9mence-Pinaud-ebook/dp/B087BD8BY4/ref=sr_1_2?dchil d=1&keywords=pinaud+clemence&qid=1631534050&sr=8-2. Access: 1 February 2021.

Poggo, Scopas S. 2009. *The First Sudanese Civil War: Africans, Arabs, and Israelis in the Southern Sudan, 1955–1972.* New York: Palgrave Macmillan.

Reeve, Richard. 2012. *Peace and Conflict Assessment of South Sudan 2012,* International Alert. Available online: https://www.international-alert.org/sites/default/files/ SouthSudan_PeaceConflictAssessment_EN_2012.pdf. Access: 20 January 2016.

Reilly, Benjamin. 2012. 'Centripetalism: cooperation, accommodation and integration', in *Conflict Management in Divided Societies: Theories and Practice,* Stefan Wolff & Christalla Yakinthou (eds). London & New York: Routledge.

Renan, Ernest. 1994. 'Qu'est-ce qu'une nation?', in *Nationalism,* John Hutchinson & Anthony D. Smith (eds). Oxford & New York: Oxford University Press.

Republic of South Sudan. 2012. 'The Presidential Decree No. 03/2012 for the Appointment of full-time and part time members of the National Constitutional Reeview Commission, (NCRC), 2012 A.D.' Available online: http://www. sudantribune.com/IMG/pdf/Constitution_Commission.pdf. Access: 9 May 2017.

Reuters. 2016. 'UN official says at least 50,000 dead in South Sudan war', 2 March. Available online: http://www.reuters.com/article/us-southsudan-unrest-un-idUSKCN0W503Q. Access: 15 May 2017.

Ringmar, E. 2016. 'The Making of the Modern World', in *International Relations,* S. McGlinchey (ed.). Bristol: E-IR Foundations.

Rittel, Horst W. J. & Melvin M. Webber. 1973. 'Dilemmas in a general theory of planning', *Policy Sciences,* 4(2), pp. 155–69.

Rolandsen, Øystein H. 2005. *Guerrilla Government: Political Changes in the Southern Sudan during the 1990s.* Sweden: The Nordic Africa Institute.

Rolandsen, Øystein H. 2011. 'A quick fix? A retrospective analysis of the Sudan Comprehensive Peace Agreement', *Review of African Political Economy*, 38(130), pp. 551–64.

Rolandsen, Øystein. 2015. 'Another civil war in South Sudan: the failure of Guerrilla Government?', *Journal of East African Studies*, 9(1), pp. 163–74.

Ruay, Deng D. Akol. 1994. *The Politics of Two Sudans: The South and the North 1821–1969.* Uppsala: Nordiska Afrikainstitutet (The Scandinavian Institute of African Studies).

Rubin, Barry M. 2010. *Guide to Islamist Movements.* Armonk, New York: ME Sharpe.

The Sentry. 2016. *War Crimes Shouldn't Pay: Stopping the looting and destruction in South Sudan.* September. Available online: https://thesentry.org/wp-content/uploads/2016/08/Sentry_WCSP_Final.pdf. Access: 31 December 2016

Sudan African National Union (SANU). No Date. 'Southern Sudan Nationalist Movement and Call for African Unity: An Appeal to African Leaders.' Retrieved from Sudan Open Archive: https://sudanarchive.net/cgi-bin/pagessoa?e=01off---v----100125--1-0-SectionLevel-0-0-1-1&a=d&cl=CL1.7.1.1&d=DwmrgdN13_20. Access: 28 November 2016.

Sawant, Ankush. 1998. 'Ethnic Conflict in Sudan in Historical Perspective', *International Studies*, 35(343), pp. 343–63.

Schultz, Ulrike. 2014. '"There it will be better . . ." Southern Sudanese in Khartoum imagining a new "home" away from "home"', *Identities: Global Studies in Culture and Power,* 21(3), pp. 305–19.

Seri-Hersch, Iris. 2017. Education in Colonial Sudan, 1900–1957. Spear Thomas. Oxford Research Encyclopaedia of African History, Oxford, Available online: https://halshs.archives-ouvertes.fr/halshs-01514910. Access: 10 March 2021.

Sharkey, Heather J. 2008. 'Arab Identity and Ideology in Sudan: the Politics of Language, Ethnicity and Race', *African Affairs*, 107(426), pp. 21–43.

Sidahmed, Abdel Salam & Alsir Sidahmed. 2005. *Sudan.* London & New York: RoutledgeCurzon.

Sikainga, Ahmad Alawad. 2000. 'Military Slavery and the Emergence of a Southern Sudanese Diaspora in the Northern Sudan, 1884–1954', in *White Nile, Black Blood: War, Leadership, and Ethnicity from Khartoum to Kampala,* Jay Spaulding & Stephanie Beswick (eds). Lawrenceville, NJ & Asmara, Eritrea: Red Sea Printing Press, Inc.

Smirich, Linda & Gareth Morgan. 2011. 'Leadership: The Management of Meaning', in *Leaders and the Leadership Process: Readings, Self-Assessments and Applications,* Jon L. Pierce & John W. Newstrom (eds). New York: McGraw Hill.

Smith, Anthony D. 1998. *Nationalism and Modernism*, London: Routledge.

Smith, Anthony D. 1999. *Myths and Memories of the Nation.* Oxford, New York: Oxford University Press.

*South Sudan News Agency* (SSNA). 2016. 'South Sudan's Machar says Kiir's 28 states expansion plan is a violation of peace deal', 25 May. Available online: http://www. southsudannewsagency.com/index.php/2016/05/25/south-sudans-machar-says-kiirs-28-states-expansion-plan-violates-peace-deal/. Access: 15 October 2017.

South Sudan Resistance Movement. No Date. *The Anya-Nya Struggle: Background and Objectives.* Headquarters, South Sudan. Retrieved from Sudan Open Archive: https://sudanarchive.net/cgi-bin/pagessoa?e=01off---100125--1-0-SectionLevel-0-0-1-1&a=d&cl=CL1.4.1.1&d=Dpdrgd22_6. Access: 28 November 2016.

Sudan People's Liberation Movement (SPLM). 1994a. *'This Convention is Sovereign': Opening and Closing Speeches by Dr. John Garang de Mabior To the First SPLM/SPLA National Convention. 2 April.* SPLM Secretariat of Information Centre. Retrieved from Sudan Open Archive: https://sudanarchive.net/cgi-bin/pagessoa?e=01off---v----100125--1-0-SectionLevel-0-0-1-1&a=d&cl=CL1.7.1.1&d=Dn1d222. Access: 28 November 2016.

Sudan People's Liberation Movement (SPLM). 1994b. *A Major Watershed: SPLM/SPLA First National Convention: Resolutions, Appointments and Protocol.* 12 March. Chukudum: SPLM Secretariat of Information Centre. Retrieved from Sudan Open Archive: https://sudanarchive.net/cgi-bin/pagessoa?e=01off---v----100125--1-0-SectionLevel-0-0-1-1&a=d&cl=CL1.7.1.1&d=Dn1d221. Access: 28 November 2016.

Sudan People's Liberation Movement (SPLM). 1996. Statement on the State of Education Services in the Liberated Areas of the Sudan Today: Presented to the Conference on Civil Society and the Organization of Civil Authority in the New Sudan By Lawrence Lual Akuey. Retrieved from Sudan Open Archive: https://sudanarchive.net/cgi-bin/pagessoa?e=01off---v----100125--1-0-SectionLevel-0-0-1-1&a=d&cl=CL1.7.1.1&d=Dn1d257. Access: 28 November 2016.

Sudan People's Liberation Movement and Sudan People's Liberation Army (SPLM/SPLMA). 2003. SPLM Preparations for War-To-Peace Transition. 4 November. General Headquarters. Retrieved from Sudan Open Archive: https://sudanarchive.net/cgi-bin/pagessoa?e=01off---v----100125--1-0-SectionLevel-0-0-1-1&a=d&cl=CL1.4.1.1&d=Dslpd24. Access: 28 November 2016.

Stewart, Frances. 2008. 'Horizontal Inequalities and conflict: An Introduction and some Hypotheses', in *Horizontal Inequalities and Conflict: Understanding Group Violence in Multiethnic Societies,* Frances Stewart (ed.). Houndmills, Basingstoke, Hampshire & New York: Palgrave Macmillan.

*Sudan Tribune,* 2015. 'South Sudan's Kiir appoints governors of 28 new states', 24 December. Available online: http://www.sudantribune.com/spip.php?article57484. Access: 29 January 2015.

Tayar, Graham. 1964. 'A shaky peace in the Sudan', *The Observer*, 13 October 1964. Retrieved from Sudan Open Archive: https://sudanarchive.net/cgi-bin/ pagessoa?e=01off---v----100125--1-0-SectionLevel-0-0-1-1&a=d&cl=CL1.4.1.1& d=DwmrgdN10_14. Access: 28 November 2016.

Thomas, Edward. 2015. *South Sudan: A Slow Liberation*. London: Zed Books. Kindle e-book edition. Available online: https://www.amazon.co.uk/gp/product/ B00RVXT62W/ref=oh_aui_d_detailpage_o08_?ie=UTF8&psc=1. Access: 8 June 2015.

Tier, Akold Ma'an; Ambrose Riiny Thiik; Ben Lou Poggo; David Deng; Gabriel Shadar; Henry Swaka; Jacob Akol; Joanna Oyediran; Jok Madut Jok; Marcia Dawes; Merekaje Lorna; Paleki Matthew Obur & Zacharia Diing Akol. 2013. *My Mother Will Not Come to Juba: South Sudanese Debate the Constitution*. Juba University Lectures. London & Nairobi: Rift Valley Institute. Available online: riftvalley.net/download/file/fid/2741. Access: 14 May 2017.

Ting, Helen. 2008. 'Social Construction of Nation – A Theoretical Exploration', *Nationalism and Ethnic Politics*, 14(3), pp. 453–82.

United Nations (UN). 2016. 'Statement to the Security Council by Adama Dieng, United Nations Special Adviser on the Prevention of Genocide, on his visit to South Sudan', Press Release, 17 November. Available online: http://www.un.org/en/ genocideprevention/documents/our-work/Doc.8_2016-11-17.AD.Statement%20 to%20SC.South%20Sudan%20-%20final.pdf. Access: 18 January 2017.

United Nations General Assembly (UNGA). 1970. Declaration on Principles of International Law concerning Friendly Relations and Co-operation among States in accordance with the Charter of the United Nations, Resolution 2625 (XXV). A/RES/25/2625. Available online: http://www.un-documents.net/a25r2625.htm. Access: 01 November 2017.

United Nations Mission in the Republic of South Sudan (UNMISS). 2015. Attacks on Civilians in Bentiu & Bor April 2014. 9 January. Available online: http://www. ohchr.org/Documents/Countries/SS/UNMISS_HRDJanuary2015.pdf. Access: 25 October 2017.

United Nations Mission in the Republic of South Sudan (UNMISS). 2017. *A Report on Violations and Abuses of International Human Rights Law and Violations of International Humanitarian Law in the Context of the Fighting in Juba, South Sudan, in July 2016*. Jointly published by UNMISS and OHCHR. Available online: https://www.ohchr.org/Documents/Countries/SS/ReportJuba16Jan2017. pdf. Access: 17 January 2017.

UN News Centre. 2016. 'As deadline slips in South Sudan, UN chief urges African partners to revive peace process', 25 January 2016. Available online: http://www.un. org/apps/news/story.asp?NewsID=53087#.VqskCFN97GI. Access: 29 January 2016.

UN News. 2021. South Sudan: UN rights commission welcomes 'first steps' towards transitional justice institutions. 1 February 2021. Available online: https://news.un.org/en/story/2021/02/1083492. Access: 29 March 2021.

Van Leeuwen, Mathijs, Marlie Van de Kerkhof & Yves Van Leynseele. 2018. 'Transforming Land Governance and Strengthening the State in South Sudan', *African Affairs*, 117(467), pp. 286–309.

*Voice of the Nile Republic*. 1969a. 'El Nimeiry's Bluff', 10 (October 15). Retrieved from Sudan Open Archive: https://sudanarchive.net/cgi-bin/pagessoa?e=01off---v----100125--1-0-SectionLevel-0-0-1-1&a=d&cl=CL1.7.1.1&d=Dpdrgd30_4. Access: 28 November 2016.

*Voice of the Nile Republic*. 1969b. 'The alleged military coup d'état', 8 (August 15). Retrieved from: https://sudanarchive.net/. Access: 26 November 2016.

*Voice of Southern Sudan*. 1969. 'It is now the NILE REPUBLIC', 5 (May 15). Retrieved from Sudan Open Archive: https://sudanarchive.net/cgi-bin/pagessoa?e=01off---v----100125--1-0-SectionLevel-0-0-1-1&a=d&cl=CL1.7.1.1&d=Dpdrgd30_2. Access: 28 November 2016.

von Bogdandy, Armin; Stefan Häußler, Felix Hanschmann & Raphael Utz. 2005. 'State-Building, Nation-Building, and Constitutional Politics in Post-Conflict Situations: Conceptual Clarifications and an Appraisal of Different Approaches', in *Max Planck Yearbook of United Nations Law*, 9, pp. 579–613.

Young, John. 2003. 'Liberation Movements, Regional Armies, Ethnic Militias & Peace', *Review of African Political Economy*, 36(97), pp. 423–434.

Young, John. 2005. 'John Garang's Legacy to the Peace Process, the SPLM/A and the South', *Review of African Political Economy*, 32(106), pp. 535–48.

Young, John. 2012. *The Fate of Sudan: The Origins and Consequences of a Flawed Peace Process*, London: Zed Books, Kindle e-book edition. Available online: https://www.amazon.co.uk/gp/product/B00A76X0V8/ref=oh_aui_d_detailpage_o03_?ie=UTF8&psc=1. Access: 2 October 2015, p. 3.

Young, John. 2019. *South Sudan's Civil War: Violence, Insurgency and Failed Peacemaking*, Zed Books, ProQuest Ebook Central, http://ebookcentral.proquest.com/lib/kcl/detail.action?docID=5581278. Access: 02 August 2021.

Young, John. 2021. 'South Sudan: The Fractured State', in *The Nation State: A Wrong Model for the Horn of Africa*, John Markakis, Günther Schlee & John Young (eds). Online version at https://www.mprl-series.mpg.de/studies/14/. Access: 02 August 2021.

Weber, Max. 1978. 'The Three Pure Types of Authority', in *Economy and Society*, Guenther Roth and Claus Wittich (eds.), Berkeley and Los Angeles: University of California Press.

Weber, Max. 1994. 'The Nation', in *Nationalism*, John Hutchinson & Anthony D. Smith (eds), Oxford, New York: Oxford University Press.

Weber, Max. 2014. 'Politics as Vocation', New York: Oxford University Press/Moulin Digital Editions.

Weilenmann, Hermann. 2010. 'The Interlocking of Nation and Personality Structure', in *Nation Building in Comparative Contexts,* Karl W. Deutsch & William J. Fotz (eds). New Brunswick, New Jersey: Transaction Publishers.

Wild, Hannah; Jok Madut Jok & Ronak Patel. 2018. 'The militarization of cattle raiding in South Sudan: How a traditional practice became a tool for political violence', *Journal of Humanitarian Action,* 3(2), pp.1–11.

Wilson, Jacqueline. 2014. *Local Peace Processes in Sudan and South Sudan.* Washington DC: United States Institute of Peace. Available online: https://www.usip.org/publications/2014/05/local-peace-processes-sudan-and-south-sudan. Access: 28 January 2016.

Wolff, Jonathan. 2006. *An Introduction to Political Philosophy,* Revised Edition. Oxford, New York: Oxford University Press.

Wolff, Stefan. 2012. 'Consociationalism: power sharing and self-governance', in *Conflict Management in Divided Societies: Theories and Practice,* Stefan Wolff & Christalla Yakinthou (eds). London & New York: Routledge.

Wöndu, Steven. 2011. *From Bush to Bush: Journey to Liberty in South Sudan.* Nairobi, Kenya: Kenway Publishers.

Zambakari, Christopher. 2015. 'Sudan and South Sudan: identity, citizenship, and democracy in plural societies', *Citizenship Studies,* 19(1), pp. 69–82.

# Index

The letter *f* following an entry indicates a page that includes a figure.

www.ingramcontent.com/pod-product-compliance
Ingram Content Group UK Ltd.
Pitfield, Milton Keynes, MK11 3LW, UK
UKHW020701280225
455688UK00004B/203